Smart Growth

Form and Consequences

Copyright © 2002 by the Lincoln Institute of Land Policy
All rights reserved
Printed in Canada

Acknowledgment is given for permission to reprint copyrighted material:
Dolores Hayden, "What is Suburbia?: Naming the Layers in the Landscape, 1820-2000."
Copyright © 2000

Library of Congress Cataloging-in-Publication Data

Smart growth: form and consequences / edited by Terry S. Szold and
Armando Carbonell.
    p. cm.
Includes bibliographical references.
ISBN 1-55844-151-4 (pbk.)
1. Regional planning—United States. 2. Land use—United States.
3. Cities and towns—United States—Growth. 4. Regional
planning—Environmental aspects—United States. I. Szold, Terry S.,
1960- II. Carbonell, Armando, 1951-
HT392 .S557 2002
307.1'2'0973—dc21
                              2002007600

Project management: Ann LeRoyer, Lincoln Institute of Land Policy
Project assistance: Kathy Foulger, Lincoln Institute of Land Policy
Copyediting: Mary Jane Higgins
Design and production: Wilcox Design
Printing: Webcom Ltd., Toronto, Ontario, Canada

Edited by
Terry S. Szold and **Armando Carbonell**

Smart Growth

Form and Consequences

Contents

Foreword
John P. DeVillars — vi

1. **Introduction and Overview:**
   And Then There Was Smart Growth — 2
   Terry S. Szold

2. **What Is Suburbia?**
   Naming the Layers in the Landscape, 1820–2000 — 16
   Dolores Hayden

3. **How They Lost Their Way in San Jose:**
   The Capital of Silicon Valley as a Case Study of Postwar Sprawl — 46
   Glenna Matthews

4. **Electronic Cottages, Wired Neighborhoods and Smart Cities** — 66
   William J. Mitchell

5. **How Do We Know Smart Growth When We See It?** — 82
   Arthur C. Nelson

6. **Seven Wise (Though Possibly Impractical) Goals for Smart Growth Advocates** — 102
   Alex Krieger

7	**Smarter Standards and Regulations:**	
	Diversifying the Spatial Paradigm of Subdivisions	110
	Eran Ben-Joseph	

8	**Smart Growth:**	
	Legal Assumptions and Market Realities	128
	Brian W. Blaesser	

9	**The Constitution Neither Prohibits nor Requires Smart Growth**	158
	Jerold S. Kayden	

10	**Ethical Principles for Smart Growth:**	
	Steps Toward an Ecological Ten Commandments	180
	Timothy C. Weiskel	

11	**Smart Growth and Urban Revival**	192
	Harvey Gantt	

Afterword — 200
Armando Carbonell

Contributors — 205

About the Lincoln Institute — 209

Foreword

When most people think about the ideal community where they would like to live, more often than not they envision an old New England town—New Ipswich, New Hampshire; Old Lyme, Connecticut; North Hero, Vermont; South Bristol, Maine; Great Barrington, Massachusetts; or Little Compton, Rhode Island. These are places with a town green, houses close enough for children to visit one another without needing to be driven, and plenty of open space, woods and farmland nearby. Or, they may think of a vibrant urban neighborhood such as Cambridge's Harvard Square, Portland's Old Port, College Hill in Providence, or Beacon Hill in Boston—places full of elegant architecture on a human scale.

Many of these communities are national models, and numerous smart growth planners use the phrase "New England town" to describe the kind of place they want to recreate across the country. These communities and the open spaces and natural beauty that surround them are an important part of our love for New England. For many of us, they are the reasons we live here instead of somewhere else. Walt Whitman said of New Englanders, "to know us, go to our mountaintops and ocean shores." These landscapes define our sense of place, our spirit, our character.

But today those mountaintops and ocean shores and the communities that surround them are under siege, threatened by unplanned and unchecked development, by what we often call sprawl. Sprawl is hard to define, but, as Justice Potter Stewart said of obscenity, "We may not be able to define it, but we know it when we see it." And see it we do. It is the endless shopping malls and parking lots lining Route 9 and Route 1 leading into Boston, New England's capital city. In the last 15 years, the population of the Boston metropolitan area has grown less than 5 percent, but the amount of developed land has increased nearly 25 percent. That's a land loss per person ratio three times the national average.

This foreword is adapted from John DeVillars' keynote address given at the symposium, "Smart Growth: Form and Consequences," in Cambridge, Massachusetts, on March 10, 2000.

Foreword

We see sprawl in virtually every part of our small corner of America, as we lose open space at the alarming and accelerating rate of 1,200 acres per week. If you travel to the White Mountains, you see it in the strip malls and traffic jams along Route 16 in North Conway, New Hampshire, where in that once bucolic village there is now three square feet of mall space for every man, woman and child in the entire state. In Rhode Island over the last 30 years, more residential, commercial and industrial land has been developed outside the state's urban centers than in the state's entire 325-year history. Southeastern Massachusetts is now one of the fastest developing areas in the region, where population has risen by 28 percent but land use has increased by 200 percent. This rapid, haphazard growth is consuming more and more of our countryside and, in too many cases, draining the vitality of once-proud cities.

As the Trust for Public Land has said, sprawl is often ugly, but the problems it creates are more than skin deep. The environmental impacts of poorly planned, in many instances unplanned, development are very real. More than half of our water pollution is now due to nonpoint sources—not industry or malfunctioning treatment plants but the parking lots, roads and other impervious surfaces that are the face of sprawl. The habitat destruction and fragmentation associated with unplanned development is now the principal threat to more than 80 percent of the endangered species in New England. Sprawl makes the job of providing clean air harder as well. We New Englanders drove one-third more miles in the 1990s than we did in the 1980s, and we drove one-third more miles in the 1980s than we did in the 1970s. Even with cars that are 98 percent cleaner, that increased travel represents nearly half of the smog problem that causes us to exceed health-based air standards more than 20 days per year in parts of New England.

Sprawl doesn't come cheap, either. The cost to our economy and to our taxpayers is as significant as it is to our environment. Talk to Jim Dodge, who founded Grow Smart Rhode Island in part because even though the customer base of his company, Providence Gas, was growing at only about 1 percent annually, he was forced to spend $18 million each year on new pipelines and equipment, because that customer base was moving farther out to previously undeveloped areas.

The average New England family feels the cost of sprawl. As commutes lengthen, we spend more money and time in our cars, and less on the things we value—our families and friends, vocations and avocations. According to the Council on Environmental Quality, transportation expenses are now the second highest expense in the family budget after housing, more than food and more than taxes of all kinds, even in Massachusetts.

Sprawl costs New England taxpayers dearly as well. For every $1.00 of revenue a new low-density housing development brings to a town, it costs the local taxpayers $1.50 in increased expenses for schools, sewers, police and other services. The taxpayers of Maine feel the pinch in their school systems. The number of public school students declined by 27,000 over the last 25 years, yet taxpayers have spent $727 million for new school construction, most of it in fast-growing suburbs. Maine taxpayers end up paying twice—once to renovate old schools in older neighborhoods that are losing population and again to build new schools in the expanding suburbs.

Much of the cost of sprawl falls on our poorest, most vulnerable citizens as land in our cities is abandoned in the flight to greenfields. The percentage of Rhode Islanders living in traditional population centers has now fallen to 30 percent, and, as a result, in the last decade alone total property values in Rhode Island's five largest cities have declined by $3.3 billion, necessitating an increase in effective tax rates of some 44 percent.

To be sure, sprawl costs us big time, environmentally, economically and fiscally. But, in the end, the real effect of sprawl is to lessen how much we value and enjoy our lives. The New England tradition of small-town democracy, civic pride and joining together with one's neighbors was built around the town green, where people could meet one another, swap a story or two, get to know one another. And it was built on a respect for our natural resources and what they can teach us.

When public greens disappear as a center of town life, when tranquility is stolen from our open spaces, when parts of New England become just a blur of strip malls, shopping centers and cookie-cutter housing developments, our traditions are lost. In too many places, too often and too quickly, we are discovering, as Gertrude Stein did with development in the East Bay near Oakland, California, that "when you get there, there is no *there*, there."

We New Englanders like to think that we are ahead of the curve. We believe that when it comes to economic or social or public policy challenges our innovative spirit and entrepreneurial ethic will point the way for the rest of the country. But, when it comes to this challenge of growing our communities in a well-planned, thoughtful, visionary fashion, we find we are not leading the way. In fact, we lag behind many other places—cities like Portland, Oregon, and Milwaukee, Wisconsin; states like Maryland and Georgia. As our economy

Foreword

booms, as development capital floods our landscape, we are woefully unprepared to handle it.

The Environmental Protection Agency, among many other agencies, could have done more about sprawl a long time ago. Our state environmental agencies also have been slow to respond. And most important, our local communities, the frontline infantry in this battle, are virtually unarmed. Woody Allen once lamented, "Never has the world faced greater choices. We are at a crossroads. Down one path is utter despair and hopelessness; down the other, total extinction. Let us choose wisely."

I believe, Woody notwithstanding, and the enormity of the challenge notwithstanding, that there is cause for optimism, that we will in fact choose wisely. The genesis for much of my optimism is the good sense and mounting frustration of the American people, nowhere more so than here in New England. We see it in countless ways. Armando Carbonell sees it in the classrooms at the Lincoln Institute and Harvard Design School, where planners from nearly every state are talking with him about what they are doing to promote more sustainable development. Terry Szold and I see it in the bright eyes and eager minds of the graduate students in urban studies at MIT, who are prepared to devote their careers to pursuing a better path.

We find optimism in the fact that in January 2000 more than 30 of our nation's governors spoke to the issue in their state of the state messages, emboldened no doubt by a prairie fire of citizen unrest that led to approval of nearly 200 ballot initiatives in the previous 15 months, approving more than $7 billion in new state and local funding to protect open space. We must tap that support, build on it, honor it through smart, effective action both as individuals and on behalf of the institutions and communities we represent. That illustrious philosopher, Jerry Garcia, once said, "Somebody has to do something, and it's just incredibly pathetic that it has to be us."

To that end, I offer some further ideas for action. We must help our governors and state legislators get their fiscal priorities in order. When it comes to sustainable development, we are spending too much on the wrong things and not enough on the right things. It makes no sense whatsoever, for example, to encourage large companies such as Fidelity Investments, as Rhode Island's leaders did recently, to expand their operations into farm and pasture land in the town of Smithfield and to fuel that expansion with tens of millions of dollars in public highway funds, when beautiful, structurally sound mill buildings in Providence and Pawtucket sit abandoned.

It makes no sense whatsoever for this Commonwealth of Massachusetts to spend $60 million to construct a new interchange on Route 3 to facilitate traffic into what is proposed to be the largest mall in New England, when we know that development will increase traffic on that roadway between Cape Cod and Boston by 37 percent, turning what is now a parking lot for several hours a day into even greater gridlock. That same project, while bleeding downtown shopping areas and neighboring malls, will also draw down some 750,000 gallons a day from an aquifer that is already tapped 250,000 gallons a day beyond safe levels. The absurdity of this kind of misallocation of resources is even starker when one notes that we, as taxpayers, will spend more on that interchange than we will invest in open space for the entire Commonwealth this year.

We need more enlightened leadership to think differently about the impacts of such development plans and to uphold the New England traditions that still exist in many communities across the region. State leaders, with our help, must address another fundamental fiscal barrier to sustainable development—overreliance on the property tax. Our dependence on local property taxes to fund basic services places an unhealthy and unfair pressure on our older cities because of their low property values and disproportionate share of tax-exempt institutions. I would suggest that the best and brightest in our land grant institutions, working with the New England Governors Conference, identify recommendations for fiscal reforms that can create incentives to encourage development where we can afford it and to discourage it on our ever-dwindling farmland and open space

The second and related battle is the effort to make our urban centers a more attractive alternative for people to raise a family and for private investors to place their capital. Here an increasingly dynamic group of mayors from big cities and small are on our side. They know as you do that livable communities begin with better schools and safer streets, and the trends are in our favor—charter schools are flourishing and introducing healthy competition for K through 12, test scores are up and crime rates are down.

But there are two other areas critical to urban revitalization that need more creative and sustained focus—brownfields redevelopment and affordable housing. Governors and state legislative leaders, as well as private capitalists, have key roles to play. Public leaders can start by taking a lion's share of the funding that today is paying for new infrastructure that is turning open space into malls and that wonderful oxymoron "office parks" and instead redirecting those investments to urban infrastructure—mass transit services, strategically placed parking garages, storefront upgrades, urban greenery, traffic calming sidewalks and all the rest. Frankly Massachusetts was doing that in the 1980s. Most of the initiatives that turned Lowell into a model city and put proud cities like New Bedford and Fall River and Springfield on the right track toward sustainable rebirth languish today, unloved, unimplemented, unfunded. We need to reverse that course and bring the urban investment ethos back to this state and to states across America.

Public investment is key but we are not going to rebuild our cities and stem the assault on greenfields without substantial *private* investment, and that must begin with investment in brownfields. You need look no further than Burlington, Vermont, to understand why. The city has 45 acres of developable land; 43 of them are contaminated. We can either support and advance projects on those parcels or we can continue to see the forests and farmland of Chittendon County carved up by the developer's bulldozers. That's why in the last several years in Burlington and 40 other communities across New England EPA has invested more than $25 million in the assessment and clean-up of contaminated urban properties. It's why EPA and the states have adopted common-sense reuse standards and liability protections for developers. Now it's up to private capital to finish the job. Real estate developers, fund managers, property brokers and others in the trade need to set their sights on the very real and very rich investment opportunities that await them on contaminated sites in our urban areas.

In a labor-short economy those who live in our inner cities are eager and available to join the workforce. The cities are where the water and sewer and transportation infrastructure is in place and, contrary to conventional wisdom and suburban stereotypes, where huge purchasing power exists. Over $2 billion from Boston inner-city neighborhoods alone is being spent each year outside the city because the retail and commercial opportunities are so limited in those neighborhoods. Smart, urban-biased developers who invest in these communities will do well by doing good.

To accelerate the renaissance of our cities we need to address a second social challenge—the cost of housing. Affordable housing is not just a human services program, it is a staple of economic development and, if managed properly, it can be a key ingredient in our battle against sprawl. Massachusetts has the third highest housing costs in America. A recent analysis by MassINC (Massachusetts Institute for a New Commonwealth) makes clear that this is the number one barrier to expanded economic growth in our state.

We have at best a modest strategy to tackle it and virtually no strategy at all to tackle it in our cities. If you go to downtown Chicopee, to Lawrence and to

Lowell, you'll see people living in historically protected, reused schools and mills—literally tens of thousands of units across Massachusetts alone. That was a high priority of state government in the 1980s, but in the 1990s that work stopped. If we're going to retain and attract new workers, if we're going to stop planting houses in cornfields and pasture lands, we need to restart that work, and there is no better place to do it than in our cities.

More enlightened state leadership and more responsible private capitalists are essential to winning the war on sprawl but in the end, especially here in New England, land use decisions are made at the local level—largely by volunteer boards overwhelmed by the volume and complexity of development proposals flooding their towns.

Let's turn our attention back to Southeastern Massachusetts. From Boston to the Cape and inland 15 miles or so are 50 communities that comprise one of the five fastest growing areas of America. Since the construction of the Southeast Expressway in the 1950s, the population of those 50 towns has increased a relatively modest 28 percent, but the amount of land consumed is greater than all the land consumed since the Pilgrims landed at Plymouth Rock. Yet, more than half of those communities do not have a full-time planner, only 20 have master plans, and only five of those have been updated in the last five years. These towns and hundreds of communities like them across New England need help. Our challenge is to develop the tools and financing mechanisms to give those planning boards and citizen volunteers, and the citizens and communities they serve, a fighting chance.

EPA has made a good but modest start with its Sustainable Development Challenge Grant program, smart growth training programs, circuit riders to offer technical assistance and other tools, but the demand far exceeds the supply. There is $4.6 million available this year for those challenge grants for the entire country. In New England alone EPA received requests from 107 communities totaling more than $14 million—3 times what is available for the whole country from just one tiny corner of America.

Simply put we are not investing anything close to what is necessary to help our communities plan their futures. Nor are we meeting the need when it comes to another essential weapon in our battle against sprawl—open space acquisition and protection. In this red-hot economy, with tax coffers overflowing, with a proposed tax cut of $1.4 billion a year here in Massachusetts, with candidates for president considered pikers if they don't offer tax cuts of at least $250 billion annually, we have abandoned a bipartisan commitment to open space protection that dates back to Teddy Roosevelt.

In Massachusetts we're investing only one-half what we did 10 years ago to permanently protect forests and farmland, wildlife habitat and other valuable open space. In New Hampshire, one of the fastest growing states in America, not 10 cents of state money is put to this purpose. In Washington, DC, the Congress refuses to act on a Better America Bonds program that through tax credits would forego $1 billion in revenue to the Treasury in order to leverage $10 billion in open space investment across America.

Senator Muskie of Maine used to say, "You have a God given right to kick the government around—don't hesitate to do so." That's my final thought, as well. Get out there and do some kicking:

- To redirect public financing away from new highway interchanges and $100 tax cuts toward open space bonds and affordable housing in our cities.
- To get that Better America Bonds program through the Congress.
- To encourage private developers and pension fund managers to invest in the redevelopment of urban brownfields.

In these and many other ways we can make a difference, although there are powerful forces arrayed against us:

- A special-interest dominated Congress;
- State legislatures more beholden to the lobbyists than their constituents;
- Too many governors with too narrow a vision;
- A wealthy and powerful real estate industry that not only fears but fails to understand our cities and the people who live in them.

But our agenda makes sense. We have the support of an increasingly less silent majority, and it is clear that many people working every day in their communities have the energy and commitment to carry forward this vision and hope for a better future. We are in a prosperous age. We have the opportunity and obligation to see to it that the legacy of that prosperity is not in fact a burden to our children but instead an inheritance of vibrant downtowns and livable neighborhoods and forever protected open spaces.

Lewis Mumford, one of the great figures in urban planning, wrote, "the final test of an economic system is not the tons of iron, the tanks of oil or the miles of textiles it produces; the final test lies in its ultimate products: the sort of men and women it nurtures and the order and beauty and sanity of their communities."

Let us use this collection of conference papers and the work that follows from them to ensure that here in New England, and across this great country, we meet that test.

John P. DeVillars
Lecturer, MIT Department of Urban Studies and Planning
Executive Vice President, Brownfields Recovery Corporation, Boston
Former Administrator, U.S. Environmental Protection Agency, New England
(1993-2000)

Introduction and Overview

And Then There Was Smart Growth

Terry S. Szold

Introduction and Overview

Dickens' classic characterization, "It was the best of times, it was the worst of times," describes the consequences of growth in the United States at the turn of the twenty-first century. The economic boom that marked the close of the 1990s was accompanied by one of the worst possible environments for attempting to slow the rush to develop new commercial and residential real estate. Even the economic slowdown that followed the nation's celebration of the new millennium has had little impact on our overall land consumption habit.

Most of the chapters contributed for this collection were submitted for publication well before the terrorist attacks of September 11, 2001. Therefore, most authors were unable to speculate about whether the post-September 11 world poses an additional challenge for smart growth and the growth management arena in general. Some may speculate that our propensity to develop in lower densities and spread out more horizontally has now been given a potent *raison d'être*. Regardless of how well- or ill-informed such speculation is, recent evidence on housing starts in the U. S. suggests that public officials, community planners and academics still need to discuss and debate the array of possible interventions to change both *how* and *where* we grow. In my view, the rationale for convening this collection is no less persuasive now, in 2002, than it was a few years ago.

Popular use of the term *smart growth* emerged in the mid-1990s, and will likely be used with greater frequency over the next few years. A diverse coalition of interest groups has given it both credibility and momentum. Some states' planning initiatives are based on smart growth principles, but, other than its inherent definition of being the opposite of stupid growth, what does it mean?

To some, smart growth is simply a euphemism for better choices about future development and land use. To others, however, smart growth principles are specifically those that embody viable alternatives to prevailing suburban sprawl. These principles when put into practice promote compact, mixed-use, transit-oriented, and environmentally sound development and land use patterns. But if we hold up the term smart growth as the all-purpose umbrella for antisprawl policies, is there any room underneath for the many other issues and questions that underlie the choices to be made about our future settlement patterns?

What smart growth is, and how it should direct us in future planning and development, remain cryptic and unclear to many observers, including decision makers in the public arena who must learn a new vocabulary and offer more than rhetoric to citizens hungry for strong policy, planning and design solutions. Whether one sees smart growth as a slogan, a catch phrase, a call to the barricades or perhaps even the battle flag waved by the enemy, it raises questions that we need to answer:

- Have the most important lessons from past development practices been fully absorbed and learned?
- In striving to advance alternatives to low-density, haphazard forms of development, where are viable models to be found?
- Have practical, ethical and distribution considerations been appropriately brought to bear on proposed smart growth interventions?
- Are the components of what we call smart growth constitutionally permissible?
- What consequences might unfold to affect various stakeholders and constituencies?

During the summer of 1999, Armando Carbonell of the Lincoln Institute and I began discussions about the need for a symposium that would bring together academics, planning and design practitioners, citizen planners and others to engage in fruitful discussion about what had become the planning and development subject du jour.[1] Smart growth still had the cachet of a relatively new movement and the least of our symposium planning worries was too little attendance. Of great concern, however, was our ability to ensure that our audience would be offered something unique and more substantial than other conferences and gatherings about the subject.

News about smart growth abounded that summer, and legislative initiatives wrapped in the banner of smart growth seemed to be sprouting up throughout the nation. This was highlighted by discussion about smart growth during the early presidential primary season by candidate Al Gore. To ensure the result we envisioned, we sought out and were gratified to find people who could provide the intellectual leadership necessary to address the scope associated with evaluating this subject, and were significantly invested and actively involved in the evolution of land use regulations, urban design and development practice.

The presentations at the symposium met our expectations and those of the attendees, and the eclectic and wide-ranging essays collected here represent the themes and issues discussed. They take the reader through the history of suburban

---

1   The symposium "Smart Growth: Form and Consequences" was cosponsored by the Lincoln Institute of Land Policy and the Department of Urban Studies and Planning at the Massachusetts Institute of Technology (MIT) on March 10, 2000, in Cambridge, Massachusetts. The chapters in this volume are based on the papers presented at that meeting to an audience of nearly 400 people.

growth to the spatial and temporal consequences of the current state and stages of growth and technological change, and across the normative assumptions about design, urban and suburban neglect and revival, private versus public property rights, and environmental ethics.

How We Got Here from There: History and Some Suggested Principles

The concept of smart growth developed from statewide growth management legislation dating from the 1970s and 1980s. Specific smart growth legislation began with Maryland Governor Parris Glendening's pioneering legislation in 1997, and continues today to extend to other initiatives from New Jersey to the West Coast. A common thread in the different statewide initiatives is the array of incentives and requirements to direct public and private investment away from the creation of new infrastructure and development that spreads out from existing built areas (Porter 1998).

The term *smart development* has been used with some frequency in recent years, and could be viewed as a close cousin to smart growth, since it refers to actual development practices that alter the current and prevailing growth pattern (APA 1998). Additionally, the term *best development practices* came into vogue around the mid-1990s (Ewing 1998). Advocates of such practices implicitly recognize the market preferences of consumers who prefer low-density lifestyles, often in greenfield settings, and the growing appeal of more traditional neighborhood development and design.

However, best development practices enjoy only a limited acceptance with true smart growth believers, since the suggested gross density of development is often similar to conventional suburban development, and such strategies are frequently applied to greenfield locations. In contrast, proponents of smart growth and smart development strive to offer something of relevance and importance to both suburbs and central cities.

In order to offer something of value, however, it is clear that to define smart growth means first to agree on some unifying principles. Without them, it is difficult to differentiate *better development* from *smart growth*. Arthur (Chris) Nelson, in Chapter 5, offers a list of smart growth principles to which he suggests all development and growth strategies must adhere:

- Preserve public goods;
- Minimize adverse land use impacts;

- Maximize positive land use impacts;
- Minimize public fiscal costs; and
- Maximize social equity.

Most other contributors to this volume would likely agree with these principles, not as an all-inclusive or exhaustive list, but as guidelines worthy as a common starting point for analyzing a program or project's worthiness in relation to having authentic smart growth "genes."

Past Development Practices: Causes and Effects

Bruce Katz (2001) points out in a recent opinion piece that suburban and exurban development continues to change the spatial and social patterns of the nation. The suburbs, as the 2000 U.S. Census tells us, are far from a monolithic form, though low-density development is the signature element. Suburbs serve as major employment centers, house a greater total population than cities, and are becoming more ethnically and racially diverse.

Dolores Hayden (Chapter 2) reminds us that suburbia is not just a place where most Americans live, but is the "dominant U.S. cultural landscape." She believes examining how existing suburbs have evolved is "central to calculating the prospects of ending sprawl." Hayden names and cites the origins of suburbia's historical layers, the eras of development that have merged the multiple connections between home and work, taking us from the borderlands of 1820 to the e-space fringes of the 1990s. The American dream includes "house, nature and community," a place where ordinary folks continue to settle and where family and community can thrive jointly.

Of course, today the size of the suburban house is booming, as is the desire of developers for large, unregulated amounts of land available at low cost, all of which is part of the dilemma for those who would grow—if not smaller—then certainly smarter. At the same time, the existing layers, such as the sitcom suburbs of the 1960s, have not all disappeared fully in a spatial sense, but are evolving. Unlike Joel Garreau's (1991) statement about edge cities representing "the search for the future inside ourselves," we may fail to find our desired future if we continue to segregate ourselves from the layers and enclaves we previously formed, naively marching to a socially and environmentally less tenable, remote exurban e-fringe. Rather than repudiate suburbia, smart growth seeks to shape it, and as necessary, preserve, renovate and reshape it.

Hayden includes in her essay some strong words for new urbanists who, she says, believe "getting the design right is essential to making society work." An analysis of suburban layers reveals contradictions that may defy easy reconciliation, and makes it clear that different kinds of interventions are useful in different places. What is not so clear is whether Hayden's clarion call for activists to mobilize ordinary citizens in the face of the sustained political pressure of real estate, banking and automotive interests will bear fruit.

Glenna Matthews (Chapter 3) presents a narrower focus on past development: a case study of postwar sprawl. She describes the evolution of San Jose, California, from a period when the landscape was devoted to orchards and fruit processing to its recognition as the putative capital of the mythic Eden of Silicon Valley. Here, as the electronics industry established root in what would flower into what we call high technology, was a situation driven by a city with a "deliberate and mindful political commitment to expansion." Further driven by the success of its new industrial economy, San Jose stretched itself over 130 square miles, with 1,500 high-tech firms eventually located within the city limits.

Not surprisingly, San Jose has found itself dealing with both the benefits of surging postwar growth and the long-term costs of being the epicenter of the high-tech economy. As Matthews makes clear, there should be an "ethical test for socially desirable growth." San Jose must confront the jobs/housing imbalance, failing levels of service on roadways, environmental degradation, and perhaps most compelling, the inadvertent erasure of its history. Matthews's concluding caution about wishful thinking in relation to growth planning might well be phrased as an admonition for policy makers and planners anywhere.

Place-Making in a Digital World

Will technology and digital communications make us grow smarter? Considering what happened to San Jose, one might assume not. In a recent article in *Urban Land*, Jim Miara (2000) identifies high-tech "smart firms" as significant culprits in fueling sprawl nationally. Many such firms have selected greenfields and former pastoral settings as preferred locations for their headquarters and offices. How can the highly educated and purportedly environmentally savvy employees and executives of such e-firms be unwitting contributors to the further extensions of edge cities, sprawl and suburbia?

William Mitchell (Chapter 4) examines the relationship between the new digital telecommunications infrastructure and the opportunities and challenges it presents for reexamining our world. He describes the loosening of spatial and temporal linkages, taking us beyond a discussion of smart growth in traditional land use and transportation terms.

Now that people are capable of working anywhere, at any time, office workspace may become increasingly fragmented. Similarly, retail space has become more fragmented by the world of e-commerce. Mitchell suggests that smart distribution systems of information and goods "force planners to rethink the relationships of land uses, land values and service network infrastructure" and think more precisely in terms of complex, dynamic human behaviors. In order to fashion future interventions, we will need to dispense with the former land use planning and design regimes and realms of practice.

Mitchell also argues that the deployment of the new infrastructure "does not simply produce featureless urban sprawl." But he warns that a "wired Walden" may indeed be bad news for smart growth. It is possible that the loosening of spatial connections could lead to what Robert Putnam (2000) characterized as civic disengagement. Reflecting upon this issue, Jonathan Weiss (2000) of the George Washington University Center on Sustainability and Regional Growth suggests that the social consequences of the physical fragmentation of our daily lives leads to a lack of participation and a "weakening of democracy." Clearly, however, as Mitchell counsels, there are multiple choices to be made about the future form of our settlement patterns, and "locational freedom does not mean locational indifference."

Implicit in Mitchell's provocative narrative is a suggestion for planners and designers to be wary of categorizing the growth of e-topia in normative terms. This is why Mitchell (1999) was careful to title his recent book on the future of our digital world as *E-topia* rather than utopia or dystopia, because the evolution of our built and natural environment in relation to this e-trend is very much a work in progress.

Mitchell's predictions have a bit of a shared flavor with Edward Bellamy (1982), the nineteenth-century American visionary, who was looking backward, coincidentally at the year 2000. Mitchell is looking forward at the new century up close, as if under a microscope, in its nymphal stage. Both Bellamy and Mitchell share optimism about an imagined future time and the civilizing potential of technology, but neither offers actual guarantees. As futurists and twentieth-century historians note, technology can be viewed as both liberating and enslaving, leaving ample room for joyous or cataclysmic prophecy by utopians and dystopians, respectively. Mitchell's speculation about "What's left of face-time?" remains only one of the unanswered questions about our evolving sense of what community—let alone utopia—means.

Goals, Principles, Commandments and Some Not-So-Golden Rules
As Chris Nelson (Chapter 5) notes, one of the primary challenges of defining smart growth is that, to this point, it has remained formless. Smart growth does not presuppose a particular built landscape, as do the various movements of City Beautiful, Garden City, growth management and sustainable development. He seeks to characterize smart growth "in a way that allows us to separate charlatans from the real thing."

Powered by this noble quest, he provides a useful set of smart growth goals and principles, presenting how its genesis can be traced to Maryland's trail-blazing legislation. Nelson augments the initial list of principles by advancing a more detailed set that can be applied to three different scales: individual development projects, communities and regions. By applying the Nelson list of principles summarized earlier in this chapter, we have a beginning from which to objectively measure outcomes. For example, projects that preserve natural resources or minimize the unnecessary extension of infrastructure may be laudable, but not genuinely worthy of what one might call a four-star, smart growth medal, because there is little jobs-housing balance or life-cycle housing.

Nelson is not suggesting that we strip away awards from places such as the Kentlands, Maryland, or Boulder, Colorado. His own observations of the examples he presents point out positive outcomes relative to growth-as-usual. But, while it is possible for us to award high marks to certain purportedly smart growth communities for quality design, design alone will not enable such projects or places to be included in the smart growth pantheon, particularly if only the wealthiest of us can reside in these places. Readers familiar with the examples can reconsider them through the lens Nelson provides.

He suggests that we not shy away or recoil at a notion that planning can shape or help to form a better place to live. He makes the case or at least forecasts that a substantial amount of our land will be recycled or reused, and sensibly concludes that there is much opportunity to create a new canvas—one that can be shaped by principles from which we can evaluate a new and improved quality of life.

Alex Krieger (Chapter 6), for his part, wants to stir up trouble. He wishes to peel away the disingenuous regalia that we have draped around our less-than-altruistic motivations and pretensions about growth. His seven not quite Swiftian goals for smart growth lead off with taxing redundancy—second homes—in a graduated fashion, as one moves farther away from a city. Also making the list of his self-styled commandments is a regional tax sharing and suburban renewal program.

Doubtless most readers of this volume are well aware of the deceptive shroud that can be draped around smart growth initiatives, providing a potential cover for NIMBY motivations and its attendant advocacy. One need read no further than Krieger's first impractical proposal to realize the discomfort he wishes us to feel if we dare seek refuge in the assumption that the growth created by the choices of others is the real problem—in fact, it is the growth of our own making.

Krieger eschews the euphoria and celebration of smart growth referenda and grassroots ballot initiatives around the nation because many such initiatives involve preserving open spaces or farmlands, rather than heralding or reinforcing urban virtue or successfully modifying development behavior. Perhaps a more significant reflection offered by Krieger relates to the danger posed by continuing to embrace notions of "enhanced livability" in decentralized places. As he recently observed elsewhere "…the urge to spread out is deeply embedded in our culture" (Krieger 1999). Discussing the normative and spatial ideology of Frank Lloyd Wright in relation to "wanderers" and "cave-dwellers (who became modern-age cliff-dwellers and city builders)," Krieger concludes, "…it is the cliff-dweller, not the wanderer, who builds community." But as Krieger cautions here, our willingness to see places of human concentration as "enjoyable rather than mandatory" may hold the key to a smarter future. Is the call to tax second homes really so outrageous? Perhaps it is no more outrageous than our willingness to live in flood zones, endure horrible commutes and carry previously unthinkable mortgage debt, all in the name of what we think is a better—although not necessarily smarter—place to live. A truly outrageous proposal, but one that's tempting to make after reading Krieger, would be to suggest that our government seriously entertain legislation to mandate the rationing of unbuilt or open space, perhaps based on a formula that considers per capita land consumption in each of the states.

After a focus on principles and goals, one might well easily dismiss the impact of adjusting design and engineering standards for laying out subdivisions. In the aggregate, however, Eran Ben-Joseph (Chapter 7) makes clear that when one considers that millions of people continue to select single-family residential lots as the preferred settlement pattern, the impact of revising the spatial requirements for setbacks and road widths—what may be the not-so-golden rules of Nelson's growth-as-usual—is truly staggering.

As an illustrative figure in Ben-Joseph's chapter points out, at least one-third of all development is devoted to roads, parking lots and other motor vehicle infrastructure. On close examination, one sees that local policy makers and officials have little excuse for not adjusting standards based on flawed assumptions of necessity, efficiency and liability. Ben-Joseph argues that the mere existence of dual standards—one for private development and another for public development—provides ample evidence "…that what should guide change is actual performance and good design." Beyond the issue of spatial patterns, Ben-Joseph has observed that the elite and gated enclaves located at the fringe are actually an emerging laboratory for better and smarter regulations and standards.

Probing beyond the veneer of superficial preference and established market appeal may reveal that the predominant configuration of the subdivision is actually not a preference at all. The lack of variation may simply represent the inadequacy of planners and designers to effectively animate and represent the range of improved spatial patterns and choices available. Smart growth advocates have only begun to utilize imaging technology to support public understanding and inform better choices about land use and design. Even if only used in a comparative way, imaging technology offers a powerful tool for citizens and planners to employ in reflecting the sharp contrast between alternative development scenarios that are shaped by imposition of different standards and guidelines. Since we now posses the means to portray, in robust and tactile fashion, the visual and spatial impact of alternative development choices, better and smarter development paradigms should not be out of reach.

Legal Assumptions, Market Realities, Constitutional Limitations

On the topic of regulating private property in the public interest to achieve smart growth objectives, Brian Blaesser (Chapter 8) suggests that sprawl, "the product of American affluence," is not a pejorative for everyone. He goes on to share his perspective about the likely emerging conflicts and tensions between smart growth and protections guaranteed by the Constitution.

Most planners and designers exposed to basic training in land use regulation are aware that if a regulation goes too far, it may be found to be a taking under the fifth and fourteenth amendments of the Constitution. But the circumstances in which a regulatory taking may be found have been subject to evolving principles involving the scope, nature, purpose, degree of connection between the objectives of the regulation itself and its application to specific properties. Blaesser navigates us through the wilderness of regulatory and constitutional principles that are applicable to recent growth management initiatives and, by extension, smart growth interventions.

The particular vulnerability that Blaesser sees for smart growth regulatory interventions relates the Supreme Court's evolution from its findings in the *Penn Central* case to its post-*Lucas* formulation that a taking may be found in cases where total deprivation caused by a regulation is not complete. Most garden-variety zoning regulations limit build-out potential and require no development in setback areas, for example. As more ambitious and exotic regulations come to fruition as a result of smart growth initiatives, however, such regulations may be subject to greater scrutiny and limitation from the courts. Traditional neighborhood development (TND), urban growth boundaries and other efforts to control the quality, amount and location of development may all require strategic examination through the lens of Blaesser's certainty and consistency doctrine.

Jerold Kayden (Chapter 9) views the scope of latitude provided in the regulatory envelope more generously than Blaesser. With confidence he tells us, "The Constitution of the United States neither prohibits nor requires smart growth." Kayden discusses the evolving framework of takings principles from the 1920s until today, looking at the classic legal cases and setting forth his own tests that can be applied to smart growth strategies. In Kayden's regulatory universe, euphoria may need to be jettisoned, but not optimism. Planners and designers may need to sharpen their "implementing instruments of smart growth," but they need not check their full stride as they attempt to reshape the built and natural environment.

Are the legal perspectives of Blaesser and Kayden completely contradictory? It is clear that Kayden will not accept a case where a regulation results in a 50 percent diminution of property value, but Blaesser will. Is the glass half full (Kayden) or half empty (Blaesser)? Politics and normative judgments about the role of property rights come into play here. Nonetheless, each perspective suggests that smart growth initiates something of value. Each offers some caution and ebullience.

Ethics and Equality

Ethics and planning have a long history. The earliest planners were reformers who believed in the transformative power of improved living conditions and recreational opportunities for city residents. Frederick Law Olmsted (1870) believed that parks could be places where city residents of all classes could recreate together. Indeed, parks could be great democratizers. By manipulating human surroundings, Olmsted believed, one could improve people's lives, be it in a park or in planned communities.

Almost 30 years later, Ebenezer Howard (1898) envisioned worker-owned cities surrounded by greenbelts that would move workers out of the crowded polluted cities into the countryside, combining the best of the city and the country. Implicit in Olmsted's and Howard's ideas, and in those of reformers who came after them, was the notion that improved living conditions meant improved lives. While environmental determinism may be a tricky and challenging ethical stand today, in the late-nineteenth century it was a commonly held idea.

Timothy Weiskel (Chapter 10) tells us that the very nature of the paradigm that planners use to evaluate growth strategies is flawed. He questions the myopia and arrogance of any growth theory—whether smart or stupid. He asks, who gets to call what smart? An altogether different paradigm is needed, according to Weiskel, one in which we implicitly recognize that there is pathology associated with any growth regime, whether smart or not, and particularly a regime that ignores, at its peril, the limits of environmental carrying capacity.

Weiskel's epistle is consistent with analysis by Timothy Beatley (1994), who implores planners to look at decisions about the use of land and, by extension, the nature of growth and development choices as inherently moral decisions. It is clear that both the planning profession and Western culture itself have been badly and arrogantly transgressing Weiskel's ecological principles, his version of ten commandments for responsible environmental behavior. Despite its initial baleful or Malthusian caste, Weiskel embraces the notions of Ben-Joseph and Nelson that rules and design guidelines matter a great deal. Our object should not be piety or absolution, but individual and collective action.

Social equity is another ethical issue, one that planners and designers sometimes neglect. Myron Orfield (1997), for example, is concerned that a move of resources to the suburbs takes away from the city. The increase of property wealth in the suburbs and the decrease of property wealth in the inner city and inner suburbs represent a shift in the tax base from some of the poorest communities to some of the most affluent. He argues that the forces of decline and sprawl are too large for individual cities and suburbs to confront alone, and suggests a regional agenda that promotes both community and stability.

Harvey Gantt (Chapter 11) shares his concerns about where ethical borders of equity are found after the application of smart growth, specifically in relation to leaving center-city neighborhoods behind. He supports better physical planning of places and neighborhoods, but sees both opportunity and danger within smart growth strategies. Will it go no further than a better way to organize sprawl?

Shouldn't it be more than well-planned streets? Shouldn't it deal with social development issues, not just the pattern of physical development?

Gantt, an architect and former mayor of Charlotte, North Carolina, knows that to grow intelligently in ways that encourage more diversity, fuel revitalization and promote infill development will take the "political will to encourage such a vision." If smart growth is unmasked as nothing more than traditional growth management repackaged, trouble will surely follow, particularly if its exclusionary attributes come into sharper focus. Without a broadened, equity-based mission, providing equal attention to both edge and center, smart growth within a metropolitan region may have fleeting, if any, impact on urban areas crying out for effective intervention.

Summary

We may witness the end of the smart growth movement at some point in the very near future. And, to borrow from T.S. Eliot, it may end with a whimper rather than a bang. We must be prepared for the reality that, however ambitiously conceived, smart growth may remain too all-inclusive, too elastic and perhaps too naive to be taken seriously.

On the other hand, even though Garden City was never built in complete accordance with Howard's vision, important elements and principles of Garden City do remain and are enshrined, at least in some form, in the planner's lexicon and consciousness. Principles of growth management have likewise been built upon in recent years, and have shown remarkable endurance. With this history in mind, consider the essays in this volume and be challenged by them. In time, smart growth could lead to another discernable layer in the U.S. landscape. Others in the future will be looking backward, and will surely judge just how smart this form of growth actually was.

References

American Planning Association (APA). 1998. *The principles of smart development.* Report no. 479. Chicago, IL: American Planning Association Planning Advisory Service.

Beatley, Timothy. 1994. *Ethical land use: Principles of policy and planning.* Baltimore, MD: Johns Hopkins University Press.

Bellamy, Edward. 1982. *Looking backward, 2000–1887.* New York, NY: Modern Library College Editions.

Ewing, Reid. 1998. *Best development practices: A primer for smart growth.* Washington, DC: Smart Growth Network: International City/County Management Association.

Garreau, Joel. 1991. *Edge city: Life on the new frontier.* New York, NY: Doubleday.

Howard, Ebenezer. [1898]1998. *Tomorrow: A peaceful path to real reform.* London: Routledge/Thoemmes Press.

Katz, Bruce. 2001. Welcome to the exit ramp economy. *Boston globe* (May 13).

Krieger, Alex. 1999. Beyond the rhetoric of smart growth. *Architecture* 88 (6):53-61.

Miara, Jim. 2000. Fueling sprawl. *Urban land* 78–79; 109.

Mitchell, William. 1999. *E-topia: Urban life, Jim—but not as we know it.* Cambridge, MA: MIT Press.

Olmsted, Frederick Law. [1870]1971. Public parks and the enlargement of towns. In *Civilizing American cities: Writings on city landscapes*, S.B. Sutton, ed. New York, NY: Da Capo Press.

Orfield, Myron. 1997. *Metropolitics: A regional agenda for community and stability.* Washington, DC: Brooking Institution and Cambridge, MA: Lincoln Institute of Land Policy.

Porter, Douglas R. 1998. The states: Growing smarter? In *ULI on the future—Smart growth: Economy, community, environment*, 28-35. Washington, DC: Urban Land Institute.

Putnam, Robert D. 2000. *Bowling alone: The collapse and revival of American community.* New York, NY: Simon & Schuster.

Weiss, Jonathan. 2000. Civic participation and smart growth: Transforming sprawl into a broader sense of citizenship. Funders' Network for Smart Growth and Livable Communities. Translation paper no. 4. Washington, DC: George Washington University Center on Sustainability and Regional Growth (November).

2

Dolores Hayden

What Is Suburbia?

Naming the Layers in the

Landscape, 1820–2000

What Is Suburbia?

Since the early nineteenth century, suburbs have been part of the process of urbanization, growing along with the crowded centers of cities. For almost 200 years, Americans have idealized life in single-family homes in natural settings, while paradoxically creating more and more urbanized landscapes to contain these demands for private space. The production of millions of model suburban houses—involving massive investments by the federal government, huge expense to individual families, and extraordinary profits for private real estate developers—has configured the landscapes where most Americans live and work. Recent debates about the costs of sprawl in dispersed metropolitan configurations reveal both a new critique and persistent attraction to low-density residential settlement.[1] Americans keep reinventing the idealized outer reaches of countrified suburbia, while older suburban layers are often dismissed as having "urban" problems.

Anyone who wants to write a new history has to ask, what is American suburbia? A demographer might answer, "the non-center city areas of metropolitan regions," but that is a negative definition, subordinating suburbia to inner city. Suburbia is, first of all, where most Americans now live. It is the dominant U.S. cultural landscape, combining cherished natural and built environments, yards and single-family houses. Second, suburbia is where millions of square feet of commercial and residential real estate are financed and built. (Although currently it is abysmally planned, designed and constructed, this has not always been the case.) Third, suburbia is the location of most of the unpaid labor of nurturing and parenting, reflecting both social and environmental practices. Fourth, suburbia is where the majority of American voters now live. Understanding how existing suburbs have been organized, financed, designed, constructed, marketed and inhabited is central to calculating the prospects for ending sprawl.

Layer by layer, the metropolitan regions of the United States have filled out with suburban construction, some in the form of individual houses, some in tracts of houses, some in planned and designed communities. The United States is home to diverse suburbs—blue-collar and elite, bare and leafy, WASP and African American, and Chinese American. But is there a larger suburban ideal, uniting diverse residents? The suburban house is booming. The average size of a new one was 800 square feet in 1950, 1,500 in 1970, 2,190 in 1998 (U.S. Bureau of the Census 2000; Separated by Design 2000). Some analysts say the suburb as settle-

---

1   The literature is vast. Sharpe and Wallock (1994) is a review essay with responses from the humanities. See Transit Cooperative Research Program (1998) for an extensive review of social science and professional literature. Overviews of suburban history include Hayden (1984), Jackson (1985), Fishman (1987), and Palen (1995).

Photograph © Alex S. MacLean/Landslides.

ment form is thriving also. Others claim the suburban frontier is closed, and rush to find new terms to describe the current spatial configuration: out-town, ruburbia, techno-burb, the galactic city, postsuburb, exopolis.[2]

Do we need new words? Let's keep the term *suburbia* and rename its layers. One can trace the history of suburban construction over seven eras. The Borderlands began about 1820, the Picturesque Enclaves about 1850, the Streetcar Buildouts around 1870, the Mail-Order and Self-Built Suburbs about 1900, the Sitcom Suburbs about 1950, the Edge Nodes around 1970, and the E-Space Fringes about 1990. All of these layers continue to exist, and many are still being built, in the metropolitan regions of 2002.

Most histories of the suburb are categorized by transportation—railroad, streetcar, auto—but the older transit networks are often gone today. This analysis shifts to a cultural landscape approach, stressing land use and using aerial photography as documentation. Most histories of suburbia deal with male perspectives on middle- and upper-middle-class suburbs. This essay compares working-class suburban configurations of house and yard with affluent ones, and looks at how both have been presented in popular culture. It also asks how women and children have experienced suburban spaces.

The dream for suburbia is house, nature and community. Model houses have been idealized at some times, and model communities at others, but most people hope for a house and yard, as well as a connection to a public social world. Model houses are often compromised by context; model towns often fail because of expense and social conflict. Perhaps the most common problem is that individual houses have often been promoted as if they were situated in model communities, when they were not. Similarly, tracts of houses have often been hyped as perfect towns, complete with appropriate public facilities and infrastructure, when they were not towns at all. While many intellectuals and designers have sneered at suburban residents as credulous, this is a simplistic, disrespectful response. Ordinary people are hopeful about their family and community life, and they struggle to supply what is lacking in order to make places work. Disentangling the strands of suburban development leads to a clearer sense of which traditions are negative and which are positive.

In my 1984 book, *Redesigning the American Dream: The Future of Housing, Work, and Family Life*, I argued that by the 1950s the American suburban house

---

[2] Terms suggested by Paul Goldberger, Leo Marx, Robert Fishman, Peirce Lewis, Jon Teaford, Edward Soja, respectively.

had become a private utopia, replacing the model town that had engaged many Americans' hopes a century earlier. In the mid-nineteenth century, developer Llewellyn Haskell promoted his expensive suburban enclave at Llewellyn Park, New Jersey, as "an Eden . . . away from the common haunts of Man" (Henderson 1987). But by the 1890s, when streetcar suburb builder Samuel E. Gross of Chicago depicted an angel with a sword labeled justice delivering a small cottage to a workman with a dinner pail, heaven was a modest house. The theme of a working-class suburban house as heaven is picked up again in D.J. Waldie's poetic evocation of Lakewood, California, entitled *Holy Land*.[3]

Perhaps middle-class Americans held on to the dream of the exclusive model community until World War II, but in the aftermath, a scramble for houses resulted. In 1946, a cover of the *New Yorker* showed a large neo-Colonial house descending on pink clouds to an affluent husband, wife and child. (But not everyone was in heaven—outside the back door, an African American maid encountered a Fuller brush salesman.) Currently, middle-class residents are being wooed back to a revival of faith in the model suburb, promoted with zealous architectural determinism. In 1992, new urbanist architects Andres Duany and Elizabeth Plater-Zyberk (1992) announced "the second coming of the American small town."[4] Michael Eisner of Disney predicted grateful people will exclaim, "Thank God for Celebration!" (Frantz and Collins 1999, 8). Yet Celebration, the new town in Florida, is a highly publicized example of the difficulties of creating a model community by building neotraditional Greek Revival and Victorian houses. Controversies about its schools and its rigid management style have filled the popular press, while most of the workers in nearby Disney World cannot afford to live there (Drew 1998; Rymer 1996). A brief look at each era of U.S. suburban development reveals architectural forms for which Americans may feel nostalgia, but it also situates the larger spatial and economic patterns behind the current concern about sprawl.

Borderlands, 1820

Beginning about 1820, some households sought a more rural lifestyle than growing urban centers like New York or Boston could offer. Historians John Stilgoe (1988) and Henry Binford (1984) have defined the borderlands as places where families might choose to set up housekeeping in pastoral settings outside the

---

3   D.J. Waldie's *Holy Land* (1996) is 316 prose segments, some as short as a sentence, about the author's life in Lakewood, from his boyhood to his present job as a city official there.
4   See also their book, with Jeff Speck, *Suburban Nation* (2000).

Borderland landscape in the foreground, with commuters approaching a ferry dock, in this "View of New York, from Weehawken," a steel engraving from a drawing by W.H. Bartlett, in Nathaniel Parker Willis, *American Scenery, Vol. II* (London: G. Virtue, 1840). Image courtesy of Beinecke Rare Book and Manuscript Library, Yale University.

growing cities. The city commute was possible by steamboat, on horseback or in a private carriage, and later by railroad. All classes lived in the borderlands, but the rich had two houses, one rural, one urban, while the poor were farmers or farm workers with small rural homes. Only middle-class men and women wanted to have it all, country and city, with just one house. They struggled with the difficult commutes while popularizing life among the trees and flowers, removed from the pollution, epidemics and economic stresses of the city under industrial capitalism.

Borderland families had two inspirational leaders who wrote best sellers. Andrew Jackson Downing, son of a nurseryman, built his practice along the Hudson River as a landscape consultant in Newburg, New York, helping to define the picturesque styles of country homes he felt were best suited to borderland scenery and life. His *Treatise on the Theory and Practice of Landscape Gardening…with Remarks on Rural Architecture* illustrated how to convert an ordinary farm into a gentleman's estate with 10 years of planting and work (Downing 1841, 92–93). *Cottage Residences* elaborated the architectural choices in 1842.

Catharine Beecher, author of a *Treatise on Domestic Economy* in 1842, and coauthor of *The American Woman's Home* in 1869, also wrote for a borderland audience. She urged women to take charge of the suburban house and family, which she called "the home church of Jesus Christ," by instructing them to stay home and master efficient house design and gardening, as well as the spiritual nurturing of large families. The gendered, pious approach to middle-class suburban life, first laid out by these two authors, with man nurturing the land and woman the family, has remained influential, although women complained of "Lonelyville."[5] But the advice-givers could not solve one problem of the borderland, the advance of the city. Once-remote houses in pastoral locations in 1820 were invaded by industries and their workers, as well as crowded by the shanties of squatters, who might keep goats or pigs on lawns, and steal their middle-class neighbors' timber.[6]

Picturesque Enclaves, 1850

Borderland values of scenery and family were codified and expanded when landscape architects and architects began to design entire new suburban communities as picturesque enclaves. Beginning in the 1850s, romantic Gothic Revival and Greek Revival houses appeared on winding roads laid out in lush landscaping. Often there was centrally reserved parkland, and some shared community activities and rituals took place in the common space. Idealism about the sanctity of the model suburb connects enclaves to other mid-nineteenth century town-making efforts whose founders believed that building a model community led to the reform of society. In 1840, Emerson commented, "Not a reading man but has a draft of a new community in his waistcoat pocket," referring to communitarian socialists such as the Shakers, the Oneida Perfectionists, or the followers of Charles Fourier at the North American Phalanx, near Red Bank, New Jersey, or at Brook Farm, in West Roxbury, Massachusetts. All of these communitarians thought of themselves as building "patent office models of the good society" because they believed that the founders of other new towns would copy their example (Hayden 1976, 8–31). Many early suburbs were conceived with the same religious fervor and environmental determinism. At Llewellyn Park, New Jersey, Haskell, the developer, was himself a religious Perfectionist, and his architect, Alexander

---

5   For an estimate of Beecher's influence, see Hayden (1977), and for the debates about these issues, see Hayden (1981).
6   Frederick Law Olmsted, letter of 1860, quoted in Fishman (1987, 120–121).

Picturesque enclave with shared common space. "May Festival at Llewellyn Park, Orange, N.J., on May 30, 1860" from *New York Illustrated News*, June 23, 1860.

Jackson Davis, had a simultaneous commission for a Fourierist Phalanx in New Jersey (Wilson 1979).

Unlike the communitarians' towns, or the Methodists' camp meetings, which breathed religious excitement, the early picturesque enclaves were rich (E. Weiss 1987). Llewellyn Park, in Orange, New Jersey, designed in the 1850s, transported wealthy businessmen, social reformers and religious enthusiasts from city centers and placed them closer to nature. Davis, two decades earlier, had produced a guide to *Rural Residences*, including an "American cottage," a "farmer's house," and a "villa" with wife on the porch and husband wheeling the infant stroller (Davis 1837; Wilson 1979, 79–90; Schuyler 1986, 149–166).[7] When Haskell first hired him to remodel an older building, Davis got on so well with his client that the job turned into a model community. Haskell's mountainous land had views, cliffs and ponds. And Haskell and his friends—businessmen, social reformers, religious idealists—had the funds to work with the terrain to achieve palatial Victorian comfort with full-time, live-in servants. Llewellyn Park residents cele-

---

7   Davis worked with Downing on both publications and commissions.

brated May Day, accompanied by reporters, with an elaborate ceremony in their central park.[8] But true to many model suburbs, they never finished building the library and other community facilities promised at the start.

Enclaves were promoted in newspapers, popular magazines, novels and plays as models of American life. When Frederick Law Olmsted designed Riverside, Illinois, in 1869, he achieved a most influential design despite a flat, swampy tract of land, because he added 32,000 deciduous trees and 47,000 shrubs. What was not reported in the papers was Olmsted's sour view that his clients were perpetuating a "regular flyaway speculation," with the promoters stealing $500,000 from the city of Chicago to cover overruns and then going under in the Panic of 1873 (Fishman 1987, 130). Thirty years later, that suburb had filled out. Similar landscaped enclaves with winding streets, designed by the Olmsted office for communities from Atlanta to Buffalo, began to set the standard for many other architects, landscape architects and builders throughout the country for the next 50 or 60 years, although often in reduced form.

Enclaves for the affluent continued to be developed, some noted for their snobbishness as much as for their scenery. In 1886, architect Bruce Price designed the resort of Tuxedo Park, New York, with massive stone gates and an exclusive clubhouse on 6,000 private acres surrounded by a barbed wire fence, eight feet high and 24 miles long, guarded by private police. Price's daughter was Emily Post, prolific author on etiquette, who called it an "American rural community" (Post 1911). In the age of the automobile, Palos Verdes, California, was designed by the younger Olmsted, providing Spanish Colonial-style architecture on dramatic hills overlooking the Pacific Ocean, with golf club and nursery school. While celebrating Mexican feast days as local rituals, residents saw no irony in adopting deed restrictions to prohibit purchasers of Mexican descent (Marsh 1990, 172–173). In Kansas City, Missouri, J.C. Nichols developed the Country Club District with "1,000 acres restricted," prohibiting billboards and African American residents (Worley 1990, 78).

Historian John Archer suggests that early British colonial suburbs became sites for the "establishment and augmentation of a person's individual identity," architecturally celebrating the alienation of wealth and privilege from the process

---

8   Short Hills, New Jersey, was a similar effort, a model suburb with extensive parkland and expensive architecture developed by Stewart Hartshorn, a man who made his fortune as the inventor of the rolling window shade, and believed that Adam and Eve could have walked in the lovely precincts of his town. For additional background on British and U.S. designs during this era, see Archer (1983).

of production, although dependent upon it" (Archer 1997, 52–53). Robert Fishman (1987, 4), who has also studied many of the English precedents for American suburbs in this era, puts it more simply as the "triumphant assertion of middle-class values" accompanied by "the alienation of the middle classes from the industrial world they themselves were creating." It is a complex task to unravel the racism and snobbery of certain enclaves from the positive aspects of spaces designed with a picturesque aesthetic in mind, respecting the natural landscape, rocks, hills, rivers, lakes, wetlands and wildlife. As Mary Corbin Sies (1997) has observed, residents' effective strategies for the preservation of physical character (strategies many other Americans can learn from) were often accompanied by extremely narrow views of social coherence, with negative lessons to teach.

Streetcar Buildouts, 1870

From the 1870s on, streetcar buildouts provided a cut-rate version of the suburban ideal (Wood 1910). A natural outgrowth of the omnibus, the horsecar and the electric streetcar, these new suburbs were linear developments along expanding transit lines of single-family, two-family, and three-family dwellings, with some commercial and apartment structures. Builders marketed these dwellings to second-generation Americans, children of immigrants who had grown up in inner-city tenements. Construction proceeded on a modest scale with builders' consensus about what looked good—in New England, generally narrow lots, high lot coverage, long two- or three-story, wood frame dwellings, gable end to the street. In the Midwest and West, smaller cottages or bungalows of a single story were often preferred.

Eugene Wood (1910) explored the contradictions of quiet streetcar suburbs built out to the maximum, and crowded commutes. These dwellings were never as separated from waged and unwaged work as the enclaves pretended to be. Multiple wage workers in families included women and children; multiple units included arrangements for kin and boarders; wives also cared for chickens and grew food. At the same time, sweat equity was part of the deal. Owner-builders were common in some cities. Bands of settlement were graded by income and available transport. Often ethnic clubs and churches—Irish American, Polish American, Italian American—provided social centers. Involvement by trained architects in streetcar suburbs was minimal, but city governments' planners and engineers started to supply infrastructure (water pipes, gas light or electricity) and think about annexation.

WHAT IS SUBURBIA?

Streetcar suburb of multifamily houses in the Fair Haven area of New Haven, Connecticut.
Photograph © Alex S. MacLean/Landslides.

Today the streetcar suburbs may not be thought of as suburbs because of their density and closeness to the center of the city. People may call them "the old neighborhood." They vary in form and age in different parts of the country. In Boston, the owner-builders were often operating on a very small scale, producing two or three structures in a career. Samuel Gross in Chicago operated on a larger scale, responsible for tens of thousands of houses at varying prices, which could be purchased on long-term plans. Detroit was somewhere in between.[9] In San Francisco, in the Sunset district, an unusual streetcar suburb was made out of streetcars themselves as older models were taken out of service and converted into funky, bottom-of-the-market dwellings (Reese 1999).

Whatever the city, the small front gardens of streetcar suburbs were often intensively cultivated. Different ethnic neighborhoods could be identified by their

---

9   For Boston, see Warner (1972) and Edel, Sclar and Luria (1984); for Chicago, see Wright (1980); and for Detroit, see Zunz (1982). Warner notes the land speculators operated on a bigger scale than the builders in Boston.

Truck loaded with parts of a ready-cut house, Pacific Portable Construction Co., Inc., Los Angeles, about 1915. Photograph courtesy of Dolores Hayden.

plantings, and the varied delights of their kitchen gardens contrast with the exotic landscapes of the elite enclaves (Hayden 1995, 35). Where streetcar suburbs have been well maintained, they offer livable patterns of mixed use worth reexamining for their compact land use and good public transit. They also have offered options for the elderly and the three-generation family unmatched in other models.

Mail-Order and Self-Built Suburbs, 1900

By the turn of the century, customers could order a house from a catalogue, and here the mail-order and self-built suburbs were born. Customers first picked out plans, and then had every last piece of lumber, every nail and door knob, shipped to the site. With the rise of companies producing mail-order houses, such as Sears, Aladdin or Pacific Ready-Cut Houses, the U.S. house was disconnected from questions of site and neighborhood (Gowans 1986). In the beginning, companies hoped to appeal to do-it-yourself homeowners. But these kits were hard to put together, so many frustrated homeowners hired carpenters to help them do the job. Many companies also began preassembling discreet parts of the house, such as built-in cabinets or bathrooms, to make the job easier. Sometimes they also offered to send a crew to construct the house from the parts in 30 days (Hayden 1995, 128–132).

Other homeowners stuck to self-building, sometimes for lack of resources, building the place over time, with scavenged materials if necessary. An African American suburb, Chagrin Falls Park, outside of Cleveland, was a source of pride to those who put it together, despite the lack of infrastructure. One resident said, "I think I bettered my condition….I had nice, fresh air, and you could have vegetables and a garden" (Wiese 1999; Harris 1991).

In cities like Los Angeles, which developed 1,200 miles of streetcar lines by 1915, the largest public transit system in the country, the dense New England and Midwestern style of streetcar suburb was transformed into a giant land sale, setting the stage for the mail-order and self-built houses. Streetcar companies, many of them privately held, were also often in the land business. Subdividers in LA held huge barbecues with slabs of roasted meat to attract potential buyers to auctions of lots in empty terrain. In Chicago, developers offered circus tents with polka bands. Wagons drew up loaded with kegs of beer.

Buyers then decided how to build on their new suburban lots, and many chose the mail-order option. Spanish Colonial might rise next to a Craftsman bungalow or a New England Cape. The mail-order manufacturers recognized the loosening of neighborhood bonds here, and formed clubs that held occasional picnics for their customers. Some of them also paid commissions to customers who recruited new buyers for the company. There were also some new communities constructed entirely of mail-order houses, including company towns, boom towns and mining towns, but overall, the most powerful effect of the mail-order and self-built suburbs was the dissolution of the older, denser patterns of transit-related suburbs, both in physical form and in the availability of public transit. Not only were they stylistically diverse. Once lots were sold, many streetcar companies stopped running the transit lines. The automobile was increasing in popularity, capable of carrying people to new strip shopping centers.

Between 1929 and 1946, due to the Depression and World War II, very few new houses or new suburbs were built. In this time, however, the federal government became involved in housing, through Herbert Hoover's efforts (as secretary of commerce and then as president) to promote home ownership as a big business strategy for economic recovery from the Depression. Hoover's Commerce Department supported Better Homes in America, Inc. (Wright 1981, 197–198; Radford 1996, 51–53).[10] By 1930, this was a coalition of more than 7,000 local chapters composed of bankers, builders and manufacturers lobbying for govern-

---

10   Radford emphasizes Hoover's interest in standardization.

ment support of private developers' home-building efforts, the start of an American growth machine.

Following Hoover, the Roosevelt era saw the establishment of new town programs in the New Deal, as well as public housing legislation, but they were never as influential. After a federal plan for a model town to house war workers (designed by Eero Saarinen, George How, Louis Kahn and Oscar Stonorov) was defeated by the real estate lobby, self-built suburbs grew by default around the Willow Run plant in Michigan, where Ford produced bombers in World War II. Similar self-building occurred around naval bases in San Diego (Peterson 2002). By the mid-1940s, realtors were busily discrediting public construction of shelter as un-American, and promoting government subsidies for private housing development as essential to democracy. In their book, *Picture Windows*, Rosalyn Baxandall and Elizabeth Ewen (2000, 87–116) discuss the heavy lobbying by bankers, realtors and builders behind the hearings on housing dominated by Senator Joseph McCarthy in 1947 and 1948. McCarthy developed his sledgehammer style hassling proponents of public housing and planned towns as socialists and communists.

Sitcom Suburbs, 1950

Sitcom suburbs of the late 1940s and 1950s were constructed with multiple federal government supports: subsidized mortgages for buyers, subsidized financing for developers, and subsidized highways to reach the houses. These suburbs appeared at the same time as national television programs, and many included television sets built into living room walls. Cultural critics such as Lewis Mumford carped at the uniformity, but from the late 1940s on, vast developments of single-family houses on small lots offered the cheapest shelter available to white, male-headed families.

Mass-produced sitcom suburbs, created in large numbers for veterans returning from World War II, had few community facilities, jobs or public transit options. They resembled earlier, smaller tracts of the mail-order and self-built suburbs that required commuting by automobile. What was new was their urban scale. The first Levittown, for example, totaled about 17,000 houses, or 55,000 people. Lakewood, California, was even larger. The new developments were produced by far larger corporations that controlled vast tracts of land, worked with the federal government and sold basic, small houses to consumers, while describing themselves as community builders because they built a few swimming pools or small commercial centers (M. Weiss 1987).

WHAT IS SUBURBIA?

Sitcom suburban houses on Cove Brook Road, West Haven, Connecticut.
Photograph © Alex S. MacLean/Landslides.

While the scale and speed of production by nonunion workers in such suburbs suggested the industrial might of postwar America, the designs were nostalgic Cape Cod cottages or ranches.[11] Working-class residents were mixed by ethnicity and religion more than before—Italian American, Polish American and Russian American; Catholic, Protestant and Jewish—but all were white. Racial segregation, always part of the suburban experience, now was enforced by government loan policies and local bankers' redlining. So was gender discrimination in lending. The long-term economic effects of racial and gender exclusion were heightened by the vast scale of new tracts, and by their promotion in mass culture. Fifty years later, households headed by persons of color and women still lagged behind in their rates of home ownership.

In 1948, William Levitt made his famous comment about male homeowners who would be converting attics into spare bedrooms and mowing the lawns: "No man who has a house and lot can be a communist. He has too much to do" (Larrabee 1948). Historian Barbara Kelly (1993) has documented the way

---

11 For a more detailed analysis of the methods of construction in this era, from the steel and glass designs of the case study houses to Levitt's reliance on traditional materials, see Hayden (1989, 197–211).

Levittown residents added to their homes, echoing the activity of the self-built suburbs earlier. Now, however, there was less flexibility about multiple units and family types. The three-generation family was split. Older members remained in inner-city neighborhoods as renters; adult children were scattered into new suburbs.

In the television sitcoms of the era, only one kind of model family was presented as suitable for one kind of model house. The family had an employed dad, a stay-at-home mom and a traditional house on a suburban street in *Leave It to Beaver*, *Ozzie and Harriet*, or *Father Knows Best*. Recent films such as *Pleasantville* and *The Truman Show* satirize overly controlled places, neo-Colonial clapboard houses, neat lawns framed by picket fences, moms in high heels and dresses making dinner, and racial exclusion. Television reached all households, even the families who didn't get the houses, and because of this, many groups excluded from the sitcom suburbs of the 1950s, and from the public subsidies that supported them, still saw the house as an emblem of belonging and upward mobility. The sitcom suburb was federal policy, backed by intense corporate lobbying and reinforced by product placement in sitcoms, as well as thousands of television commercials that used the model house as the setting for all sorts of goods, from detergents to diapers, dishwashers to Dodge cars. The economic goals of Better Homes in America, Inc., and all of the lobbyists behind McCarthy had been realized.

Interplay between real developers and the makers of sitcoms and movies in this era is fascinating. In *Bachelor in Paradise*, a bachelor (Bob Hope) heads for a California tract to write an analysis of its social life, sure he will hate it. By the end of the film, he has married the only single woman within miles and moved in for good. In *Mr. Blandings Builds His Dream House* (Hodgins 1946), an advertising executive (Cary Grant) tires of New York and moves his family to an isolated, custom built, neo-Colonial suburban house, where he is overcharged for everything. (Because Eric Hodgins wrote for *Fortune* magazine, it is quite possible his novel, and the subsequent film, were meant to play alongside the McCarthy housing hearings, where private builders stressed the impossibility of making postwar housing with unionized construction trades, as well as attacked the "communistic" nature of public housing.) More than 70 model Blandings "dream houses" were constructed around the country and raffled off as publicity for the film (Jurca 1998). In Kansas City, the developer J.C. Nichols demonstrated he could build the same house for less than Blandings paid. Orders poured in.

Meanwhile, Hodgins wrote a sequel but it was never filmed. The hero gave up commuting and moved his family back to midtown Manhattan, where Blandings could walk to his job in an ad agency selling dog food and whiskey.

WHAT IS SUBURBIA?

Edge node of new office buildings and a mall adjacent to I-95, Stamford, Connecticut.
Photograph © Alex S. MacLean/Landslides.

Unfortunately, most suburbanites couldn't afford this option. They were stuck with the sitcom, which cast them as Mr. Homeowner and Mrs. Consumer. Houses kept getting a little larger, and many families tried to move up as they discovered the "mansion subsidy," tax deductions for mortgage interest that rose with the cost and size of the house. Estimated at $81 billion in 1994, the mansion subsidy remains larger than the annual budget of the U.S. Department of Housing and Urban Development (Kemper 1994).

Edge Nodes, 1960

From the 1960s on, private developers responded to the federally supported infrastructure of interstate highways, and the lack of planned centers, public space and public facilities in sitcom suburbs, by large-scale construction of commercial real estate—the basis of the edge nodes. Malls and offices sprouted adjacent to interstate off-ramps in areas hard to locate and often with names such as "intersection of 7 and 84." Terms such as *out-town* or *edge city* did not explain these places. Perhaps *taxopolis* would have been better. Historians have shown these were usually at the edge of the suburban ring because federal tax policies between 1954 and 1986 offered accelerated depreciation for new commercial real estate in greenfield locations. Developers received huge tax write-offs for "every type of income-producing structure," including motels, fast-food restaurants, offices, rental apartments and, of course, shopping centers. As Hanchett (1996, 1099) notes, "Throughout the mid-1950s, developers had sought locations *within* growing suburban areas. Now shopping centers began appearing in the cornfields *beyond* the edge of existing development." This lucrative tax write-off cost the federal government about $750 to $850 million per year in the late 1960s. Accelerated depreciation also encouraged cheap construction and discouraged adequate maintenance.

Edge nodes brought the rise of the mall and the destruction of many Main Streets. Nodes often spilled over into older arterials nearby, where loose zoning and automotive uses (billboards, fast food, gas stations, auto sales, motels) had prevailed since the 1920s. Site plans were scaled to the truck or car, never to the pedestrian. Access by public transit was minimal, and routes often reinforced segregation by race and class (Cohen 1996).

Over time edge nodes added more building types—office parks, industrial parks, big-box discount stores and power centers (groups of big boxes), plus outlet malls trying to look like villages, cineplexes and freeway churches. Building was cheap; depreciation was accelerated; obsolescence was rapid. Less and less was local. Businesses were increasingly tied to national or international chains, part of an expanding global economy, often requiring airport access as well as access by truck. Warehouselike buildings were dictated by management protocols about facilities having nothing to do with the towns where they operated (Easterling 1999).

Although they have become the most visible of U.S. suburban landscapes, edge nodes have few defenders. Those who do speak in their favor, such as Joel Garreau (1991), tend to idealize them as a temporary, rough frontier of economic growth. The presence of housing in edge nodes was often the result of a developer filling in leftover sites with affordable housing units. Nearby freeways made many of them undesirable. Unlike all of the earlier patterns, almost no one chose to call edge nodes home if there were other residential options. Millions who worked in edge nodes refused to live in places like Tysons Corner, Virginia, or Schaumburg,

What Is Suburbia?

E-fringe agricultural land subdivided for large-lot houses, Durham, Connecticut.
Photograph © Alex S. MacLean/Landslides.

Illinois, an environment documented by photographer Bob Thrall with the ironic title, *The New American Village* (1999). Instead, many Americans chose to drive to residences located even farther away, on the rural fringe (Daniels 1999).

E-Space Fringes, 1990

Sometime early in the twentieth century, starting with the mail-order suburb, and continuing with the sitcom suburb, Americans began to separate the house from its neighborhood, and to idealize the house itself. By the 1990s, consumers were focused on the house. Although jobs had moved to the edge nodes, cheap gas and subsidized freeways meant that workers could commute outside those nodes, scattering into the rural areas beyond, creating a new pattern I have named e-space fringe. The arrival of digital technologies (e-space) made it easier for the two-worker family to arrange to be in a remote location (Wolf 1999).[12] Houses might include a home office, as some workers were freed by telecommuting. Some might include two home offices. Even rural states such as Vermont have been affected by fringe development so vast it overpowers small towns and rural landscapes (Campoli, Humstone and MacLean 2001). Affluent Americans consumed a staggering portion of the world's resources to sustain larger and larger houses and the patterns of consumption they imply, with or without the home offices.

The rural fringe appeared to be a revival of the borderland aesthetic of the 1820s with its vision of pastoral life in the countryside, now supported by digital technologies. In the mid-1980s, many feminists thought that suburban housing and neighborhood spaces might be transformed by the addition of day care, elderly care, home offices and accessory units. Each of these programmatic changes responded to women's increasing involvement in the paid labor force, and the predominance of new family types, including the two-worker family and the single-parent family, with some greater flexibility than the traditional neighborhood of isolated suburban houses provided. Change did happen in Europe, with city complexes like the Frauen-Werk-Stadt of Vienna (Hayden 2002).

Only a few new American housing projects considered the need for new service elements in multifamily design. Instead, single-family houses continued to be built on the fringe, because jobs boomed in suburban office parks, malls and factories. More families hired poor women of color as nannies and maids (Ehrenreich 2000). Corporate cleaning services such as Merry Maids and Maids International paid the minimum wage while charging about $25 per worker per hour for domestic service. Advocates of digital technology touted the rural fringe as modern, but its patterns rested on a Victorian architecture of gender, on low-paid servants or unpaid female housework and male yard work. It was as old as Downing and Beecher, corsets and bustles, wing collars and frock coats.

The original borderland was Lonelyville to many women, and so is the new rural fringe. As women have worked for pay outside the home, their social contacts have increased, but children have less contact with parents, and husbands with wives. The nuclear family of the sitcom suburbs fragmented as American men and women were working long hours to pay for more remote houses, and for the cars to reach houses on former farmland or woods. Often, huge new houses lacked any design quality in their arrangements. And with mansionization came tear-downs, as older houses, some of them historic landmarks, were torn down to make way

---

12 Wolf calls workers completely free to locate anywhere "lone eagles."

for houses three or four times larger on existing, desirable sites in rural areas or older suburban neighborhoods.

A second trend has been to create new enclaves in the fringe—large-scale suburban developments, most of them expensive, some of them gated, some of them designed in historicist styles. These are greenfield developments, organized by many of the same large developers who have produced more conventional subdivisions in the past. What attracts them to the fringe is the lower cost of land, and the availability of large amounts of land not under local regulation.

Why have borderland ideas and enclaves lasted? Many pastoral dreams were revived in the 1950s, as exurbanites commuting on special club cars from towns like Westport, Connecticut, to Madison Avenue looked for ways to sell television programs and consumer goods to residents of sitcom suburbs (Spectorsky 1955). The producers and ad men liked to think of themselves as superior to the residents of mass-produced sitcom suburbs. The media men thought they were lifestyle pioneers, living two lives at once, having dynamic city jobs and country homes, cultural stimulation and natural beauty—the best of both worlds, no compromises. They passed these values on in their work, but their borderland scenarios always rested on servants or an unpaid mom. The borderland life also rested on belief in access to an endless amount of available land, and on access to new technologies of transportation and communication to overcome the friction of distance. With each successive generation, and each mile from the inner city to the outer fringe, this lifestyle became less tenable socially, ecologically and physically.

Back to Borderlands and Enclaves, or Beyond?

Many of the spatial conventions and social expectations of the nineteenth and early twentieth centuries remain to the present day—layers tangled in memory, experience and manners, as well as in the images of popular culture and the pronouncements of architects and urban planners. In the first half of the nineteenth century, residents, designers and pattern book writers forged enduring ideals of romantic houses set in picturesque terrain inhabited by elite, exclusive communities. The ideals were made three-dimensional, first for individual families, then for affluent enclaves between 1820 and 1860. When suburban houses were also mass-produced for working families in streetcar buildouts, mail-order suburbs and sitcom suburbs, they lost some of their snob appeal. Cultural critics sneered, but modest houses and yards made ordinary, working-class residents also feel connected to nature, able to rear their families, and able to form ties with other suburban residents, despite rather limited natural settings. Because of sweat equity, minimal places became more comfortable. While the working-class patterns are physically spare, they seem far more savvy, recognizing economic constraints and the multiple connections between home and work. They suggest how to go beyond the borderland and the enclave, rather than back to them.

Any analysis of the costs of sprawl must rest on detailed economic history and substantial knowledge of how the layers of suburban America have been constructed, as well as how the work of reproduction has been accomplished. Without such historical analysis, it is difficult to weigh the strengths and weaknesses of new proposals as well. Architects and developers often suggest today that new enclaves are the best way to solve suburban planning problems because they offer the fewest constraints.[13] Density in new enclaves is fine; so are good proportions and narrow streets, but not privatized gentility, high prices and greenfield locations.

Less flashy projects include far more economic savvy, such as Concord Village, a Hope VI project in Indianapolis, administered by Eugene Jones as the executive director of the Indianapolis Housing Authority, and designed by Clyde Woods of Indianapolis and Tise, Hurwitz and Diamond of Boston (Epp 1996; Eckert 1996). As part of a broad local economic development strategy, planners, architects and organizers trained small contractors to construct sections of the project, house by house. They worked at the scale of the streetcar and self-built suburbs in an African American neighborhood. Instead of contracting the whole project to a large builder, they taught and enabled small builders to create new one- and two-family units to fit in with an existing older neighborhood in scale and streetscape. For the professionals involved, such as project architects Daniel Glenn and Olon Dotson, it meant tough, unglamorous work, with lots of organizing. But they recognized the multiple dimensions of housing as a part of economic production as well as reproduction, and they recognized the importance of connecting physically to an existing community.

The history of U.S. suburbia is the history of the search for the triple dream: house, yard and community. Millions of families got houses and yards, although working-class families have often had to build their houses, or earn extra cash at home to hold onto them. The getting of community has been more uncertain. Middle-class community space is often in better supply than working-class community space. But everywhere, real community is constructed by people, not

---

13 Thoughtful works by designers include Calthorpe (1993), Calthorpe and Fulton (2001), Duany, Plater-Zyberk and Speck (2000), Garvin (1996), Girling and Helphand (1994), Rowe (1991), Southworth (1997), and Stern and Massengale (1981).

developers. Designers can offer public space that supports or constrains community, but there is no magic connection, no perfect town where architecture makes the better society. That was an idea of the 1840s, a time when designers also thought the perfect prison could eliminate crime, and the perfect hospital could cure mental illness.

Political Implications

Where there are existing houses (hard won), existing public infrastructure and existing community networks (forged over years of propinquity), it makes sense to nurture and protect older suburbs, to infill and rehabilitate rather than to design again. Communities of activists and voters are essential to this place-based process. It is time to repair each layer in the dispersed metropolitan landscape and consider how to deal with each type, remembering that government subsidies have been distributed unevenly over the decades and some greater equality is due. The first wave of subsidies came from the federal government in the 1940s and 1950s, for homeowners and residential developers. The second wave came from the federal government in the mid-1950s to the 1980s, to support commercial real estate. The third wave, the kind of transit and infrastructure subsidies tracked in Myron Orfield's *Metropolitics* (1997, 1–15), involves high property taxes extracted from low-income central cities and older suburbs to support new development in affluent outer suburbs. Orfield, a lawyer and member of the state legislature of Minnesota, argues that coalitions must be built at the level of state government to overcome the deficiencies of federal programs and local interests. He sees change as resulting from long-term political activity. Surely better planning and better design do require a new political framework. The implication is that planners and architects need to become more active as citizens who have a strong interest in the political changes necessary to support better work.

At the same time, planners and architects can assess the current state of their knowledge about developers as decision makers. Given that Americans inhabit some fairly unsatisfactory suburban landscapes constructed during eight decades of developer lobbying and five decades of developer subsidy, how should professionals in planning and architecture assess the current tools for ending sprawl through urban design and regional planning? While smart growth has gotten extensive publicity over the last few years, and one can download sprawl-busting advice from many websites, many of the claims made for the planner's toolkit are far too broad. In buoyant economic times, it is difficult to stop the developers' rush to new commercial and residential real estate. Before smart growth is seen as a solution, the growth machine should be critiqued. (Molotch 1976; Molotch and Logan 1987; Fodor 1999; Daniels 1999). Developers underlying premise is often that massive growth must occur, while older layers will disappear. What would it mean to preserve all of the existing layers, to retrofit rather than rebuild?

Similarly, new urbanist architects' desire to build greenfield developments should be balanced by commitment to preservation. William Fulton (1996) has asked, is new urbanism hope or hype? These architects are a diverse group who resist categorization. Much of what they advocate is not controversial—designers everywhere support pedestrian scale, even those who define themselves stylistically as modernists. Much new urbanist work is wonderful, but in their zeal to succeed, some new urbanists sound like architectural determinists who believe that getting the design right is essential to making society work, refusing to acknowledge that many people will struggle to create community even in the most dreary physical settings. Some seem to place excessive trust in complex charters, codes, rules, checklists and handbooks to keep streets narrow and roof pitches uniform (Calthorpe and Poticha 1993; Duany, Plater-Zyberk and Speck 2000, 247–264). At times, these rules read like the dogma of a new religion, one where heretics will be cast out.

The clients of new urbanists include many large for-profit developers who can handle the economic burdens of large-scale developments, but recent analyses suggest that these clients often create hybrids, accepting new urbanist ideas piecemeal, following the codes or checklists only when it suits them (Ewing 2000, 66–71). Other new urbanists have clients that include city and regional planning authorities. Peter Calthorpe of California favors affordable housing, transit and energy conservation. Andres Duany and Elizabeth Plater-Zyberk of Florida have done a large number of projects, including many upper-income projects, while emphasizing neotraditional architecture and the "second coming" of the small town. Ray Gindroz of Pittsburgh has built low-cost public housing, but his firm also developed the pattern book for Celebration, Disney's expensive new town. None of these firms have specialized in the delicate work of retrofitting and rebuilding existing suburbs, surely because few clients exist to sponsor such projects and make this kind of work pay.

There is a need for diverse nonprofit clients—public housing agencies, nonprofit developers, environmental organizations, economic development groups— to sponsor the physical reconstruction of suburbia as well as old centers. Historical analysis of suburban development can provide a fine-grained analysis of the seven layers of suburbia, making it clear that different kinds of interventions are useful in different places. The old enclaves may need preservation, but help should be given in exchange for public access and interpretation of their private parks and natural landscapes. The aging streetcar buildouts, self-built, mail-order and sitcom suburbs may need transit restored (if it has been disrupted) and green spaces, schools and social services strengthened or added. They might welcome tax incentives for owner improvements. In the larger and more spacious versions of these suburbs, accessory apartments can improve their flexibility to house smaller families. The edge nodes are a lesson in how Americans need to assess developers rather than subsidize them. They cry out for new landscaping requirements and tough infrastructure assessments to discourage new commercial development and to promote mixed use. And the rural fringe? A growth boundary is one tool. Development impact fees are another. Requiring dedicated public open space in new subdivisions, connected to a spine of existing open space, is a third. Farmland preservation is a forth (Daniels 1999, 211-260; Benfield et al. 1999, 137-161; Benfield et al. 2001). All of these tools are partial; each is more effective when applied in combination with the others. The whole metropolitan agenda needs to be more than the sum of the parts.

Sixty percent of Americans live in suburbs, but those suburbs form metropolitan regions. As the conversation about smart growth proceeds, programs to conserve the physical character of older suburban landscapes, to improve the houses and extend the sense of community, need to be supported by national and state policy as well as by local initiatives. Complex corporate lobbying efforts have led to the current configuration of the American landscape, with millions of private houses and relatively few satisfactory centers of public life. For decades, these lobbyists used political influence to shape a private market for shelter based on government subsidies that might have been better directed toward building public spaces and infrastructure. White male heads of working-class households benefited, but income tax deductions always subsidized the rich more handsomely than home buyers of modest means. The tax situation was compounded by federal policies that recognized the necessity of commercial development in suburban communities, but provided incentives for greenfield sites and rapid depreciation. Americans have cherished suburbia in many of its forms, but feel puzzled and frustrated by its current shape.

With good reason, a new generation hopes to start over. The problem is that many Americans believe starting over means exerting total design control over elite enclaves or placing isolated houses in undeveloped land at the fringe. So what might it really mean to be smarter? Suburbia is the hinge, the connection between past and future, between old inequalities and new possibilities. In all kinds of existing suburbs, inequalities of gender, class and race have been embedded in material form. So have unwise environmental choices. If these are to be changed, first some significant preservation, renovation and infill must take place on the suburban ground already occupied, as well as in the old city centers. Directing federal, state and local subsidies toward the less affluent, designing appropriate public transit, and requiring more environmental accountability will be difficult. Activist groups may be able to mobilize voters' commitments to existing suburban and urban places in order to mount sustained political pressure against the American growth machine—the real estate-banking-building-automotive lobby that has wielded influence for the last 80 years. A new political consensus will be essential to reconfiguring the U.S. metropolitan landscape as a place of socially and environmentally responsible development.

References

Archer, John. 1983. Country and city in the American romantic suburb. *Journal of the society of architectural historians* 42 (May):139–156.

———. 1997. Colonial suburbs in South Asia, 1700–1850, and spaces of modernity. In *Visions of suburbia*, Roger Silverstone, ed. London, England: Routledge.

Baxandall, Rosalyn, and Elizabeth Ewen. 2000. *Picture windows: How the suburbs happened.* New York, NY: Basic Books.

Beecher, Catharine E. 1842. *Treatise on domestic economy*. Boston, MA: Thomas H. Webb.

Beecher, Catharine E., and Harriet Beecher Stowe. 1869. *The American woman's home*. New York, NY: J.B. Ford.

Benfield, F. Kaid, Matthew D. Raimi, and Donald D.T. Chen. 1999. *Once there were greenfields: How urban sprawl is undermining America's environment, economy, and social fabric.* Washington, DC: National Resources Defense Council.

_____. 2001. *Solving sprawl*. Washington, DC: Island Press.

Binford, Henry. 1984. *The first suburbs: Residential communities on the Boston periphery, 1815–1860.* Chicago, IL: University of Chicago Press.

Calthorpe, Peter, and William Fulton. 2001. *The regional city: Planning for the end of sprawl.* Washington, DC: Island Press.

Calthorpe, Peter, with Shirley Poticha. 1993. *The next American metropolis: Ecology, community, and the American dream*. New York, NY: Princeton Architectural Press.

Campoli, Julie, Elizabeth Humstone and Alex MacLean. 2001. *Above and beyond: Visualizing change in small towns and rural areas.* Chicago, IL: American Planning Association Planners Press.

Cohen, Lizabeth. 1996. From town center to shopping center: The reconfiguration of community marketplaces in postwar America. *American historical review* 101(October):1050–1081.

Daniels, Tom. 1999. *When city and country collide: Managing growth in the metropolitan fringe.* Washington, DC: Island Press.

Davis, Alexander Jackson. 1837. *Rural residences*. Hand-colored folio, Beinecke Library, Yale University.

Downing, Andrew Jackson. 1841. *Treatise on the theory and practice of landscape gardening,* New York, NY: A.O. Moore.

_____. 1842. *Cottage residences.* New York and London: Wiley and Putnam.

Drew, Bettina. 1998. Celebration. *Yale Review* 86 (summer):51–70.

Duany, Andres, and Elizabeth Plater-Zyberk. 1992. The second coming of the American small town. *Wilson quarterly* 16 (winter):19–50.

Duany, Andres, Elizabeth Plater-Zyberk and Jeff Speck. 2000. *Suburban nation: The rise of sprawl and the decline of the American dream*. New York, NY: North Point Press.

Easterling, Keller. 1999. *Organization space*. Cambridge, MA: MIT Press.

Eckert, Toby. 1996. Placing hopes in Hope VI: *Indianapolis business journal* (Dec. 9-15):1.

Edel, Matthew, Elliott D. Sclar, and Daniel Luria. 1984. *Shaky palaces: Homeownership and social mobility in Boston's suburbanization*. New York, NY: Columbia University Press.

Ehrenreich, Barbara. 2000. Maid to order: The politics of other women's work. *Harper's* 300 (April):59–70.

Epp, Gayle. 1996. Emerging strategies for revitalizing public housing communities. *Housing policy debate* 7:582.

Ewing, Reid. 2000. The future of land development. *Metropolitan development patterns: 2000 Annual Roundtable*. Cambridge, MA: Lincoln Institute of Land Policy.

Fishman, Robert. 1987. *Bourgeois utopias: The rise and fall of suburbia*. New York, NY: Basic Books.

Fodor, Eben. 1999. *Better not bigger: How to take control of urban growth*. Gabriola Island, BC: New Society Publishers.

Frantz, Douglas, and Catherine Collins. 1999. *Celebration, U.S.A.: Living in Disney's brave new town*. New York, NY: Henry Holt.

Fulton, William. 1996. *The new urbanism: Hope or hype for American communities?* Cambridge, MA: Lincoln Institute of Land Policy.

Garreau, Joel. 1991. *Edge city: Life on the new frontier*. New York, NY: Doubleday.

Garvin, Alexander. 1996. *The American city: What works, what doesn't*. New York, NY: McGraw Hill.

Girling, Cynthia L., and Kenneth I. Helphand. 1994. *Yard-street-park: The design of suburban open space*. New York, NY: John Wiley & Sons.

Gowans, Alan. 1986. *The comfortable house: North American suburban architecture 1890–1930*. Cambridge, MA: MIT Press.

Hanchett, Thomas. 1996. U.S. tax policy and the shopping-center boom of the 1950s and 1960s. *American historical review* 101 (October):1082–1110.

Harris, Richard. 1991. Self-building in the urban housing market. *Economic geography* 67 (January):263–303.

———. 1996. *Unplanned suburbs: Toronto's American tragedy, 1900-1950*. Baltimore, MD: Johns Hopkins University Press.

Hayden, Dolores. 1976. *Seven American utopias. The architecture of communitarian socialism, 1790–1975*. Cambridge, MA: MIT Press.

———. 1977. Catharine Beecher and the politics of housework. In *Women in American architecture: Historic and contemporary perspectives*, Susana Torre, ed. New York, NY: Whitney Library of Design.

———. 1981. *The grand domestic revolution: A history of feminist designs for American homes, neighborhoods, and cities*. Cambridge, MA: MIT Press.

———. 1989. Model houses for the millions: Architects' dreams, builders' boasts, residents' dilemmas. In *Blueprints for modern living: Case study houses, history and legacy*, Elizabeth A.T. Smith, ed. Cambridge, MA: MIT Press.

———. 1995. *The power of place: Urban landscapes as public history*. Cambridge, MA: MIT Press.

———. 2000. Flying over Guilford. *Planning* 66 (September):10-15.

——— with photographs by Alex S. MacLean. 2001. Aerial photography on the Web: A new tool for community debates on land use. *Lotus* 108: 118-131.

———. 2002. *Redesigning the American dream: The future of housing, work and family life* (1984. rev. and expanded). New York, NY: Norton.

Henderson, Susan. 1987. Llewellyn Park, suburban idyll. *Journal of garden history*. 7:221–243.

Hodgins, Eric. 1946. *Mr. Blandings builds his dream house*. New York, NY: Simon and Schuster.

Jackson, Kenneth. 1985. *Crabgrass frontier: The suburbanization of the United States*. New York, NY: Oxford University Press.

Jurca, Catherine. 1998. Hollywood, the dream house factory. *Cinema journal* 37 (summer):29.

Kelly, Barbara M. 1993. *Expanding the American dream: Building and rebuilding Levittown*. Albany, NY: State University of New York Press.

Kemper, Vicky. 1994. Home inequity. *Common cause* (summer):14–18.

Larrabee, Eric. 1948. The six thousand houses that Levitt built. *Harper's* (September): 84.

Marsh, Margaret. 1990. *Suburban lives*. New Brunswick, NJ: Rutgers University Press.

Molotch, Harvey. 1976. The city as growth machine. *American journal of sociology* 82: 309-330.

Molotch, Harvey, and John R. Logan. 1987. *Urban fortunes: The political economy of place*. Berkeley, CA: University of California Press.

Orfield, Myron. 1997. *Metropolitics: A regional agenda for community and stability*. Washington, DC: Brookings Institution and Cambridge, MA: Lincoln Institute of Land Policy.

Palen, J. John. 1995. *The suburbs*. New York, NY: McGraw Hill.

Peterson, Sarah Jo. 2002. The politics of land use and housing in World War II Michigan: Building bombers and communities. Ph.D. dissertation, Yale University.

Post, Emily. 1911. Tuxedo Park: An American rural community. *The century magazine* 82 (October):795–805.

Radford, Gail. 1996. *Modern housing in America: Policy struggles in the New Deal era*. Chicago, IL: University of Chicago Press.

Reese, Jennifer. 1999. Streetcar suburb. *Preservation* 51 (January/February):52–57.

Rowe, Peter. 1991. *Making a middle landscape*. Cambridge, MA: MIT Press.

Rymer, Russ. 1996. Back to the future: Disney reinvents the company town. *Harper's* 293 (October): 65–71 ff.

Schuyler, David. 1986. *The new urban landscape: The redefinition of form in nineteenth-century America*. Baltimore, MD: Johns Hopkins University Press.

Separated by design. 2000. *New York Times, sect. H* (March 8):6.

Sharpe, William, and Leonard Wallock. 1994. Bold new city or built up 'burb? Redefining contemporary suburbia. *American quarterly* 46 (March):1–30.

Sies, Mary Corbin. 1997. Paradise retained: An analysis of persistence in planned, exclusive suburbs, 1880–1980. *Planning perspectives* 12:165–191.

Southworth, Michael. 1997. Walkable suburbs? *Journal of the American Planning Association* (Winter):28–44.

Spectorsky, A.C. 1955. *The exurbanites*. Philadelphia, PA: J.B. Lippincott.

Stern, Robert A.M., and John Massengale, eds. 1981. *The Anglo-American suburb*. London, England: Architectural Design Profile.

Stilgoe, John. 1988. *Borderland: Origins of the American suburb, 1820–1939*. New Haven, CT: Yale University Press.

Thrall, Bob. 1999. *The new American village*. Baltimore, MD: Johns Hopkins University Press.

Transit Cooperative Research Program. 1998. *The costs of sprawl—Revisited*. Washington, DC: National Academy Press.

U.S. Bureau of the Census. 2000. *American Housing Survey, 1999*. http://www.census.gov/hhes/www/housing (June 2001).

Waldie, D.J. 1996. *Holy land: A suburban memoir*. New York, NY: St. Martin's.

Warner, Sam Bass, Jr. 1972. *Streetcar suburbs*. Cambridge, MA: Harvard University Press.

Weiss, Ellen. 1987. *City in the woods: The life and design of an American camp meeting on Martha's Vineyard*. New York, NY: Oxford University Press.

Weiss, Marc. 1987. *The rise of the community builders: The American real estate industry and urban land planning*. New York, NY: Columbia University Press.

Wiese, Andrew. 1999. The other suburbanites: African American suburbanization in the North before 1950. *Journal of American history* 85 (March):1519.

Wilson, Richard Guy. 1979. Idealism and the origin of the first American suburb: Llewellyn Park, New Jersey. *American art journal* (October):79–90.

Wolf, Peter. 1999. *Hot towns: The future of the fastest growing communities in America*. New Brunswick, NJ: Rutgers University Press.

Wood, Eugene. 1910. Why pay rent? *Everybody's magazine* 22 (June):765–767.

Worley. 1990. *J.C. Nichols and the shaping of Kansas City*. Columbia, MO: University of Missouri Press.

Wright, Gwendolyn. 1980. *Moralism and the model home: Domestic architecture and cultural conflict in Chicago, 1873–1913*. Chicago, IL: University of Chicago Press.

———. 1981. *Building the dream*. New York, NY: Pantheon.

Zunz, Olivier. 1982. *The changing face of inequality: Urbanization, industrial development, and immigrants in Detroit, 1880–1920*. Chicago, IL: University of Chicago Press.

3

Glenna Matthews

How They Lost Their Way in San Jose

The Capital of Silicon Valley as a Case Study of Postwar Sprawl

> Santa Clara Valley, known throughout the world as "The Valley of Heart's Delight" because of its scenic attractions, mild climate, and diversified agriculture, is located 32 miles south of San Francisco....Horticulture is the leading industry of the county, and it is doubtful if there is a section of similar area in all the world that produces so many varieties or so vast a quantity of fruits....San Jose, the county seat, is the industrial center of this productive area and has long been recognized as the most extensive canning and dried fruit packing center of the world.
> *California Blue Book,* 1928

If one is interested in the causes and consequences of sprawl, there can be few cities in the country better suited to an examination than San Jose, currently the self-designated "Capital of Silicon Valley." In 1950, some 95,000 San Joseans lived in a city of nearly 17 square miles. In 2000, an estimated 910,000 live in 174 square miles. The industrial landscape has gone from being one of orchards and fruit processing plants to one of high-tech campuses—with a few remnants of the earlier orchards to inspire nostalgia. How did this extraordinary change come about, and what have been the costs and benefits?

San Jose is the county seat of Santa Clara County, a jurisdiction that stretches from Palo Alto in the north (some 30 miles below San Francisco) to the rural town of Gilroy in the south, and includes both a fertile valley and lovely foothills. For the first half of the twentieth century, the valley was home to the largest orchard the world had ever seen, with more than 100,000 acres devoted to fruit trees, primarily growing prunes, cherries and apricots. To process the local bounty, there was a plethora of canneries and dried fruit packing plants; indeed, as late as 1960, there were still 215 food-processing operations in the county. As beautiful as the Valley of Heart's Delight may have been in its heyday, it is important to emphasize that there *were* adverse environmental effects from the orchards, because rainfall alone was inadequate to keep the trees alive and healthy. As a consequence, growers turned to wells as a source of water for their crops. By 1920, the 10,000 wells had caused the water table to drop and the land to subside. By the 1930s, local voters had begun to approve what would eventually become a quite elaborate system of percolation dams designed to replenish the aquifer.

But there was more amiss in this Eden than merely the problem of how to irrigate the fruit. The Great Depression of the 1930s revealed the considerable vulnerability of prunes and apricots to the vicissitudes of world markets—and to an elastic market for specialty foods on the home front as well. So desperate were

The Valley of Heart's Delight in the 1920s. Most of the orchards have now vanished.
Photograph courtesy of the Sourisseau Academy, San Jose State University.

growers for solutions that by the end of the decade they had begun to uproot fruit trees (Matthews 1977; 1985). And if growers and processors were hurting, then the whole area was hurting, because this was by far the most important component of the local economy.

Further, even when markets were thriving, fruit was still a highly seasonal industry. By the time that World War II began, a broad range of local leaders had begun to believe in the need to diversify beyond horticulture. One leader recalled that period of transition in a talk he gave to the San Jose Rotary Club in 1972: "Half the work force was employed in canneries, bustling with activity for 13 weeks in summer and unemployed the rest of the time. When canneries went on strike [workers had achieved a union by dint of great struggle in the 1930s], everyone's hopes fell. The Chamber of Commerce called vainly for more industries, more of any kind of job excepting those intimately bound to canning…" (Starbird 1972).

Even before Pearl Harbor, a local firm had begun to secure some of the military contracts that foreshadowed the future: Food Machinery Corporation, which had built capital equipment for canners and growers, secured a contract to build amphibious landing vehicles for troops. Shortly thereafter, a small valley machine shop, the Joshua Hendy Iron Works, was tapped to build two-story engines for Liberty Ships. Together these two firms received some $289 million of federal dollars during the course of the war (Abbott 1993, 10). Adding to the hotly desired diversification of the local economy was IBM's decision in 1943 to locate a punch card factory in San Jose.

These developments were taking place in San Jose or close to it in Sunnyvale, where Hendy was located. Further north in the county, close to Stanford University, an electronics industry had been developing, an industry that would spawn Silicon Valley. Little known to most Americans, the Santa Clara Valley had been home to successful experiments in electronics well before the birth of the

The Fiesta de las Rosas Parade in downtown San Jose in 1929. Photograph courtesy of History San Jose.

semiconductor industry in the 1960s—indeed, even before the founding of Hewlett-Packard in 1938. In the late nineteenth century, scientific breakthroughs with radio waves were pointing the way to new applications, some of which would later prove to be of commercial and military value. Innovations in both realms took place in the San Francisco Bay Area, including the world's first ship-to-shore radio transmission, first commercial radio station and first television tube (Sturgeon 1992, 5).

The most important single breakthrough came in the years before World War I with Lee DeForest's invention of a vacuum tube, a means by which electrons could be controlled in an oscillating, feedback circuit, in the Palo Alto laboratory of the pioneering electronics firm Federal Telegraph. Hence, when Stanford engineering professor Frederick Terman encouraged his students William Hewlett and David Packard to launch their firm in 1938, there was already a local context for their efforts. Terman was another local leader who was eager to see economic diversification take place, at least in part because he wanted his students to be able to stay in the area rather than go East for employment.

This, then, was how matters stood in 1944: the Depression had hit the area hard, but there were the first glimmerings of the high-tech, defense-contractor future. Another contributing factor to the vast scale of postwar change lay in the Fourth Army being stationed in San Jose during the war. Countless men came through and saw a desirable place to locate after the war ended. That this played a transformative role can be inferred from the fact that the local school population began to soar even before the arrival of Lockheed and a big IBM plant in the mid-1950s, the firms that would become the two biggest private employers in the county. Indeed, between 1950 and 1957, more than 120 new schools were built in the area, and the tract homes sprang up like mushrooms.[1] San Jose would become a classic example of what Dolores Hayden calls sitcom suburbs, communities filled with new housing developments, which emerged after World War II under a combination of market incentives and federal policy.

The election of 1944 produced a San Jose City Council committed to change and able to bring the change about. That year a number of incumbents were off fighting in the war. As a result, a group calling itself the Progress Committee was able to gain a majority on the council. The newcomers quickly fired the city manager, a man who had been in office since the 1920s, and replaced

---

1   This information is contained in newsletters in the archives of the Santa Clara County Office of Education.

him with someone as dedicated to growth as they were. Not until 1950, however, did they succeed in hiring someone who was not only growth oriented, but also possessed the savvy and force of personality to achieve this end. That year, A.P. "Dutch" Hamann took office. He had no previous governmental experience, but he had excellent connections—he had been student body president at Santa Clara University in the 1930s—and very decided ideas about what a city should be:

> He [Hamann] said, if you wanted to grow and be able to pay the bill, you had to annex surrounding areas to the City. To do that you couldn't sit on your hands. Pretty soon you would become like Bakersfield and St. Louis, an enclave circled by other small incorporated cities or special service districts that would tie you up forever. If you got bottled up, your tax rate would put you out of the running for new industries; they would go to Sunnyvale or Santa Clara, your assessed valuation would remain frozen. It was as bad as being hemmed in by geographical barriers, samples of which were many in all size cities. It was really just that simple (Starbird 1972).

When accused of trying to turn San Jose into another Los Angeles, Hamann responded by saying that he welcomed the label. In addition to his grasp of a particular philosophy of growth, one that might well be called municipal imperialism, he was a superb salesman, and he had the energy to travel to New York on a regular basis to pitch San Jose bonds to easterners.

By 1950, there were powerful national factors conducive to suburban sprawl, and there were factors peculiar to San Jose that heightened the effects in that city, among them the presence of a deliberate and mindful—if not necessarily smart—political commitment to expansion. In addition, the area possessed an aura of destiny at that time, best exemplified by an article in the *Saturday Evening Post* in April 1946. Entitled "Factory in the Country," it singled out the Santa Clara Valley as embodying the possibilities of combining manufacturing with a rural atmosphere. The caption for an illustration proclaims: "The double life pays off here. When the employees of this engine plant [Hendy] in Sunnyvale, California, are not working in the shop, they are harvesting prunes, apricots or pears on their adjoining farms."

This article is a good indication of the desire to have it both ways that flourished among many San Joseans of the time. As another instance of this phenomenon, a special progress edition of the *San Jose Mercury* (January 19, 1958) proclaimed: "The face of the land continued to change markedly during 1957 as Santa Clara County proceeded to overlay urbanization on the traditional base of

Downtown San Jose at mid-century, view looking east. There has been a great deal of development in the vicinity of the foothills in the intervening decades. Photograph courtesy of the California Historical Society.

agriculture. The trees, blossoms, and crops are still here, but so are more homes, more and better roads, more water conservation, sewerage, and drainage projects." In other words, the progress would exact no cost. Such attitudes—flagrant examples of wishful thinking—provided a poor context for sound planning decisions.

In the meantime, the locomotive of growth, with Dutch Hamann as the engineer, rolled on. It should be pointed out that Hamann had some very useful allies in his quest to turn San Jose into "one of the four or five most important areas of the West Coast."[2] The most influential was Joe Ridder, whose family bought the leading local newspaper, the *San Jose Mercury*, in 1952.[3] Ridder shared Hamann's vision for the city, and he was quite prepared to pull out all the stops to aid the pro-growth campaign. Reputedly he said, "Prune trees don't buy newspapers." Whether or not he actually said this, he behaved as though this philosophy animated him, and his newspaper lobbied hard to get public support for various bond measures that were necessary to keep the momentum going by paying for new infrastructure.

During Hamann's 19 years as city manager, his Panzer Divisions, as his annexation squad became known, achieved a grand total of approximately 1,400 annexations, while the city grew from 16.98 square miles to 136.7 square miles. According to the authors of a book about power in San Jose, the city's chief advantage lay in the sewage outfall to the bay constructed in the late nineteenth century to accommodate the canneries: "San Jose's greatest weapon in the annexation wars was its control of the sewer system. What water was to Los Angeles, sewage was to San Jose….San Jose used this sewage monopoly in its battles with adjacent cities and with adjacent landowners" (Trounstine and Christensen 1982, 97). The county had vast stretches of unincorporated land. San Jose could offer a developer a quick solution to the sewage problem as well as lower lot sizes and less stringent construction requirements if he opted for annexation. Hence there was a congruence of interest between Dutch Hamann and what he was trying to achieve—a city that was not hemmed in—and those who wanted to reap the profits of housing the tens of thousands of newcomers.

Many other problems had to be dealt with along the way to San Jose's becoming a metropolis, such as getting the local taxpayers to continue footing the bill for the new infrastructure required for a city of several hundred thousand inhabitants, and securing enough water to accommodate the growth (Matthews 1999). The problem that has had the most significant long-term impact, I would argue, owing to the nature of the solution that was arrived at, was the vexing issue of how to get the myriad local school districts to go along with annexation. At the time that Hamann took office, California law called for the boundaries of a unified school district to be coterminous with those of the city it served. San Jose had an abundance of small districts in its hinterland, school districts that would lose

---

2   Quote from the San Jose Master Plan (1958, 17).
3   The *San Jose Mercury* merged with the *San Jose News* in the 1980s to become the *San Jose Mercury News*.

their identity and be swallowed up by San Jose Unified, should annexation take place. Not surprisingly, they became the staunchest foes of annexation. In 1953, State Assemblyman Bruce Allen of San Jose carried successful legislation that divorced school districts from political boundaries. As a direct consequence, there are today 24 districts that lie within the city limits of San Jose. Over the years, there have been wildly divergent tax bases among the various districts: in the mid-1960s, for example, an assessed valuation of $5,130.94 lay behind each child in Alum Rock, the poorest district, with $56,936.81 behind each child in Orchard, the richest district. State public policy has mandated a narrowing of such gaps, but they have by no means disappeared entirely (Vance 1966, 141). In short, inequity in school finance was built into the system as a cost of expansion.

Another immediate cost of the rampaging sprawl was the precipitous decline of downtown San Jose. With new shopping centers being built to serve the new developments in outlying areas, downtown San Jose quickly lost its retail primacy and became a virtual ghost town. This abandonment was enhanced when the city moved its offices from downtown to a location about one mile to the north, and the *San Jose Mercury* also left downtown for the outskirts. Indeed, San Jose had always had an inferiority complex relative to Palo Alto, its more glamorous neighbor to the north, and this situation was growing worse, not better, as the orchards vanished and the civic identity represented by a prosperous central business district vanished too.[4]

One sign that San Joseans were growing disaffected lay in the election of Virginia Shaffer to the San Jose City Council in 1962. An ardent opponent of Hamann and his policies, Shaffer was a deeply conservative woman who campaigned to end the growth so as to end the burden for taxpayers who were footing the bill. By 1969, Hamann was gone. By 1974, San Joseans had elected Janet Gray Hayes to be mayor, the country's first woman mayor of a city larger than 500,000 in population. Significantly, Hayes rode to office on a wave of voter dissatisfaction with unchecked development. Her successor, Tom McEnery, then dedicated himself to rebuilding downtown, an ambitious and protracted process.

While these changes were unfolding in San Jose—and while the hundreds of housing developments, the new shopping centers, a larger airport and new roads were being built—building of a different sort was going on in some of San Jose's

---

[4] I have been a close student of San Jose for several decades. While I was attending San Jose State University in the late 1960s, and immediately before beginning graduate studies at Stanford University, I hosted a weekly public affairs program on Channel 36 in San Jose. I also served on an official committee to evaluate the local antipoverty program.

sister cities to the north. As we have seen, Hewlett and Packard founded their pathbreaking firm in Palo Alto in 1938. Ten years later, the Varian brothers and a few others founded Varian Associates, which would become the first occupant of Stanford Industrial Park in 1951. Both of these firms antedated the semiconductor industry, and both eschewed the consumer market at first. Indeed, the presence of large defense contractors such as Lockheed—which at its height employed around 33,000 people—meant that military end use constituted the first large market for the nascent local electronics industry. From the beginning, defense and high-tech workers found their best source of affordable housing in San Jose, though the plants themselves were locating elsewhere.

In 1947, William Shockley and two others had invented the transistor at the Bell Laboratories in New York. This was followed a few years later by Texas Instruments's substitution of silicon for the germanium used as a semiconductor in the first transistors, a choice subsequently endorsed by the nascent industry. In 1955, Shockley decided to set up his own firm, the Shockley Transistor Corporation, near his hometown of Palo Alto. (He was able to fabricate semiconductors because a consent decree from the Justice Department had placed some of the technology developed by Bell Laboratories in the public domain.) Shockley, a famously difficult person, would soon see eight of his top people—the "traitorous eight"—leave to work for their own enterprise, Fairchild, and from the latter came the spin-offs that created Silicon Valley (Moore 1996, 166).[5] In 1969, Intel appeared—the firm that would perfect the microprocessor and become the industry standard—and two years later the region's nickname became Silicon Valley. It should be pointed out that little of this first wave of semiconductor development came within the city limits of San Jose, though by this time there was a large IBM plant in South San Jose.

By 2000, the situation was very different: there were some 1,500 high-tech firms within the expansive city limits of San Jose, including the giant Cisco Systems. A massive investment in downtown was fueled by the city's ability to leverage its property tax income in bond markets—and the city was being widely hailed as a downtown revitalization success story ("A Down Downtown Coming Up," *New York Times,* December 7, 1997). San Jose now has a larger population size than San Francisco (and is third in size in the state to Los Angeles and San Diego). It also has been developing a splendid set of cultural amenities, including

---

5   Moore was one of the eight, and he has explained that they decided to work within the corporate framework of Fairchild Camera and Instrument, which then founded the Fairchild Semiconductor Corporation.

Downtown San Jose in the late twentieth century, view looking west. In the foreground is the Plaza de Cesar Chavez; the domed building is the Tech Museum of Innovation. Photograph courtesy of Ken Heiman, San Jose Silicon Valley Chamber of Commerce.

the Children's Discovery Museum, the Tech Museum of Innovation, the San Jose Repertory Theater, and an opera, ballet and symphony. The San Jose Museum of Art has completed an expansion project. The city built a handsome sports arena and, in consequence, was able to attract a major league franchise, the San Jose Sharks of the National Hockey League, an addition to the local scene that has greatly enhanced civic pride. Finally, the council voted to relocate City Hall back to the downtown, and certain corporations are beginning to locate headquarters there, too, beginning with Adobe Systems in 1996, the first such corporate decision since 1951.

Perhaps most noteworthy is the fact that this city, with an overwhelmingly European American population at the time downtown died, became home to many non-European immigrants in the late twentieth century: it went from being

7.6 percent foreign born in 1970, to 26.5 percent foreign born in 1990, with most of the newcomers arriving from Asia and Latin America. Strikingly, the reinvented downtown reflects these new demographics as well as the interests of native-born people of color. At the heart of downtown is Cesar Chavez Plaza, named in honor of the renowned labor leader, who was living in the East San Jose barrio at the time he began his career of activism. On one side of the plaza is an upscale hotel, and on the other is the Tech Museum, further confirmation that this naming opportunity has not been relegated to a marginal locale. The main public library is named in honor of Martin Luther King. There is a magnificent monument to another labor leader, Ernesto Galarza, near the plaza. There is a statue of the Aztec deity Quetzalcoatl at the tip of the plaza. The Federal Building can boast a splendid bas relief by Ruth Asawa that details the Japanese American experience in California. Moreover, signage for the rapid transit system is tri-lingual, English, Spanish and Vietnamese, the latter reflecting the presence of one of the nation's largest and most influential communities of immigrants from Southeast Asia. Most telling about the clout of people of color in San Jose is the fact that the Latino community prevented a statue of the Anglo conqueror of Mexican San Jose, Thomas Fallon—a statue that was the pet project of former mayor Tom McEnery—from being installed in the downtown area. Much of this downtown diversification owes to the visionary leadership of Susan Hammer, McEnery's successor as mayor.[6]

A more down-to-earth example of the way public policy in San Jose reflects the interests of less affluent residents is the city's permission of the widespread establishment of home businesses in immigrant neighborhoods, especially in East San Jose, where the barrio has been. The country and the world know about successful immigrant entrepreneurs in high tech, such as Jerry Yang of Yahoo. Less well known is the fact that small-scale immigrant entrepreneurs in the Valley are converting garages, living rooms and parlors to store fronts. Beauty shops are a particular favorite, but other types of businesses include florist shops, tailoring establishments and gift shops. This phenomenon has, in turn, enabled many families to survive (*San Jose Mercury News,* March 19, 2000). In short, the diversity of people living—and voting, once they become naturalized citizens—within the city limits of San Jose has produced a city with an impressive record of responsiveness to a broad array of interests. This is not to say, of course, that San Jose does not contain

---

[6] Interview with Bob Brownstein of the local labor think tank, Working Partnerships, July 12, 2000.

its share of the desperately poor, along with other U.S. cities of similar size. And enlightened local public policy cannot redress the inequalities caused by the vast number of poorly paid jobs in the uniformly nonunion high-tech industry.

Another direct benefit of postwar growth lies in the extent to which there is now metropolitan governance in the realm of water. As newcomers flooded into the Valley in the postwar years, multiple and antithetical interests had to be satisfied in the quest to provide an adequate water supply for growth. A fierce struggle ensued about whether water for the valley should come from the state of California or the federal government and about who should govern the system of wholesale distribution. Out of this contentiousness and strife came the Santa Clara Valley Water District, coterminous with the county, and thus a regional solution to the problem. The district pools water and prices it, irrespective of the diverse costs of obtaining it. In short, in this policy area San Jose and Santa Clara County would seem to embody David Rusk's argument for the superiority of "elastic" cities on the basis of their allegedly greater fairness.[7]

Thus the advantages conferred by growth have been substantial. Above all, it should be emphasized, San Jose has found ways to capture benefits from the high-tech revolution that actually originated some miles to the north. Had the city not grown so large physically, it could not conceivably be home to so many high-tech installations now—nor could it be calling itself the "Capital of Silicon Valley," a sobriquet that has done wonders for its ability to attract international tourism. Palo Alto may now be claiming to be the "Birthplace of Silicon Valley," but no other jurisdiction is disputing San Jose's claim to be the capital.[8]

If the benefits of postwar growth have been substantial, so, too, have been the long-term costs of San Jose becoming a metropolis at the epicenter of the high-tech economy. Some are merely more intense versions of problems that are endemic in prosperous areas in the early twenty-first-century United States, and some are specific to San Jose and Silicon Valley. In the first category are surreal home prices and nightmarish traffic, interrelated difficulties caused by the explosion in tech jobs. Indeed, between 1992 and 1998, the Silicon Valley region saw the creation of more than 200,000 new jobs, accompanied by the building of only 38,000 new housing units.[9]

---

[7] See Rusk (1996) for a discussion of the beneficial role that annexation can play in a city. For more details about the history of water supply, see Matthews (1999).

[8] Sunnyvale now bills itself as the "Heart of Silicon Valley," and Union City (in southern Alameda County) bills itself as the "Gateway to Silicon Valley."

[9] See Joint Venture: Silicon Valley Network (October 1998). Joint Venture is a consortium made up of business, government and educational leaders.

As an instance of the inflation in the cost of housing caused by this pattern, an inflation that is less pronounced in San Jose than in ritzier areas to the north, but is still extraordinary, the *San Jose Mercury News* (December 12, 1999) published an account of the price history of one three-bedroom bungalow in the Willow Glen neighborhood. Purchased originally for $9,500 in 1947, it sold in the spring of 1999 for $533,000. Not surprisingly, the couple who bought it both work in high tech, and they used their companies' stock plans to finance the purchase.

Where do the less affluent go for housing? One answer is suggested by the following. In the twelve months ending in July 1998, there was $1.4 billion of new construction in San Jose, a record. In the words of the *Mercury* (July 21, 1998): "Permits for new apartments showed the strongest growth as builders rushed to meet the region's extraordinary demand for housing within the confines of city policies that call for high-density 'infill' development within existing urbanized areas."

In addition to the highly paid high-tech professionals, the valley is home to 40,000 to 50,000 assembly workers, a number of whom work for the minimum wage or less, and many cannot afford adequate housing at all.[10] One recourse they have is to double- and triple-up in housing until together a group of people can afford the rent. In fall 1999, I interviewed two undocumented workers from Oaxaca, Mexico, who explained that someone who is here legally signs a lease and then others claim beds or even space on the floor until they can cover expenses.

For many people—an estimated 150,000, in fact—the solution to the problem of how to find affordable housing lies in a lengthy commute, a solution that, in turn, intensifies the problem of increasingly clogged freeways. Indeed, so many Silicon Valley workers are currently living in the Central Valley that, in October 1998, the Altamont Commuter Express (ACE) was launched as a daily train to the valley over the Altamont Pass from the interior of the state.[11] The ACE originates in Stockton, with eight stops along the way before it reaches its final destination in San Jose, a trip of 2 hours and 25 minutes in length (*San Jose Mercury News*, October 20, 1998). But only 1,200 or so of the thousands with long drives can be accommodated in this fashion.

---

10 These workers are the primary focus of my work-in-progress, *Silicon Valley Women and the California Dream*, under contract to Stanford University Press.
11 The Valley community that has undergone the most change is Tracy, 60 miles east of San Francisco, and 60 miles south of Sacramento. Tracy's population grew from 18,500 in 1980 to 53,000 in 2000, and the rampant development that earlier took place in the Santa Clara Valley is flourishing there. See the *Los Angeles Times* (May 13, 2000).

One gauge of the severity of the traffic problem lies in the statistics that rate freeways on their congestion. An *F* rating is the worst possible and means that traffic flows at below 35 miles an hour. Between 1994 and 1998, the number of freeway miles in the region receiving an *F* during afternoon peak traffic nearly tripled, going from 11 percent to 31 percent of the total miles in the county (Joint Venture 1999). It is clear that no matter what the investment in improved transportation—and more than a billion dollars of spending has been authorized by local taxpayers—the problem will not be meaningfully addressed until there is greater balance between growth in jobs and in housing starts.

Then there is the issue of building community around a sense of a shared past. Like many other Sunbelt cities undergoing ultrarapid growth, San Jose has seen various negative consequences that stem from having so many citizens without a long-term connection to the area, including an underinvestment in its own history. Despite the wealth of cultural amenities being constructed in downtown San Jose, there has been no similar rush to invest in the preservation and/or display of archival records. The Tech Museum of Innovation has received a massive infusion of money, highly appropriate under the circumstances, but no concomitant resources have been devoted to how the Valley has developed. To quote an article in a commemorative magazine published by the *San Jose Mercury News* on October 25, 1998, to honor the opening of the Tech, "The city [like] the museum of innovation is a paean to change." Tragically, one of the era's most historically significant regions will be difficult for scholars to study adequately in the twenty-first century because of this underinvestment.[12]

Inflated housing prices, worsening traffic, and the undermining of community willingness to commit resources to local history are not unique to San Jose. But the peculiar toll taken on the environment by the growth of high tech in an area perforated by 10,000 agricultural wells is perhaps an idiosyncrasy in San Jose and Santa Clara Valley. For the first decade or so of the semiconductor industry, the full story of potential environmental degradation remained hidden from public view. The orchards were rapidly disappearing, but such was considered the price of progress and the conventional wisdom at the time.

---

12 Various big firms have their own archives, though not all of them grant the public access. Stanford University has a commitment to documenting the tech history in its hinterland, but nowhere is there an areawide vision or areawide fundraising to achieve that vision. The oral histories I have conducted—and taped—with surviving San Jose leaders from the immediate postwar period are the only extant record of the personal experiences of some of the key players in the transformation.

Then in the early 1980s, matters took a turn for the worse. In September 1980, workers had found chemical leaks in the soil near the IBM plant in South San Jose, with a few more such discoveries being made near other plants in succeeding months. In December 1981, the news got worse, because this time the leak of the solvent TCA, used to clean chips—a leak for which Fairchild was responsible—had produced traces of contamination in a well owned by the Great Oaks Water Company. A few weeks later, a housewife who lived in one of the neighborhoods served by this water company, who had read the newspaper accounts, wrote a letter to Great Oaks providing the names of eight women in her Los Paseos neighborhood, including herself, who had suffered miscarriages or given birth to children who were stillborn or who had birth defects, all within a three-year period.[13]

From these beginnings was born the Silicon Valley Toxics Coalition, a grassroots organization to pressure the government to regulate the industry. The pollution became a major national story, and this led eventually to the Environmental Protection Agency's designating 29 Superfund sites in the valley. It turned out that the problem of chemical leakage was widespread among even the blue-chip companies, exacerbated by the fact that the agricultural wells served as perfect conduits for toxins to penetrate into the aquifer.

This is not the place to go into the full history of the Silicon Valley Toxics Coalition. Suffice it to say that, though the group has enjoyed many successes, its long-term leader, Ted Smith, thinks it is impossible to "get ahead of the curve" on regulation because the industry innovates so constantly that the production processes, including the selection of chemicals, also change constantly. Activists no sooner win a victory against one toxin, than another, whose impact may well be unknown, takes its place.[14]

The loss of so many orchards in the rush to development and the concern to preserve existing open space—as well as the alarming news about the pollution potential of high tech—have combined to produce a mobilized environmental community in San Jose and the valley. In April 1996, this community succeeded in inducing the San Jose City Council to establish a greenline that would contain

---

13   See the *San Jose Mercury News* (February 2, 1982) for the original story about Lorraine Ross's letter to Great Oaks. The *Mercury* of July 10, 1983 contained several pages about the issue, including detailed information about the problem plants.
14   Interview with Ted Smith, March 1, 1999.

development within well-defined boundaries. But the efficacy of this policy in redressing the problems is dubious. It is not enough to establish such boundaries when the imbalance between sensible housing solutions and explosive job creation continues. All that happens is that another jurisdiction will be dealing with the problems and/or that the cost of housing will soar (see Nelson, this volume).

Further, the greenline boundary has been drawn in such a way that it will permit a huge high-tech installation in the still rural Coyote Valley, in the southern part of the city, an installation that is bound to aggravate some of the existing difficulties. The city considered whether to permit Cisco Systems to build a 385-acre campus with a projected 20,000 employees in the northern tip of Coyote Valley. In an editorial advocating that the Cisco project be approved, the *San Jose Mercury News* (March 19, 2000) explained the reasons as follows:

> ...[S]ince the birth of Silicon Valley, San Jose has provided the bulk of the housing, without adding enough industry to keep it financially stable. Even today, with the tremendous industrial growth in North San Jose since the mid-1990s, the city still has some 56,000 more homes than it would need to house the people who work here.
>
> This is why it's not only important to allow Cisco to build in Coyote, but also appropriate to invest some public money to help pay for things like freeway interchanges and flood control that historically have been handled by the public sector in areas like these.
>
> Open space is important to the quality of life in San Jose...but North Coyote is inside [the] urban growth boundary.

In other words, though the newspaper's editors surely understand the regional impact this project will have on one of the country's most inflated housing markets, it is perceived as being too good to pass up. Simply put, the city has already done its duty as a bedroom community, while other jurisdictions benefited from an industrial tax base, and now it's San Jose's turn.

As we look at those costs of expansion peculiar to San Jose, it is clear that the fragmentation of schools has had significant long-term consequences. The barrio neighborhoods in East San Jose, though within the city for the most part, are incorporated within independent, underfunded school districts lacking the resources to give their students a first-rate education. That only 56 percent of the city's Latino population currently graduates from high school no doubt owes something to this situation. Inasmuch as Latinos now constitute about one-quarter of the city's population, this educational shortfall is both a personal tragedy for the individuals involved and a contributing factor in the ongoing shortage of skilled workers in the high-tech industry. The nonprofit consortium Joint Venture: Silicon Valley Network announced in 1999, for example, that the valley's workforce gap costs local firms an estimated $4 billion a year in recruiting expenses and in lost productivity. About 160,000 jobs, or one-third of the Silicon Valley workforce, were filled by workers recruited from outside the region or by people who were commuting long distances (*San Francisco Chronicle,* May 18, 1999).

It is particularly noteworthy that in this region, known around the world, whose glamour has made the dot-com kids into virtual celebrities, high-tech jobs are not particularly attractive to local young people. Concerned about the workforce gap, Joint Venture sponsored a survey of 1,200 valley students in grades 8 to 11. The students' top career choices were lawyer, doctor/nurse, secretary and farmer. Many "were intimidated by the belief that all computer jobs required extensive educations at four-year universities," when, in fact, there are also good jobs going begging, for which one can prepare at a community college.[15]

Harvey Gantt (this volume) has cautioned that growth that leaves a city's poorest residents stranded in declining neighborhoods can never be called smart. This is not exactly the way things have played out in San Jose, yet the consignment of the poorest students to schools that cannot conceivably do an adequate job—because the schools' permanent impoverishment was a cost of expansion—constitutes evidence that, despite all the prosperity and the revitalization of downtown, San Jose flunks the ethical test for socially desirable growth. Scholars have repeatedly documented that the region's prosperity is highly maldistributed—with the inequalities growing, by all accounts—and the educational system is seemingly unable to play a creative role in redressing the inequality.[16]

Then there is the toll on the landscape. There is still open space, there are still lovely and unspoiled foothills, but the orchards have virtually disappeared. The city of Sunnyvale maintains one city block as an Orchard Heritage Park. As trees die in this apricot orchard, the city has pledged to replace them, so remnants of the glory that was the Valley of Heart's Delight can live on—an orchard heritage park and a

---

15 Interview on March 1, 1999, with Kay Mascoli, who supervised the survey.
16 On April 16, 2000, the *San Jose Mercury News* ran its annual list of the top firms in the valley. The number six firm was Solectron (the top five being Hewlett-Packard, Intel, Cisco, Sun and Oracle), a company that supplies temp workers for high tech. That Solectron is so big and so prosperous is a good indication of why inequality is growing. For all the media attention to the dot-com prosperity stories, there are many thousands who work in the valley in low-wage jobs.

Potemkin orchard. Among the strangest anomalies in today's valley is IBM's position as one of the largest fruit growers. The firm owns 80 acres of orchards near its South San Jose plant. When visiting dignitaries arrive from around the world, they can be shown this orchard as an example of the beauty of the Valley of Heart's Delight. The two brothers who maintain it state explicitly that it is run for show and not for profit.[17] Can postmodern irony go much further?

The larger problem is that the high-tech industry that has brought such prosperity has also brought the use of chemicals so toxic that in conjunction with the practices and the land use patterns of the agricultural past, they constitute an ongoing threat to the well-being of the community. A mobilized group of environmentalists must constantly monitor the industry, prodding the federal government and various local jurisdictions to regulate the chemicals stringently

In sum, to study the history of San Jose is to realize that growth on a massive scale *can* produce benefits for a broad array of residents. But this history also provides a cautionary tale about what kinds of costs should be avoided—above all, in this case, decisions to the detriment of educating the poor and protecting the landscape. We have seen that wishful thinking about how the city could preserve the beauty of the pastoral landscape while encouraging rampaging development in the late 1940s opened the door to a host of unnecessary problems. In the early twenty-first century, that wishful thinking persists as the city considers allowing Cisco Systems to build a plant projected to employ 20,000 people in a hitherto agricultural setting without, at the same time, planning a realistic way to house them. Wishful thinking is the key to understanding how they lost their way in San Jose.

---

17   The orchard is maintained by the Lester brothers, from a family of pioneering orchardists (*San Jose Mercury News,* April 5, 1998).

References

Abbott, Carl. 1993. *The metropolitan frontier: Cities in the modern American West*. Tucson, AZ: University of Arizona Press.

Joint Venture: Silicon Valley Network. 1998. *Silicon Valley 2010*. San Jose, CA: Joint Venture: Silicon Valley Network (October).

―――. 1999. Index of Silicon Valley. San Jose, CA: Joint Venture: Silicon Valley Network.

Matthews, Glenna. 1977. A California Middletown: The social history of San Jose in the Depression. Ph.D. thesis. Stanford, CA: Stanford University.

―――. 1985. The apricot war: A study of the changing fruit industry during the 1930s. *Agricultural history* 59 (January):25–39.

―――. 1999. The Los Angeles of the north: San Jose's transition from fruit capital to high-tech metropolis. *Journal of urban history* 25 (May):459–476.

Moore, Gordon. 1996. Some personal perspectives on research in the semiconductor industry. In *Engines of innovation: U.S. industrial research at the end of an era,* Richard S. Rosenbloom and William J. Spencer, eds. Cambridge, MA: Harvard Business School Press.

Rusk, David. 1996. *Cities without suburbs, second ed., rev*. Baltimore, MD: Johns Hopkins University Press.

San Jose Master Plan. 1958. Institute of Governmental Studies Library, University of California, Berkeley.

Starbird, George. 1972. The new metropolis: San Jose between 1942 and 1972. Talk delivered to San Jose Rotary Club, San Jose Public Library, March 1, 1972.

Sturgeon, Tim John. 1992. The origins of Silicon Valley: The development of the electronics industry in the San Francisco Bay area. M.A. thesis. Berkeley, CA: University of California, Berkeley.

Trounstine, Philip J., and Terry Christensen. 1982. *Movers and shakers: The study of community power*. New York, NY: St. Martin's Press.

Vance, Glen W. 1966. School district organization in the metropolitan area of Santa Clara County, California. Ed.D. thesis. Tuscon, AZ: University of Arizona.

4

William J. Mitchell

**Electronic Cottages,
Wired Neighborhoods
and Smart Cities**

What is the relationship between new digital telecommunications infrastructure and smart growth?[1] Does this emerging infrastructure create an opportunity to structure urban growth in new, more intelligent and responsible ways? Or will it simply contribute to urban sprawl?

Experience with earlier types of network infrastructure suggests that, for good or ill, the relationship will be a strong one (Graham and Marvin 2001). We know that urban growth generates demand for additional capacity for road, water supply, sewer, electric power and telephone networks. Conversely, extension of these sorts of networks produces urban growth opportunities. We should expect a similar reciprocal relationship between digital telecommunications networks and growth patterns.

The following paragraphs recount a designer's speculations and questions about this relationship. There is not yet much rigorous, empirical social science backup for my remarks since the conditions and systems that concern me are just beginning to emerge. Perhaps, though, I can provide some useful ways to begin thinking about some of the key issues.

Loosening Spatial Linkages

In general, the effect of new network infrastructures is to loosen spatial and temporal linkages among urban activities. Significantly, such loosening is selective rather than universal; some linkages weaken or disappear, but others remain and may attain new importance as a result. This sets in motion a process of fragmentation and recombination of established building types and urban patterns.[2] Eventually, new types of urban fabric emerge.

Consider, for example, a traditional village clustered around a well—still a very common pattern in many parts of the developing world. The houses must be within water-carrying distance of the well, and this imposes strong constraints on the village's size and shape. Because inhabitants must regularly come to the well, it establishes the location of the village's principal public space, and this space serves as a venue for being seen in the community, for exchanging news and gossip, for business and social transactions, and for cementing social ties. A public bathing place may be associated with it, further supporting these social functions. But what happens to all this when a piped water supply system is installed? The village can

---

1   For a comprehensive introduction to the social, cultural and political implications on new digital telecommunications infrastructure, see Castells (1996).
2   The phenomenon of fragmentation and recombination is explored in more detail in Mitchell (1995; 1999). See also Horan (2000) and Kotkin (2000).

Photograph courtesy of William J. Mitchell.

Digital telecommunication networks are the latest among infrastructure networks to be superimposed on cities. A new fiber optic backbone follows the long-established route of El Camino Real in Palo Alto, California. All photographs in this chapter courtesy of William J. Mitchell.

now grow larger and take on a different shape, by extending itself out along the water supply lines. The old village well loses its attraction, and so, therefore, does the surrounding public space—at least partially. (Maybe a cafe will emerge to compensate.) And the public bathing place fragments to recombine with domestic space, as houses get private bathrooms.

Think also of the old mill towns of the northeastern United States. Since early technologies for transmitting power (systems of belts, gears and other types of mechanical linkages) could only operate effectively over very short distances, the mills were tightly clustered around sources of water and steam power. Then came the electric power grid and electric motors, breaking this tight linkage between power generation and application, and allowing the convenient application of power to production tasks wherever it might be needed. Industrial production space fragmented and redistributed itself in response to other imperatives—ready availability of raw materials, proximity to labor, access to transportation, and so on. Even in the home, mass-produced electric appliances enabled the industrialization of many household tasks. Mill towns became obsolete.

Closer to our own time, transportation and telephone networks were crucial in the formation of the typical twentieth century urban pattern. High-speed transportation enabled separation of industrial zones from garden suburbs. Telephone connections allowed distancing of management from production; managers and clerical staff could cluster with one another, in a comfortably white-collar culture, in downtown high-rise office buildings. Department stores could take advantage of downtown's superior accessibility. Out of all this came the coarse-grained pattern of cities like Chicago and many others, with their dense central business districts, rings of industrial and warehouse zones, leafy residential suburbs, extended transportation networks, and morning and evening commuter rush hours as people moved in large numbers from one more or less single-purpose zone to another.

These are, of course, simplified versions of some very complex and nuanced stories. And the path dependencies and details, in particular contexts, do matter. But, they certainly illustrate a general truth about the spatial effects of urban networks.

Today, digital telecommunication networks—the latest among the infrastructure networks to be superimposed upon cities—are sparking a similar process of fragmentation and recombination. Their most immediate effect is, obviously enough, upon spatial linkages that have existed primarily to facilitate the transfer of information. For example, the nine-to-five office workplace emerged not only to provide conveniently located space, but also to enable ready circulation of information among office workers, between office workers and files (on paper) and between office workers and their clients. Now, remotely accessed digital files, together with efficient person-to-person electronic communication and portable access devices such as laptops, cell phones, and PDAs, allow office work to be performed almost anywhere—in the home, in hotel rooms, on airplanes and in airport lounges, and at client sites. Thus, office work space begins to fragment and recombine with many other settings.

Similarly, you once had to go to a music store to transfer recorded music into your possession, but now—much to the consternation of the music industry—you can download MP3 files over the Internet. As a result, retail space also fragments and recombines with locations—homes, dorm rooms, offices, and the like—that are equipped with Internet connections.

Loosening Temporal Linkages

Just as transportation and telecommunication technologies selectively loosen spatial linkages among urban activities, so storage technologies selectively loosen temporal linkages—particularly linkages between production and consumption. For example, primitive tanks and cisterns for rain water storage allowed water to be consumed long after the rain had fallen, thus allowing habitation of localities through dry periods. Modern water supply systems combine extensive catchment and reservoir systems with network distribution; large cities would be impossible without them.

Similarly, granaries and early road transportation systems loosened the temporal and spatial linkages between food production and consumption; they allowed cities to draw upon their agricultural hinterlands and to subsist from harvest to harvest—even, perhaps, building up reserves against bad harvests. Railway networks, grain silos and grain transportation ships vastly increased the scope and scale of this sort of system. Refrigeration further extended the principle to perishable foods such as meat, fish, fruit and vegetables—allowing Australia, for example, to become a meat exporter to distant Europe.

In the domain of information, it was writing that first loosened the temporal linkages between intellectual production and consumption. Ancient libraries, like the famous one at Alexandria, became storehouses of information, magnets for scholars and sites for the intensive asynchronous transfer of information. Later, the extensive copying and circulation of manuscripts, printing and mail systems contributed to the development of a decentralized, asynchronous, global system of scholarly production and consumption.

Today, packet switching, the Internet and the World Wide Web combine digital electronic storage of information with electronic network distribution. (Servers are like grain silos, and network backbones are like railroad tracks.) They do so with enormous efficiency, and they make very effective use of distributed electronic intelligence—thousands upon thousands of servers, routers, clients, etc.—to control the whole system. Electronic mail, Web transactions and the like now accomplish asynchronous information transfer on an almost incomprehensively vast scale, and so greatly reduce the need to coordinate activities. Successful placement of a telephone call requires the other party to be available, so schedules, working hours and time zones matter, but asynchronous transfer through voice mail or e-mail does not require worrying about these things. Similarly, a traditional retail store requires customers, sales staff and purchase items to be present in the same place, at the same time, during opening hours, but a Web retail site does not; it can operate 24/7/365. Activities that once required scheduling and coordination, due to the need for some kind of synchronous exchange, can now take place at any time.

Miniaturization, Dematerialization and Ubiquity

This digitally mediated, selective loosening of spatial and temporal linkages among activities is reinforced by another striking effect of the digital electronic revolution—the miniaturization and dematerialization of many of the artifacts that accumulate and circulate within urban systems.

Electronically serviced spaces can support new functions and establish new relationships among activities. A sidewalk cafe in Adelaide, South Australia, serves as an Internet access point and informal workplace.

Telephones vividly illustrate this phenomenon. Once they were large, heavy, electromechanical devices attached to walls or located within special telephone booths and boxes; consequently, you called a specific *place*. Then telephones became smaller, lighter and more electronic than electromechanical. They moved to the desktop and the bedside table, and they were plugged into modular wall jacks; their connection to the architecture became looser. Finally, they became small enough to fit in your pocket, and they became wireless; now you call a *person*, without necessarily knowing or caring where that person currently happens to be located. As a result, the act of conversing by telephone is no longer confined to a relatively few, highly specialized locations. Today—sometimes to our great annoyance—*any* place can potentially be a place for telephone conversation.

It is much the same with computers. When I was a graduate student, computers had to be moved around on big trucks, and you had to go to a campuswide computer center to get your computational work done. By the time I was a junior faculty member, they were becoming small enough to move around on hand trolleys and cheap enough to move into offices. Now, like many other people, I carry a laptop computer with me all the time. Thus, any place becomes a place for word processing or checking e-mail—even a taxi on the way to the airport.

Wireless, portable access devices mobilize activities. Any place can become a workplace.

With increasing network bandwidth, and the growing ubiquity of networked computers, you will not even need to carry the laptop. You will just need a smart card to provide identification, and you will have all your files and software served instantly to whatever machine happens to be at hand—in an office, hotel room, waiting area or anywhere else (anywhere in the world) with electricity and networking. The information resources that you need will simply follow you around through the global digital network.

Consider the performance of recorded music. Once you needed a specialized piano and rolls of perforated paper. Then came portable gramophones and records. Compact disks made the records smaller, and the Walkman made the gramophone wearable. Most recently, recorded music has completely dematerialized; it has been separated from its material substrates and taken the form of MP3 files. It now resides on servers and is distributed through the Internet to tiny MP3 players. You can get whatever music you may want, pretty much whenever and wherever you may want it.

Of course, not everything can be miniaturized, dematerialized and made available ubiquitously. Our cities still contain lots of large, heavy, hard-to-move, material things. There are still things that you have to go *to*. But the effects of electronic miniaturization and digital dematerialization are, nonetheless, increasingly significant. In the buildings and urban patterns of the twenty-first century, we will see less emphasis on specialized, fixed-purpose workplaces, service sites and entertainment sites, and more emphasis upon flexible spaces that can serve different purposes at different moments—depending upon the people and electronic devices currently present and the information currently flowing.

Intelligent Distribution Systems

Digital networking also transforms the structure and behavior of distribution systems. The elementary idea of a distribution system is that you have a central storage or generation site—a village well, a reservoir, a granary, a warehouse, a power plant, or whatever—and you distribute to surrounding areas through networks of pipes, wires or wheeled transportation routes. Collection systems are the inverse of this; the flows run from the hinterland to the center. The sizes and efficiencies of such systems depend basically upon the impedances of the network channels; you can pump out more water, over larger areas, if you have bigger pipes. Much geographic and location theory is grounded upon these very simple ideas. But the Internet works in a different way.

The Internet does not have one, central information storage point (like old-fashioned time-sharing computer systems), but millions of servers scattered around the globe. The network does not have a simple radial structure, but is a highly redundant web that generally offers numerous alternative paths from node to node. It is not centrally controlled, but depends upon the distributed intelligence of countless servers, switches, routers, and so on. And, services like that provided by Akamai employ sophisticated algorithms to optimize the flow of information from servers to clients.

As distributed intelligence is embedded in other types of distribution networks, they will, increasingly, start to behave much like the Internet—with profound consequences for the relationship between network infrastructures and land use.[3] Road vehicles, for example, can now be equipped with GPS-based navigation systems that can compute the shortest path from the origin of a trip to the destination, the fastest path, the path that maximizes use of freeways, the path that minimizes use of freeways, and so on. Furthermore, roads can be equipped with sensors that provide real-time information on traffic flows. Through use of transponders in vehicles and appropriate sensing devices at street intersections and other strategic locations, electronic road pricing schemes can be implemented—as, for instance, they have been in Singapore. Put all this together and you can have

---

3   For an introduction to the relevant technology, see Gershenfeld (1999).

An electronic road pricing system efficiently manages use of transportation resources in Singapore. The cost of driving down Orchard Road varies with the size of the vehicle and the time of day.

a transportation system in which road prices vary dynamically, in a fine-grained way, in response to current traffic conditions (that is, it costs motorists more to drive down congested streets than empty ones), and vehicle navigation systems can take account of current prices when computing optimal routes. Thus, vehicles begin to behave much like packets in a packet-switching network, demand can be managed in a sophisticated way and road resources can be allocated efficiently and fairly through an automated market mechanism.

Now consider warehouses and distribution centers embedded in such a network. Orders can be placed, and inventories can be managed, electronically. Consumer sites within the network can be served efficiently from distribution centers at appropriate intervals. If you are selling compact, high-value, nonperishable items such as books and electronic devices, you can achieve wide and effective coverage combined with economies of scale by creating huge, national and international distribution centers at major airline hubs; this is what Internet retailers, such as Amazon.com, have done. If you are selling more perishable, bulkier items such as groceries, you can still take orders electronically, but you need regional dis-

In Lisbon, Portugal, an electronic system tracks buses and displays their expected arrival times at bus stops.

tribution centers. If you are an online pizza seller, then you need production and distribution centers at the local scale. Whatever you are selling, you need electronically dispatched vans or bicycles (as in urban delivery systems such as that operated by Kozmo.com) to get from the distribution centers to customer locations.

The emerging logic of advanced electrical distribution systems is similar. Electric supply grids now integrate multiple power plants rather than a single, central plant. Now imagine extending this principle by integrating buildings that can sometimes "run the meter backwards" by operating photovoltaics, fuel cells, wind generators and the like. Introduce dynamic electricity pricing that can vary instantaneously according to demand. And introduce smart appliances and building service systems that can optimize power use by minimizing consumption when prices are high and performing heavy tasks when prices are lower. The result, once again, is a system that can potentially achieve dramatic efficiencies through distributed intelligence and automated market mechanisms.

Sometimes, within such intelligent distribution systems, multiple consumers may compete for scarce resources. Consider two "smart" cars converging on a vacant "smart" parking space, for example. The system controlling and charging for

Advanced electrical distribution systems can integrate multiple, nontraditional power sources, provide dynamic pricing and support smart appliances. A photovoltaic installation captures solar power in the outback of Australia.

the space (a descendent of the primitive parking meter) might run an automated auction and sell it to the highest bidder. Motorists could set their bid limits according to how urgently they needed to park, or how long they had been looking for a space.

The prospect of such smart distribution systems raises many interesting policy issues, of course. It must suffice here to observe that these systems will force planners to rethink the relationships of land uses, land values and service network infrastructure. It will be increasingly inadequate to conceive of these relationships in terms of fixed network configurations, schedules and costs (the traditional way of thinking about a rail transportation system, for example) and increasingly necessary to think in terms of very complex dynamic behaviors. The dynamics of the Internet, and of today's electronically mediated global financial system, illustrate what is to come.

In summary, the "smart" in smart growth has been understood in too limited a way. It should imply not only intelligent land use and appropriate configuration of transportation and utility networks, but also the large-scale use of electronic intelligence and telecommunications networking to manage and distribute resources, in more sophisticated and efficient ways, within the urban fabric.

What's Left for Face-time?

What (if anything) drives spatial clustering in a world of remote and asynchronous electronic transactions, miniaturization and dematerialization, and highly dynamic smart supply systems? What holds buildings, neighborhoods, cities and regions together as coherent spatial entities?

One obvious part of the answer is that network infrastructure (including digital telecommunications infrastructure) still requires significant investment and is still costly to operate over large and sparsely settled areas. These well-known imperatives have not been repealed.

A second part of the answer is that locational freedom does not mean locational indifference. People do *care* where they are when they send e-mail or surf the Web. Scenic, climatic and cultural qualities of place still matter and remain attractors. Places that have these sorts of qualities (in other words, qualities that cannot be pumped through a wire) tend to become nuclei of development as traditional locational determinants are weakened by electronic interconnection.

A third part of the answer is that synchronous, face-to-face interaction—though often costly and inconvenient by comparison with electronic alternatives—remains very highly valued. People will put their scarce and precious face-time into what matters most to them, and will relegate less critical, less valuable and less enjoyable interactions to electronic means in order to facilitate this. Hence different types of architectural and urban clusters will emerge from different priorities for use of face-time.

New Architectural and Urban Patterns

If you want to pursue the agrarian dream, for example, the isolated electronic cottage may seem attractive. You can create a wired Walden by constructing a dwelling that is largely self-sufficient through rain water collection, photovoltaic power, and so on, but connected (perhaps via satellite link) to the global digital network. You might work as a writer, or designer, or stock trader, while spending most of your time face-to-face with nature. This pattern is only sustainable on a very limited scale, of course; it puts pressure on scenic and recreational areas, achieves only very low densities of development and is generally bad news for smart growth.

There are variants on the electronic cottage theme, based upon different social value propositions. The counterculture communal variant revisits the utopian ideal of like-minded people living and working together—but maybe as Web designers rather than as farmers. The anti-urban survivalist version values separa-

Concentrations of specialized knowledge and talent continue to exist in an electronically interconnected world. New York's Times Square is now a major node of news, entertainment and financial networks. Exterior electronic displays make this activity publicly visible.

tion from the conflicts and corruption of the city, puts face-time mostly into the traditional nuclear family, makes use of the Web as a resource for home schooling, and emphasizes ruggedly individualistic, free-agent, electronic trading of skills and services.

If you value neighborhood life, and the Putnamesque accumulation of social capital, then a networked version of a traditional neighborhood might seem far more appropriate. Such a neighborhood might consist of electronically serviced live/work dwellings that support flexible work patterns, putting more face-time into child care or elderly care, working at home by the disabled and immobilized, or even full-time telecommuting. Since commuting away is sharply reduced, these dwellings generate 24-hour demand for local services such as cafes and restaurants, local child care and elderly care centers, health clubs, business centers, and the like. These services can become the attractions of a neighborhood center (much like the old village well) and can create opportunities for lots of face-time with the neighbors—rather than with coworkers at the office. This all becomes a way of providing an economic engine for new urbanist, neotraditional developments that do not have to be recreational or retirement villages (Duany, Plater-Zyberg and Speck 2000; Calthorpe and Fulton 2001; Urban Villages Forum 1992).

If you believe Alfred Marshall's famous remark that specialized knowledge is "in the air" in certain places, you will want to put a lot of your face-time into hot spots for your interests—Silicon Valley for electronics and software, Hollywood for entertainment, Lower Manhattan for the financial industry, and so on. By virtue of their concentrations of knowledge and talent, combined now with electronic connections to the wider world, these hot spots are becoming specialized global hubs. All the evidence seems to show that their dominance is strengthened, not weakened, by global interconnectivity. They attract many expatriates, who put their face-time into being at the world center of things rather than into maintaining traditional family and cultural ties.

A New Agenda for Research, Education and Practice

The selective loosening of spatial and temporal linkages among activities, as a consequence of deploying digital telecommunications infrastructure, does not simply produce featureless urban sprawl. It has the more complex and subtle effect of allowing a wide variety of new spatial patterns to emerge. These varying patterns derive primarily from differing priorities for use of face-time, and differing choices of what to relegate to electronic interaction.

Any serious effort to promote smart growth must take account of these patterns, their potentials and their problems. They will be increasingly prominent features of many future urban landscapes. So it no longer suffices to frame the discussion of smart growth in traditional land use and transportation terms.

For the universities, this suggests a new research and teaching agenda. First, urban planners and designers need to develop a much more sophisticated understanding of digital telecommunications technology and associated institutional and policy issues—probably through cross-disciplinary efforts with information technology specialists. Second, there is a need to integrate this understanding, at a theoretical level, with our current understanding of land use and transportation issues; we need cogent theorization of the interrelationships among land use, transportation *and* telecommunication. Finally, as the effects of digital telecommunication on urban form and functioning become increasingly observable, there is an urgent need for empirical research upon which to ground theorization and teaching.

For practicing architects, urban designers and spatial planners, there are new classes of problems to investigate and new prototypes to invent. How should a wired, live/work dwelling be configured? What should an electronically serviced neighborhood be like? How should retail, educational, medical and other facilities be redesigned and relocated in response to the conditions of the digital electronic era? How can we create successful public space under these conditions? How can we take advantage of these conditions to gain efficiencies, curtail urban sprawl and enhance sustainability?

For developers, there are new challenges and opportunities. Projects that are designed to take clever advantage of digital telecommunications infrastructure to enhance their attractiveness while reducing unnecessary resource consumption are likely to have an increasingly decisive edge on the competition. Conversely, projects that ignore digital telecommunications will be at a competitive disadvantage—much like projects with inadequate or expensive transportation access, water supply and sewers and electrical supply.

For policy makers, the new challenge is to establish frameworks for development that encourage desirable new patterns made possible by digital telecommunications. For example, zoning practices may need to be amended not just to minimally tolerate or allow live/work dwellings, but to actually promote such arrangements. Telecommunications policy must be coordinated with land use and transportation policy. And transportation policy must begin to take account of changes in living and working patterns, new logistical strategies, and intelligent control systems made possible by distributed intelligence and digital networking.

Conclusion

In conclusion, I suggest that we must reframe the discussion of smart growth, at these various levels of discourse, to integrate sophisticated, well-grounded consideration of the emerging effects of the digital telecommunications revolution. Doing so does not, of course, guarantee the replacement of sprawl by smart growth. But failure to do so dooms us to falling into avoidable traps and missing some crucial opportunities.

Urban designers and planners, developers and public officials must now *learn* about new telecommunications infrastructure and its uses; they can no more afford to ignore it than they can afford to ignore the automobile. They must *think* about the new building types and development patterns—both desirable and undesirable—that are emerging as a consequence of this infrastructure's large-scale deployment. They must *evaluate* the social, economic, cultural and environmental implications of these new types and patterns. And finally, they must *act*—through design innovation, land use and transportation policy, infrastructure investment and other means that may be at their disposal—to encourage those new types and patterns that offer the most attractive combinations of economic and cultural vibrancy, social equity and long-term environmental responsibility.

References

Calthorpe, Peter, and William Fulton. 2001. *The regional city: Planning for the end of sprawl.* Washington, DC: Island Press.

Castells, Manuel. 1996. *The rise of the network society.* Oxford, England: Blackwell.

Duany, Andreas, Elizabeth Plater-Zyberg, and Jeff Speck. *Suburban nation: The rise of sprawl and the decline of the American dream.* New York, NY: North Point Press.

Gershenfeld, Neil. 1999. *When things start to think.* New York, NY: Henry Holt.

Graham, Stephen, and Simon Marvin. 2001. *Splintering urbanism: Networked infrastructures, technological mobilities and the urban condition.* London, England: Routledge.

Horan, Thomas. 2000. *Digital places: Building our city of bits.* Washington, DC: Urban Land Institute.

Kotkin, Joel. 2000. *The new geography: How the digital revolution is reshaping the American landscape.* New York, NY: Random House.

Mitchell, William J. 1995. *City of bits: Space, place, and the Infobahn.* Cambridge, MA: MIT Press.

———. 1999. *E-topia: Urban life, Jim—But not as we know it.* Cambridge, MA: MIT Press.

Urban Villages Forum. 1992. *Urban villages: A concept for creating mixed-use urban developments on a sustainable scale, second ed.* London, England: Urban Villages Group.

5

Arthur C. Nelson

How Do We Know Smart Growth When We See It?

The New Urban Canvas

This chapter is about characterizing smart growth in a way that allows us to separate charlatans from the real thing. It seems that every idea that some consider leading to better outcomes than the status quo is deemed a form of smart growth. That may be true, but the trick is to develop a set of goals and principles within which all good ideas fall (and bad ideas are excised). Before we do this, however, we need to have some perspective on the next generation of development so we know whether changing the form of new development is worth the effort.

In the United States today, we have about 110 million housing units and, by my reckoning, about 22.2 billion square feet of office space, 16.5 billion square feet of retail space, 7.7 billion square feet of warehouse space and 14.8 billion square feet of manufacturing space. Nearly half of all this development is more than 40 years old. Much of it will be replaced over the next generation. Residential areas will be replaced by commercial and mixed-use development. Office buildings and factories will be torn down and replaced, or converted to other land uses. What few people realize is that over the next generation most existing development will be replaced or converted to other land uses. This is on top of building new structures to accommodate new growth.

To amplify this point, consider the nation as a whole. Between 2000 and 2025, the nation's population will grow from 281 million to 340 million, and employment will grow from 166 million to 222 million. If we assume that two-thirds of the built environment is devoted to residential land uses and one-third to employment-based land uses, roughly 25 percent of all development seen in 2025 will have been built between 2000 and 2025 to accommodate new development (Table 1).

What about existing development? Existing development deteriorates and existing uses in such development become obsolete. There are no good figures on the extent to which existing development is torn down and replaced, though some assumptions are reasonable. Suppose we assume, to be conservative, that all land uses survive 100 years before being replaced (though not necessarily torn down). This may be high or low depending on the area, but it seems a useful point of departure. Using this assumption, about 20 percent of the development seen in 2025 will be existing development in 2000 that is replaced (Table 1). For the nation as a whole, nearly 50 percent of the built environment in 2025 will have been built (or reconfigured) between 2000 and 2025. For some large, rapidly growing metropolitan areas, such as Atlanta, Las Vegas, Orlando, Phoenix and

Table 1
Development Needs 2000 to 2025

Area	New Development Needed (%)	Conversion @ 100-Year Useful Life (%)	Total Development Needed (%)
United States	24.7	20.1	44.7
Atlanta	43.9	17.4	61.3
Baltimore	23.2	20.3	43.5
Boston	12.3	22.3	34.5
Chicago	16.4	21.5	37.9
Cleveland	5.0	23.8	28.8
Dallas	39.6	17.9	57.5
Denver	39.6	17.9	57.5
Detroit	10.7	22.6	33.3
Houston	37.7	18.2	55.9
Kansas City	25.7	19.9	45.6
Las Vegas	71.1	14.6	85.7
Los Angeles	10.1	22.7	32.8
Miami	23.8	20.2	44.0
Minneapolis-St. Paul	34.9	18.5	53.4
New York	3.4	24.2	27.6
Oakland	28.7	19.4	48.1
Orlando	55.7	16.1	71.7
Philadelphia	8.5	23.0	31.6
Phoenix	58.8	15.7	74.6
Pittsburgh	5.0	23.8	28.8
Portland (Oregon)	49.0	16.8	65.8
St. Louis	14.5	21.8	36.3
San Diego	39.9	17.9	57.7
San Francisco	13.8	22.0	35.7
San Jose	23.5	20.2	43.8
Seattle	32.8	18.8	51.7
Tampa-St. Petersburg	31.7	19.0	50.7
Washington, DC	28.7	19.4	48.1

Source: Nelson (2001).

Portland (Oregon), this figure exceeds 60 percent. Even the slowest growing metropolitan areas, such as Cleveland and Pittsburgh, will see new development and conversion exceeding 25 percent. To be more specific, between 2000 and 2025, the United States will add, roughly:
- 60 million people;
- 24 million households; and
- 56 million jobs, of which half will be in business, professional and personal services.

In rough terms, this equates to:
- 45 million housing units (half of which will replace existing units);
- 10.0 billion square feet of retail space, of which 5.3 billion will be newly added;
- 25.0 billion square feet of office space, of which 12.2 billion square feet will be newly added; and
- 2.0 billion square feet of industrial space, of which 1.0 billion will be newly added.

Incomes will rise, opportunities expand, the role of technology broaden, and quality of life improve for most people—maybe everyone. For planners and analysts and the communities for which they work, this suggests that there is a real opportunity to reshape development patterns over the next generation. We have before us a new canvas. The question is, how shall we paint it? Smart growth promises that this canvas will be different from the past, and better. But how can we tell whether what is claimed to be smart growth, is?

Smart Growth in Historical Context

The Chicago Exposition's "City Beautiful" (Scott 1969) and Ebenezer Howard's "Garden City" (Fishman 1989) launched the modern U.S. city planning movement at the turn of the last century. Half a century later, *growth management* (Nelson and Duncan 1995), then a quarter-century after that *sustainable development* (Jenks, Burton and Williams 1996) became the new watchwords for planning. Now *smart growth* is the popular term for improving development patterns. What they all have in common is shaping the built environment to achieve social, economic and environmental objectives. City Beautiful promised clean cities with wide boulevards, gardens and economic prosperity set amidst an attractive environmental backdrop. Howard believed that garden cities could solve all social and economic ills while creating an idyllic countryside outside dirty, congested and ungodly London.

Growth management was a backlash first against rapid suburbanization of northeastern cities, followed in short order by California, the Northwest and Florida. That movement aimed to recreate a regional landscape wherein development would be directed to where facilities could serve it, and away from open spaces that society desired to preserve. Its central premises were that if growth could be accommodated in a landscape configured to preserve open spaces, economic efficiencies could be achieved, the environment protected and society's well-being elevated. Sustainable development probably elevated growth management principles without explicitly meaning to by adding the codicil that growth per se must achieve a renewable level of resource consumption.

Now we have smart growth. Like all previous movements, it promises environmental preservation, economic well-being and social advancement. Unlike other movements, however, it is formless. It does not presuppose a particular built landscape, at least not the kind represented by City Beautiful (gleaming white buildings surrounded by gardens), Garden City (satellite new towns surrounded by greenbelts), growth management (clear separations between urban and rural land uses, although the actual form of development depended on many factors) and sustainable development (advocating at some level compact urban areas). Smart growth can achieve all, some or none of these outcomes. The trouble with smart growth is that it is difficult to know it when we see it.

Popular Characterizations of Smart Growth

Smart growth first came to the nation's attention in the mid-1990s, when Maryland Governor Parris N. Glendening launched that state's Smart Growth and Neighborhood Conservation Program. It has three straightforward goals:

1. Preserve remaining natural resources;
2. Support existing communities and neighborhoods by targeting state resources to support development in areas where infrastructure is already in place or planned; and
3. Save taxpayers from the unnecessary cost of building infrastructure required to support low-density, land-extensive development beyond where infrastructure already exists.

To the International City/County Management Association, on the other hand, smart growth: ...invests time, attention, and resources in restoring community and vitality to center cities and older suburbs. New smart growth is more town-centered, is transit and pedestrian oriented, and has a greater mix of housing, commercial and retail uses (than the status quo). It also preserves open space and many other environmental amenities. (Anderson 1998, 1).

Apparently, smart growth can mean other things too. To the National Association of Home Builders, it means favoring new development over redevelopment because, in part, the economic multiplier is higher for new construction than rehabilitation (NAHB 2000). To its credit, however, the NAHB's vision of smart growth also means providing a wider range of housing options to meet changing needs. Moreover, in true smart growth spirit, it is the lead organization with HUD and others intent on building one million new residential units in central cities within a decade.

More examples of smart growth concepts could be given, but most if not all would lead to the same assessment: smart growth as popularly conceived prefers (1) building where infrastructure and development already exist, as opposed to building on greenfields, especially where infrastructure does not exist, and (2) connecting land uses within built landscapes with transportation alternatives to the single-occupant vehicle. Allow me to now characterize smart growth goals and principles.

Smart Growth Goals

To devise smart growth goals, we begin with the growth management literature of the 1970s, which proffers goals that are, for the most part, identical to the smart growth goals posed in Maryland. Ervin et al. (1977), for example, described three growth management goals:

1. Preserve public goods;
2. Minimize taxpayer exposure to costs; and
3. Minimize adverse land use interactions.

Notice that the first two are essentially restatements of Maryland's three goals (whose second and third goals relate to minimizing cost). Missing is whether smart growth aims to minimize adverse land use interactions, which I believe it does.

Popular characterizations of smart growth go beyond goals of growth management. Smart growth also aims to provide for a greater mix of housing than the status quo. In this respect, smart growth is more than growth management. In consciously expanding housing choice by providing for a mix of housing, presumably wherever development is directed, at least some characterizations of smart growth introduce social equity.

Finally, smart growth aims to create positive interactions between land uses, as Anderson implies, in the sense that the only way to truly offer multiple means of access between land uses is to integrate them. Where growth management aimed merely to minimize negative interactions, smart growth attempts to maximize positive ones. Smart growth, thus, has at least five straightforward goals:

1. Preserve, if not advance, public goods such as air, water and significant landscapes. Certain resources are available to everyone (such as air), so no one can be excluded, and adding one more person does not deprive another of its enjoyment. Yet polluting the air does deprive people of its enjoyment.
2. Minimize, if not prevent, adverse land use impacts. Certain land uses have adverse effects on others, such as placing a landfill in the midst of an area planned for new community development.
3. Maximize positive land use impacts. Some land uses have synergistic effects on other land uses, such as neighborhood schools on residential development.
4. Minimize public fiscal costs. Smart growth should minimize the cost per unit of development to provide public facilities and services.
5. Maximize social equity. Smart growth should maximize jobs/housing balances within small areas; provide equal accessibility to work, shopping, services and leisure; ensure life-cycle housing opportunities within neighborhoods; and offer socioeconomic balance within neighborhoods.

Smart Growth Principles

At the risk of being too simplistic, given the potentially unfathomable nature of smart growth, I offer a set of smart growth principles for the goals listed above.

1. Preserve public goods.
   - Prevent further expansion of the urban fringe.
   - Use a systems approach to environmental planning—shifting from development orientation to basins or ecosystems planning.
   - Preserve contiguous areas of high-quality habitat, as large and circular as possible if it is at or outside the urban fringe.
   - Design to conserve energy.

2. Minimize adverse land use impacts.
   - Prevent negative externalities between land uses.
   - Separate auto-related land uses from pedestrian-oriented uses.

3. Maximize positive land use impacts.
   - Achieve jobs/housing balance within three to five miles of development.
   - Design the street network with multiple connections and relatively direct routes.
   - Provide networks for pedestrians and bicyclists as good as the network for motorists.
   - Incorporate transit-oriented design features.
   - Achieve an average net residential density of six to seven units per acre (without the appearance of crowding). This includes clustering housing to provide open space within sites. (This density supports basic public transit.)

4. Minimize public fiscal costs.
   - Channel development into areas that are already disturbed.

5. Maximize social equity.
   - Provide for affordable single-family and multifamily homes for low- and moderate-income households.
   - Provide life-cycle housing.

These principles can be applied to policies and projects. Policies can include land use and facility plans, regulations guiding development patterns, capital improvement plans that direct public investment, building codes, and the like. Projects would typically be new development or redevelopment at a specific site. It may be difficult for most projects to meet all the principles, but they should in some way be consistent with at least one principle within each goal to be considered minimally smart growth. For example, a project that is not built in an area that is already disturbed (a greenfield) would not by this definition be considered smart growth.

The goals and their principles can also be applied to policies or projects at different scales, such as a site, a community or a region. An example of a regional project would be a transit system, and of a regional policy, a metropolitan urban growth boundary (UGB). A UGB that inhibits the market from providing affordable single-family and multifamily homes for low- and moderate-income households, and from providing life-cycle housing, would not be considered smart growth.

Applying the Principles

Let's apply these principles to examples at three projects, communities and regions.

- Projects: The Kentlands in Maryland and Ridenour in Georgia
- Communities: Boulder, Colorado, and Silver Spring, Maryland
- Regions: Ventura County, California, and metropolitan Portland, Oregon

1. Information Center
2. Old Farm
3. Barn
4. Mansion
5. Market Square
6. Market Square Shopping Center
7. Kentlands Boulevard
8. Market Square
9. Kentlands Square Shopping Center
10. Great Seneca Highway
11. Route 124 Quince Orchard Road
12. Quarry Park
13. Recreation Center
14. Upper Lake
15. Middle Lake
16. Lower Lake
17. Hill Districts
18. Rachel Carson Elementary School
19. Day Care
20. Route 28 Darnestown Road
21. Gatehouse
22. Lake Lynette
23. Lake Inspiration
24. Lake Helene

Figure 1   Plan of The Kentlands, Gaithersburg, Maryland

Source: http://www.Kentlandsuse.com/images/overview/Kentlandsmap.jpg

Projects

The Kentlands is purported to be a good example of an individual development that follows smart growth principles. It is a new urbanism community of about 1,500 homes and 800,000 square feet of retail and office space near Gaithersburg, Maryland (Figure 1). Its housing density is higher than surrounding suburban areas, and its housing choices more numerous. It has a reasonably wide range of commercial opportunities, and a variety of ways in which to get around. It is decidedly better than the standard suburban product, but is it smart growth? Probably not, in my opinion. Consider that it is an example of leapfrog development some 30 miles from the nearest urban center; commuting is likely aggravated by its distance and isolation from urban areas.

Ridenour is a mixed-use development roughly at the intersection of two arterial highways in suburban Cobb County, Georgia (Figure 2). It is an 88-acre site that will be home to 500 homes ranging from single-family detached to multifamily units, 100,000 square feet of offices, 50,000 square feet of retail, a park, a

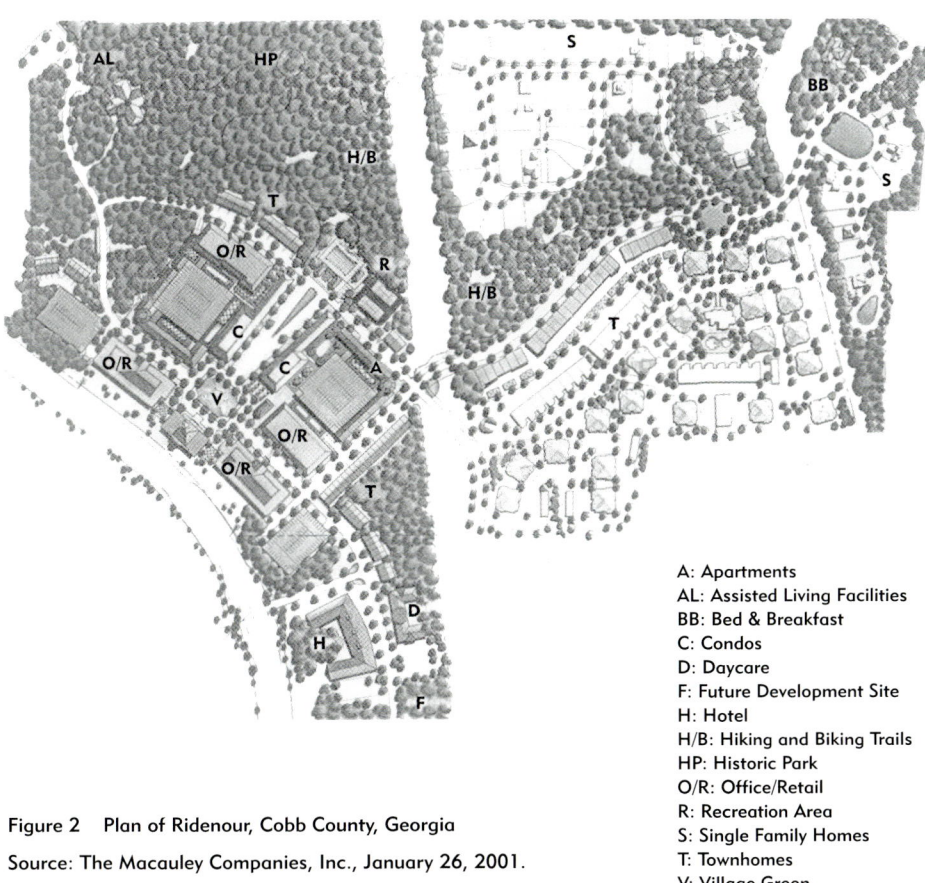

Figure 2   Plan of Ridenour, Cobb County, Georgia
Source: The Macauley Companies, Inc., January 26, 2001.

A: Apartments
AL: Assisted Living Facilities
BB: Bed & Breakfast
C: Condos
D: Daycare
F: Future Development Site
H: Hotel
H/B: Hiking and Biking Trails
HP: Historic Park
O/R: Office/Retail
R: Recreation Area
S: Single Family Homes
T: Townhomes
V: Village Green

Table 2
Comparing the Kentlands with Ridenour

Smart Growth Goal and Principle	The Kentlands	Ridenour
Preserve public goods.		
Prevent further expansion of the urban fringe.[1]	No	Yes
Shift from development orientation to basins or ecosystems planning.[2]	na	na
Preserve contiguous areas of high-quality habitat.[3]	No	Yes
Design to conserve energy.[4]	No	Yes
Minimize adverse land use impacts.		
Prevent negative externalities between land uses.[5]	No	Yes
Separate auto-related land uses from pedestrian-oriented uses.[6]	Yes	Yes
Maximize positive land use impacts.		
Achieve jobs/housing balance within three to five miles of development.[7]	No	Yes
Design street network with multiple connections and relatively direct routes.[8]	Yes	Yes
Provide networks for pedestrians and bicyclists as good as that for motorists.[9]	Yes	Yes
Incorporate transit-oriented design.[10]	No	Yes
Achieve an average net residential density of six to seven units per acre.[11]	No	Yes
Minimize public fiscal costs.		
Channel development into areas that are already disturbed.[12]	No	Yes
Maximize social equity.		
Provide for affordable single-family and multifamily homes for low- and moderate-income households.[13]	?	Yes
Provide life-cycle housing.[14]	?	Yes

Notes

1. The Kentlands is greenfield development that expands the suburban fringe into rural Maryland. Rindenour is well within the existing suburban developed region.
2. It is not clear whether the Kentlands pursues planning based on the ecosystems approach within its regional context, but in Ridenour the issue is moot since it is developed within the existing suburban fabric.
3. The Kentlands may not necessarily preserve or undermine large contiguous areas of habitat, but Ridenour, being within the suburban developed region, clearly does not threaten such habitat.
4. Energy savings attributable to designs and circulation with the Kentlands are offset by longer commutes to work and shopping. Ridenour includes energy-saving design with internal circulation and is directly connected to regional transportation systems.
5. The Kentlands imposes negative externalities on regional agricultural operations (Nelson and Duncan 1995). Ridenour fits into the existing developed suburban region.
6. Within their projects, both the Kentlands and Ridenour separate vehicles from people.
7. The Kentlands provides homes for up to 2,000 workers, but most jobs provided within the project are in retail with low wages. Ridenour will generate about 600 jobs, and its residential areas will be home to about 650 workers, in a variety of housing types and prices or rents. Ridenour will achieve a reasonable jobs/housing balance.
8. Both the Kentlands and Ridenour have street networks with multiple connections and relatively direct routes.

9. Both the Kentlands and Ridenour provide networks for pedestrians and bicyclists as good as those for motorists.
10. The Kentlands is not designed to accommodate transit connections and has no transit-oriented development relationships. Ridenour is an example of transit-oriented development, albeit done in advance of anticipated light rail or express bus systems.
11. The Kentlands net density appears to fall under this target, while Ridenour exceeds it.
12. See note 1.
13. Although the Kentlands offers homes of varying sizes, prices and types, it is not clear whether it strikes a balance such as providing for its regional fair share of housing for low- and moderate-income households. Ridenour provides this balance, with about 15 to 20 percent of its housing geared for regional low to moderate incomes.
14. In Ridenour, it will be possible for someone to be raised as a child, move into an apartment, move into single-family detached homes of difference sizes depending on family needs and income, and cycle down to smaller homes or apartments as needs change. It is not clear whether this is possible in the Kentlands.

Table 3
Share of New Metropolitan Housing Units Built in Central City Boulder and Longmont 1988–1998

Year	Population Boulder	New Unit Share of Metropolitan Area	Population Longmont	New Unit Share of Metropolitan Area
1988	81,987	28.8%	49,832	10.4%
1989	82,649	23.8%	50,694	14.3%
1990	83,312	35.2%	51,555	5.1%
1991	84,581	20.2%	52,683	10.1%
1992	85,851	26.7%	53,809	14.9%
1993	87,120	16.5%	54,937	15.0%
1994	88,389	13.6%	56,064	19.4%
1995	89,659	5.3%	57,191	28.0%
1996	90,928	7.8%	58,318	22.4%
1997	92,197	6.8%	59,446	41.4%
1998	93,467	7.5%	60,572	30.9%

Source: Adapted from U.S. Bureau of the Census, building permit annual reports (Nelson 2001).

bed and breakfast, a day care center and an assisted living center. Is this smart growth? I think so. The area has already been disturbed, it provides for jobs/housing balance, uses existing transportation systems (including buses that connect to regional rail) and provides for a system of internal open spaces. Table 2 compares the Kentlands with Ridenour.

Communities

Boulder, Colorado, home to the University of Colorado, has used an urban growth boundary since the 1970s to rein in urban sprawl and prevent development of the Rocky Mountain foothills (Figure 3). It has done little, however, to ameliorate housing needs. Although the city has an elaborate, inclusionary housing effort,

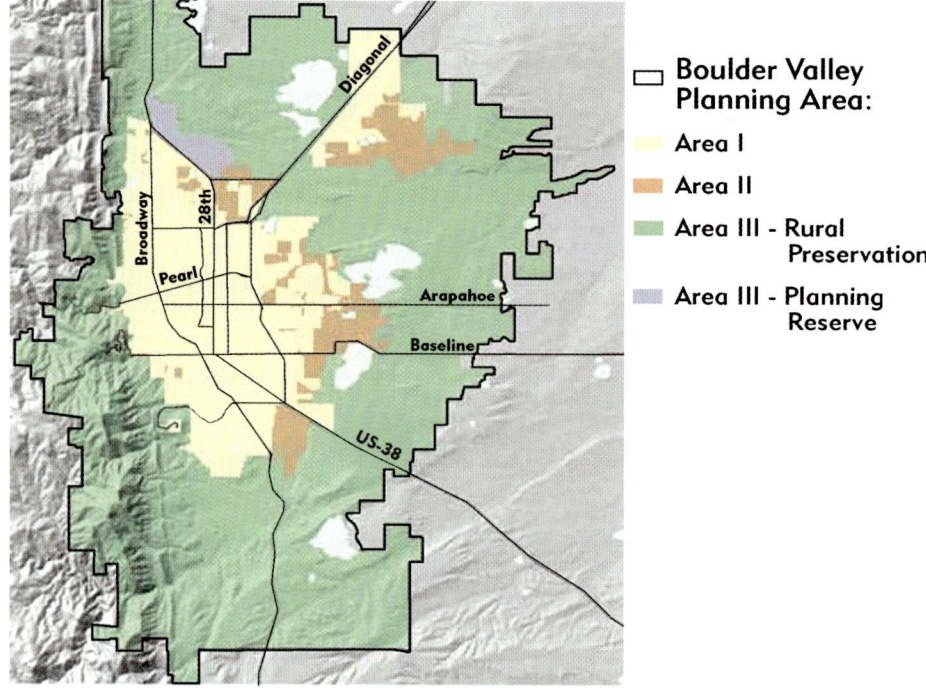

Figure 3 Map of Boulder, Colorado
Source: http://www.ci.boulder.co.us/planning/BVCP2000/bpbvcpback.htm

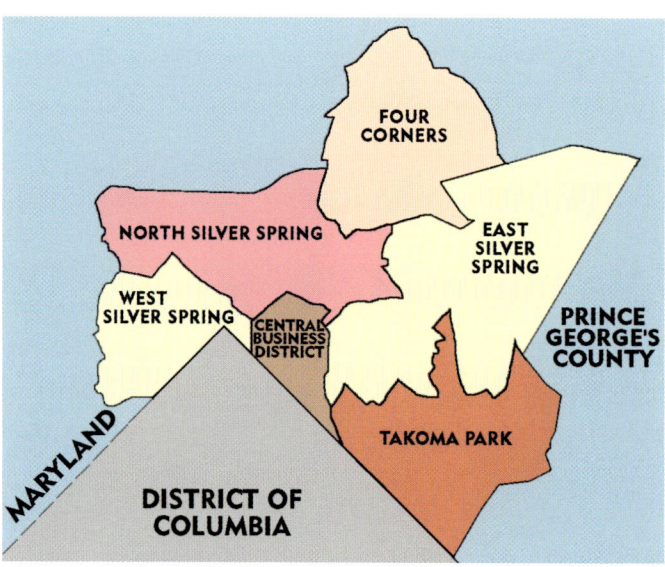

Figure 4 Six Planning Areas within Montgomery County, Maryland
Source: Adapted from PowerPoint slide provided by mayor's office, Silver Spring, Maryland, July 24, 2000.

Table 4
Households and Housing in Silver Spring, Maryland, 1997

Attribute	Single-family Detached	Townhouse	Garden	High-rise Apartment	All Types
Percent	30.1%	2.4%	26.8%	40.7%	100.0%
Household Size	2.75	2.15	1.79	1.72	2.06
Monthly Costs					
Homeowners	$1,292	$1,221	$964	$754	$1,224
Renters	$1,030	$918	$659	$794	$747
Household Income					
Under $30,000	8.7%	3.9%	23.3%	30.9%	20.4%
$30,000–$49,999	12.3%	22.7%	46.2%	35.8%	30.4%
$50,000–$69,999	16.3%	13.3%	22.7%	17.6%	18.6%
$70,000–$99,999	21.7%	18.7%	7.0%	12.0%	14.1%
$100,000+	41.0%	41.5%	0.7%	3.5%	16.6%
Median	$87,365	$80,265	$44,905	$37,990	$49,640

Source: Montgomery County Planning Board online, *http://www.mc-mncppc.org/factmap/databook/profiles/silversp.htm*.

homes in Boulder are nonetheless out of financial reach for many if not most of the people who work there. Housing demand is displaced to Boulder County's other major city, Longmont, and its surrounding rural areas (Table 3).

Silver Spring, Maryland, is located in Montgomery County, Maryland, adjacent to the District of Columbia. Composed of six planning areas, it is contained within Montgomery County's regional urban growth boundary (Figure 4). Facing development pressures comparable with Boulder's, it nonetheless appears to provide a wider range of housing more commensurate with the working population's salaries (Table 4). Table 5 compares Boulder with Silver Spring as smart growth communities.

Regions

In November 1999, Ventura County voters approved several growth control initiatives. They include a countywide measure that requires voter approval before agricultural and open space may be rezoned and converted to residential or commercial use, complemented by UGB measures in the cities of Oxnard, Camarillo, Thousand Oaks and Simi Valley (Figure 5). The city UGB measures require voter approval before land outside a city's urban boundary may be annexed into the city. While this appears in some ways to be smart growth, I believe it is not.

Since 1978, the Portland, Oregon, metropolitan area has used a UGB combined with some of the nation's most restrictive open space preservation policies to shape urban form (Figure 6). All projected needs for development are accom-

Table 5
Comparing Boulder with Silver Spring

Smart Growth Goal and Principle	Boulder	Silver Spring
Preserve public goods.		
Prevent further expansion of the urban fringe.[1]	?	Yes
Shift from development orientation to basins or ecosystems planning.[2]	Yes	Yes
Preserve contiguous areas of high-quality habitat.[3]	No	Yes
Design to conserve energy.[4]	No	Yes
Minimize adverse land use impacts.		
Prevent negative externalities between land uses.[5]	No	Yes
Separate auto-related land uses from pedestrian-oriented uses.[6]	Yes	Yes
Maximize positive land use impacts.		
Achieve jobs/housing balance within three to five miles of development.[7]	No	Yes
Design street network with multiple connections and relatively direct routes.[8]	Yes	Yes
Provide networks for pedestrians and bicyclists as good as that for motorists.[9]	Yes	Yes
Incorporate transit-oriented design.[10]	No	Yes
Achieve an average net residential density of six to seven units per acre.[11]	No	Yes
Minimize public fiscal costs.		
Channel development into areas that are already disturbed.[12]	?	Yes
Maximize social equity.		
Provide for affordable single-family and multifamily homes for low- and moderate-income households.[13]	No	Yes
Provide life-cycle housing.[14]	No	Yes

Notes

1. By failing to accommodate its proportionate share of the regional demand for development, and failing to be part of a regional approach to containing sprawl, Boulder's policies shift development away from Boulder to the rural countryside beyond its greenbelts, although they do prevent growth from occurring within its greenbelt. Silver Spring accommodates development and is part of Montgomery County's regional urban containment program.
2. Boulder has pursued an ecosystem approach by itself, and Silver Spring has done so through its coordination with Montgomery County.
3. By displacing development not guided by a regional urban containment plan, Boulder does not preserve large contiguous areas of habitat, but Silver Spring, as part of Montgomery County's urban containment plan, does.
4. Energy savings attributable to designs and circulation within Boulder are offset by longer commutes to work for the workers whose jobs are in Boulder but who cannot afford to live there. Silver Spring includes energy-saving design with internal circulation, and is directly connected to regional transportation systems.
5. By displacing development to rural areas beyond its greenbelt, Boulder imposes negative externalities on regional agricultural operations (Nelson and Duncan 1995). Silver Spring is part of Montgomery County's urban containment program.
6. Both Boulder and Silver Spring separate vehicles from people.

7. Boulder's households support about 60,000 jobs, but about 80,000 people work there, indicating that a jobs/housing balance is not met. Silver Spring's households support about 27,000 jobs, reasonably close to the 30,000 jobs found there. Neither have true jobs/housing balance, but Silver Spring is closer.

8. Both Boulder and Silver Spring have street networks with multiple connections and relatively direct routes.

9. Both Boulder and Silver Spring provide networks for pedestrians and bicyclists as good as those for motorists.

10. Although it has a small bus system, Boulder does not pursue transit-oriented development relationships. Silver Spring does.

11. Boulder's net density appears to fall under this target, while Silver Spring exceeds it.

12. See note 1. Boulder's planning displays no serious effort to accommodate its proportionate share of regional development, thereby displacing that development throughout Boulder County, although it does direct development within Boulder to areas already disturbed or within the UGB.

13. Although Boulder has homes of varying sizes, prices and types—and it has an elaborate inclusionary housing program—it is not clear whether it strikes a balance, such as providing for its regional fair share of housing for low- and moderate-income households. Silver Spring appears to provides this balance, with about 20 percent of its housing geared for regional low to moderate incomes (Table 4).

14. In Silver Spring, it is possible for someone to be raised as a child, move into an apartment, move into single-family detached homes of difference sizes depending on family needs and income, and cycle down to smaller homes or apartments as needs change. It is not clear whether this is possible in Boulder.

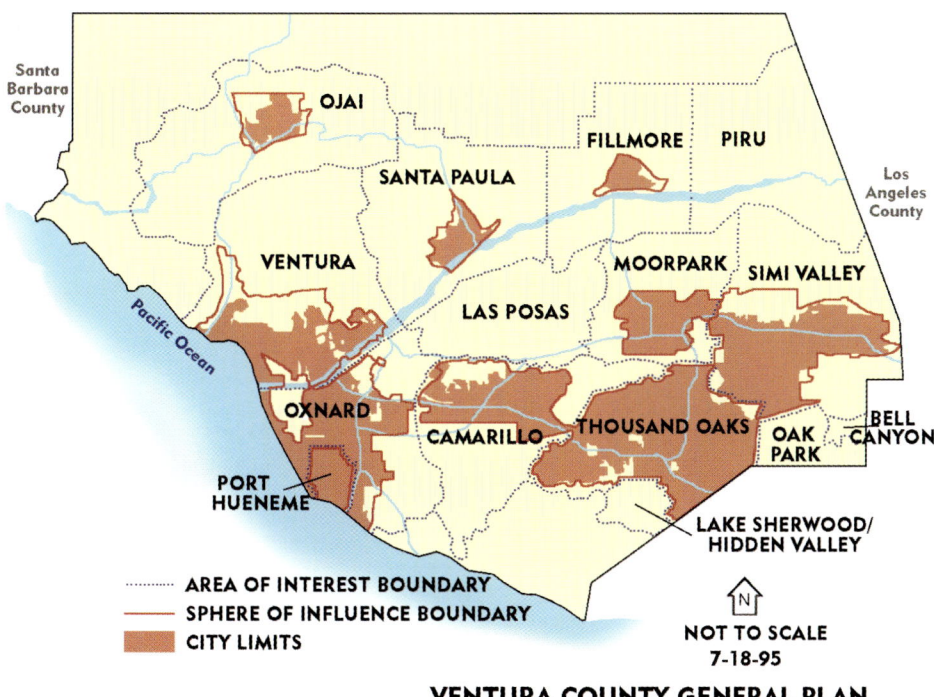

Figure 5   Ventura County, California

Source: adapted from http:elib.cs.berkeley.edu/cgi-bin/display_page??page=80&elib_id872&format=gif

Table 6
Comparing Ventura County with Metropolitan Portland

Smart Growth Goal and Principle	Ventura County	Metro Portland
Preserve public goods.		
Prevent further expansion of the urban fringe.[1]	Yes	Yes
Shift from development orientation to basins or ecosystems planning.[2]	Yes	Yes
Preserve contiguous areas of high-quality habitat.[3]	Yes	Yes
Design to conserve energy.[4]	No	Yes
Minimize adverse land use impacts.		
Prevent negative externalities between land uses.[5]	Yes	Yes
Separate auto-related land uses from pedestrian-oriented uses.[6]	Yes	Yes
Maximize positive land use impacts.		
Achieve jobs/housing balance within three to five miles of development.[7]	No	Yes
Design street network with multiple connections and relatively direct routes.[8]	Yes	Yes
Provide networks for pedestrians and bicyclists as good as that for motorists.[9]	Yes	Yes
Incorporate transit-oriented design.[10]	No	Yes
Achieve an average net residential density of six to seven units per acre.[11]	No	Yes
Minimize public fiscal costs.		
Channel development into areas that are already disturbed.[12]	No	Yes
Maximize social equity.		
Provide for affordable single-family and multifamily homes for low- and moderate-income households.[13]	No	Yes
Provide life-cycle housing.[14]	No	Yes

Notes
1. Both Ventura County and metropolitan Portland limit the outward expansion of urban development.
2. Both Ventura County and metropolitan Portland include planning provisions that address ecosystems.
3. Both Ventura County and metropolitan Portland include planning provisions that preserve large areas of habitat.
4. Energy savings attributable to designs and circulation within Ventura County are offset by longer commutes to work. Metropolitan Portland includes energy-saving design features, including shorter distances to work.
5. Both Ventura County and metropolitan Portland do a reasonably good job of preventing negative externalities.
6. Both Ventura County and metropolitan Portland have efforts that separate vehicles from people.
7. Both Ventura County and metropolitan Portland achieve jobs/housing balance on a broad scale, but while Portland extends its planning to achieve balance within each of its communities, Ventura County does not.
8. Both Ventura County and metropolitan Portland have street networks with multiple connections and relatively direct routes.
9. Both Ventura County and metropolitan Portland provide networks for pedestrians and bicyclists as good as those for motorists.
10. Ventura County does not pursue transit-oriented development relationships. Metropolitan Portland does.
11. Ventura County's net density appears to fall under this target while metropolitan Portland's achieves it.
12. See note 1. Ventura County's planning displays no serious effort to accommodate its proportionate share of

regional development, thereby displacing that development throughout the region, although it does direct county development to areas already disturbed or within the UGB.

13. Although Ventura County has homes of varying sizes, prices and types, it is not clear whether it strikes a balance such as providing for its regional fair share of housing for low- and moderate-income households. Metropolitan Portland has planning policies that give communities explicit housing targets to reach.

14. Within most if not every community in metropolitan Portland it is possible for someone to be raised as a child, move into an apartment, move into single-family detached homes of difference sizes depending on family needs and income, and cycle down to smaller homes or apartments as needs change. It is not clear whether this is possible in Ventura County.

modated within the UGB. The Portland approach explicitly addresses all smart growth goals and every principle. Table 6 compares metro Portland's smart growth planning with Ventura County's.

Observations

Are the Kentlands, Boulder and Ventura County bad communities? No. They each offer positive outcomes relative to growth as usual. The Kentlands is clearly an improvement on conventional suburban subdivision design and development. Boulder started trying to preserve what it could a generation ago, by itself, in the

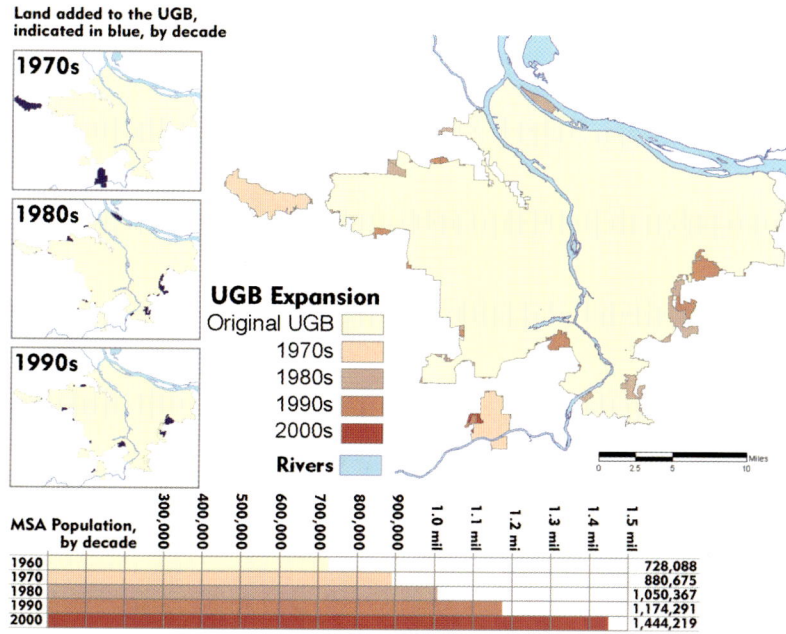

Figure 6   Metropolitan Portland Urban Growth Boundary

Portland's population has grown dramatically since the creation of the urban growth boundary in 1978; nonetheless, development has been accommodated with very few expansions to the boundary.

Source: Metro, Portland Oregon.

Growth as Usual	Better Growth	Smart Growth
Conventional subdivisions	The Kentlands	Ridenour
	Boulder	Silver Spring
Conventional land use planning	Ventura County	Metropolitan Portland

Figure 7   Smart Growth Continuum

absence of a regional framework, which is still lacking. Ventura County has contained urban development within UGBs. All efforts are noteworthy, with many receiving well-deserved awards.

But are they smart growth, strictly speaking? I would say, no. While elements of each reflect smart growth sensitivities, on balance they don't deserve the label. In contrast, Ridenour, Silver Spring and metropolitan Portland are examples of smart growth. Each clearly is based on at least one principle within each of the smart growth goals, and each is based on more principles on aggregate than their counterparts. Unlike the Kentlands, Ridenour demonstrates how to create new communities *within* the developed suburban environment. Unlike Boulder, Silver Spring is consciously designed to fit into the larger metropolitan framework, but still uses UGBs to define the urban-rural interface. Unlike Ventura County, metropolitan Portland is proactive in accommodating all development needs both throughout the metropolitan area and within each of its communities.

What emerges from this exercise is a continuum of smart growth, illustrated in Figure 7. Growth as usual is what many people today are attempting to change, with smart growth being the desirable outcome. Without a scheme to decide what is truly smart growth, though, there is no way to evaluate claims by sponsors that their products earn the term. The continuum allows for a middle ground: if something is an improvement over growth as usual but does not meet all conditions of smart growth, it can nonetheless be considered better growth.

Smart growth must have objective meaning or the concept is mere pablum. I have offered a framework within which assertions of smart growth can be assessed objectively. More work can be done to flesh out objective measures—my principles are merely starting points—but this checklist can help us recognize smart growth when we see it. Now what we need is an organization to offer a smart growth stamp of approval to assure quality control on the use of the term.

References

Anderson, Geoff. 1998. *Why smart growth: A primer.* Washington, DC: International City/County Management Association.

Ervin, David E., et al. 1977. *Land use control: The economic and political effects.* New York, NY: Praeger.

Fishman, Robert. 1989. *Urban utopias in the twentieth century.* Cambridge, MA: MIT Press.

Jenks, Mike, Elizabeth Burton, and Katie Williams. 1996. *The compact city: A sustainable urban form?* London, England: E & FN Spon.

National Association of Home Builders (NAHB). 2000. *Smart growth report: Building better places to live, work and play.* Washington, DC: National Association of Home Builders.

Nelson, Arthur C. 2001. *A new canvas: The time really is now to shape the built environment.* Atlanta, GA: City and Regional Planning, Georgia Institute of Technology.

Nelson, Arthur C., and James B. Duncan. 1995. *Growth management principles and practices.* Chicago, IL: American Planning Association.

Scott, Mel. 1969. *American city planning.* Berkeley, CA: University of California Press.

6

Alex Krieger

Seven Wise (Though Possibly Impractical) Goals for Smart Growth Advocates

Seven Wise (Though Possibly Impractical) Goals

Do environmentalists, production home builders, advocates for urban infill and cul-de-sac suburbanites all envision the same result when exhibiting enthusiasm for smart growth? It is unlikely. Indeed, it is hard not to smile at the somewhat diabolical nature of the smart growth slogan. On the one hand, it suggests the possibility of attaining what all presumably want—smarter growth—and by the mere use of the term placing oneself on the right side of the argument. On the other hand, cynics might ask, is not one reason for the popularity of the slogan its role as a cover for NIMBYism, that self-centered stance that no more growth (at least near one's own backyard) is best?

When hearing out an advocate on the subject, it is generally wise to ask, "smart growth for whom?" I offer the following seven *impractical* suggestions for pursuing a smarter growth future.

1. How About Taxing Redundancy?

By some accounts, approximately 1 in 12 houses in the United States is vacant; these houses are either abandoned, considered obsolete or beyond repair, are for sale and between occupants, are new and not yet occupied, or are sited in undesirable neighborhoods. This surprising statistic does not even include second homes owned by the same household. U.S. culture has a rather substantial capacity for constructing redundancy (not only, by the way, in middle-class housing), and prosperous times hardly impede such capacity. Let me invoke a recent *USA Today* cover story reporting on the trend toward second homes. The photograph shows a handsome middle-age couple strolling down a rather pleasant new-urbanist-looking street. The accompanying narrative describes the recent surge in second-home communities, while quoting other no doubt equally handsome couples on their explanations for why a single home is no longer sufficient. This trend is not going to help society as a whole grow smarter. However, it is unlikely that those investing in a second home perceive themselves as acting either foolishly or insensitively.

So why don't we find a way to tax redundancy, developing a graduated tax to boot. For example, second-home purchases would be taxed in relationship to geography. Using Boston as the primary address, a second home in Roxbury or Dorchester (to be used as rental property, perhaps) would produce a small premium on the owner's tax bill. A second home located, say, between Routes 128 and 495 would face a much larger tax. But a second home in the Berkshires, on Cape Cod or along the Maine coast would face a usurious tax! (On second thought, leave Maine out of this. That happens to be where my family vacations.) By the way, such a tax on redundancy should be a dedicated tax; not simply accruing to the

Photograph © Alex Krieger.

Looking down on a large subdivision of large houses. Photograph © Kathy Foulger.

general budget of a municipality, but used solely for the purpose of implementing other smart growth policies—like neighborhood reinvestment or an affordable housing fund.

Such taxing of redundancy (a historic cause of sprawl) would surely meet resistance, as it goes against the very grain of our national economic welfare. What would happen to the U.S. economy if we only purchased what we truly needed? One shudders to think, even as an examination of most Americans' closets and garages reveals countless things no longer viewed as quite so essential. The next time you encounter that frequently used indicator of national economic health—the number of annual new housing starts—consider whether all are necessary, especially where they are sprouting and for whom they are being built.

2. How About Championing an Up-zoning Amendment for the City of Cambridge?

Cambridge, Massachusetts, is a very desirable place to live, so shouldn't one make it easier to move there? As a bonus to the region, more housing in Cambridge would keep some people from buying into a greenfield subdivision somewhere west of Route 495. More housing may ease the present housing shortage, or make housing a little less unaffordable in Cambridge. It might have allowed a young

Seven Wise (Though Possibly Impractical) Goals

professor like myself to experience that live-work proximity that William Mitchell discussed in Chapter 4. (I, sadly must commute from the more affordable town of Boston.) Is not increasing density in already urbanized areas generally a good thing for smart growth, at least as a countervailing force to suburban sprawl?

What is the likelihood of convincing Cantabridgians that an up-zoning amendment is a good thing for them? How many residents of Boston's Back Bay are supporting air-rights construction above the Massachusetts Turnpike? The question of smart growth for whom is a very real one. Would an up-zoning amendment be "smart" for the present residents of Cambridge? Not if they believed (rightly or not) that it would tax municipal services or bring more traffic into their city. However, from a regional perspective it may be smarter, or from a national land use standpoint, or from an open space conservation point of view, or an ecological perspective.

Now, what about taking the perspective of a young family seeking a new home and neighborhood while calibrating issues of convenience, children's education and real estate affordability. Should they pay more to live in Cambridge, doing their part to curtail sprawl, or should they go for that relatively inexpensive distant subdivision and the promise of decent public schools, albeit at the cost of a second car? Such weighing of options leads to quite different conclusions about what is in the best interests of a community, or a region, or a family, and needs to be discussed more at conferences about smart growth.

3. What About Raising the Gasoline Tax by a Dollar?

If auto-dependence leads, as many argue, to very unsmart growth patterns, let's make those accountable—the drivers—pay by saddling them with a user fee. Two benefits might accrue to society: a reduction (somewhat) in the use of the automobile given higher operating costs, and a revenue stream (if dedicated) for worthwhile smart growth causes—affordable housing, again, or public acquisition of open space, or increased funding of public transportation systems. It's hard to gauge how unpopular such a tax would be. There is a belief that gasoline prices, like most consumer costs, are inelastic. Yet they do not seem to be so in practice. The cost of gasoline has fluctuated by over a dollar during the past year or so without a major consumer outcry, nor, by the way, any appreciable decline in per capita mileage usage. That may take another dollar or two hike. Yet it is hard to find any political leaders who seem willing to publicly champion something like a dedicated gasoline tax. While impact fees are occasionally discussed—tolls, or excise taxes, or use assessments—few seem likely on our horizon.

A classic cloverleaf separates land uses and fosters auto-dependency. Royalty-free stock photograph.

In truth, despite occasional brave words, we are not particularly courageous about pursuing the kind of policies that may actually lead to smarter growth, or at minimum, sprawl reduction. Generally, paths of least resistance are followed. Most of the so-called smart growth referenda in recent elections have dealt primarily with conservation of open space, in generally affluent communities well positioned to afford such. Is this sufficient "smarts" to alter our national land development behaviors? It is doubtful.

4. How About Regional Transfer of Development Rights?

Why shouldn't the owners of valuable agricultural or scenic land (not wishing to turn it over for development, while avoiding the economic penalty of not doing so) be able to "sell" the development value to sites in already urbanized areas? This would require the cooperation of places like Cambridge—that is, desirable places with demand for development to which such rights could be transferred. Transfer sites would have to be identified either through voluntary regional cooperation or some form of (dare one say) regional governance. Some manner of regional authority would have to balance out those areas designated for conservation against the areas ready and willing to accept additional growth. This would surely be perceived in conflict with one of the most cherished U.S. municipal rights, home rule, where intermunicipal competition for markets and tax bases often precludes cross-jurisdictional cooperation.

Furthermore, streamlined approval processes would have to exist in the areas of transfer. Well, good luck there! One of the perennial catalysts for sprawl is the ease of permitting on many greenfield sites by comparison to the layers of approvals, review and red tape governing the pace of redevelopment in most urbanized areas.

5. Then, How About Regional Tax Sharing?

Wouldn't this be a good device to balance out a region's growth pressures while minimizing the sort of competition for tax revenue among individual communities, which ultimately does not benefit any region-wide growth management efforts? Wouldn't this help first-ring suburbs no longer perceived as good areas for investment, or simply built out and therefore struggling to increase revenue or maintain services? Wouldn't it help some inner-city neighborhoods in the region to maintain their levels of service and thus minimize (or better yet, reverse) the downward spiral of poorer conditions coupled with continued loss of population and commerce? The Twin Cities in Minnesota have one of the very few such revenue sharing programs. Are there better strategies for leveling out such inequalities among neighboring communities, or is the relative scarcity of such regional cooperation another example of our uncourageous search for effective smart growth policies?

6. How About Using Some of the Federal Budget Surplus to Create a Suburban Renewal Program?

(Notice that these suggestions are not becoming more plausible.) Why not use some of the (pre-9/11) surplus to conceive a national campaign equivalent to the urban renewal programs of the mid-twentieth century. These would not be focused on slum clearance, residential displacement or top-down planning, but (having learned from the mistakes of the urban renewal era) would emphasize renovation, infrastructure enhancement, adaptive reuse, selective densification, modernization of community facilities such as schools, provision of home-based or small-scale commercial improvement subsidies, and similar strategies aimed at

Looking at the Portland metropolitan urban growth boundary from the outside in Springville, Oregon. Photograph © Kathy Foulger.

struggling older suburban areas. Again, stabilizing (or repositioning, as the development community describes it) and raising the attractiveness of areas already developed should diminish—even if slightly—the impulse to abandon and build anew farther away. This leads me to my final and likely most impractical suggestion.

7. How About Becoming Culturally Less Susceptible to the "New and Improved" Sales Pitch?

My skepticism about the new urbanism bandwagon lies not in the advocated principles, but in the often exaggerated claims of success. These are usually claimed for new development with the subliminal message of product marketing: move from the unfashionable sprawl that you currently inhabit into our brand-new, amenity-laden version. Things advertised as "new and improved" frequently seduce a consumer market and, indeed, have been the cause of much sprawl—and redundancy! Entrepreneurial (if not sustainability-motivated) home builders understand perfectly well the allure of the slightly different rather than the truly innovative. At the very moment when U.S. society is becoming interested in alternative lifestyles and dwelling places, including the old city itself, a new and improved version of the suburb should not dominate our sense of options.

Now I'm getting a bit strident, which is never very useful. Of course, better management of our land and other resources is a very smart thing to set out to do, and has been advocated by many people over time. My point is that to do so effectively will ultimately require some difficult choices and some courageous policies, not to mention acknowledging one's own responsibility for less than (societally) smart individual actions. Instead, I hear impassioned rhetoric—useful but insufficient—and, worse, echoes of quite selfish motivations involving the protection of one's own quality of life while criticizing others seeking to achieve a similar level or being able to partake of the same choices.

It seems that it is always the next subdivision, not one's own, which causes all of the traffic congestion and lack of social engagement, and chews up valuable open space. Do not, some seem to be saying, limit my ability to benefit from the sprawl of my own choosing (such as by adding a toll or impact fee), but do protect me from the impacts of future growth. Perhaps this is inevitable when a good idea such as the suburb becomes universally (or nearly so) achievable, and thus becomes subject to stresses enforceable by early advocates. When, as is said of early-twentieth-century Pittsburgh, an executive had to bring a second white shirt to work because the first would be covered in soot by midday, smart growth may, indeed, have to decamp from the overstressed industrial city. Earlier in the twentieth century, decentralization was a way to enhance livability. We are at a different point in the urbanization process today.

For me, the best hope of growing smarter at the beginning of the twenty-first century lies not in draconian land use restrictions or radical zoning changes (as useful as some of these might be), but in the reemergence of interest in city life. The recognition I consider most essential to future growth management is that today more people than in the 1950s and 1960s seem willing to seek out the virtues of city living, to see places of high human concentration not as congested or dysfunctional but as desirable, enjoyable rather than mandatory, as they were during the Industrial Revolution. That view, along with additional courage to challenge conventional wisdom and to keep asking "smarter growth for whom?", remains high on my list of smart growth endeavors.

I am just as intolerant of those city dwellers who figured out the virtues of urban dwelling a bit earlier, and are now begrudging others the opportunity to return to the city, as I disapprove of those unrepentant suburbanites seeking to deny newcomers the benefits of their suburban dreams. Insuring that broad choices in habitat are available to all may be among the most impractical but most essential kind of smart growth policies.

7

Eran Ben-Joseph

Smarter Standards and Regulations

Diversifying the Spatial Paradigm of Subdivisions

The design and building professions usually must work within a rather rigid framework of controls and standards that dictate all aspects of subdivision layout. Simple dimensions for minimum street width, sidewalks or planting strips may seem innocuous, but when applied to miles of streets in hundreds of subdivisions occupied by millions of people, they have an enormous impact on the way our neighborhoods look, feel and work for us. Take street standards as an example. The prevailing right-of-way width for a residential subdivision street, as specified by the Institute of Transportation Engineers (ITE), has remained at 50 to 60 feet for the last 55 years. In a typical suburban subdivision, with 5,000-square-foot lots and 56-foot rights-of-way, streets amount to approximately 30 percent of the total development. When typical 20-foot driveway setbacks are included, the total amount of paved space increases to about 50 percent of the development (Figure 1).

I do not mean we should abolish standards. Obviously, design and engineering standards can and often do assure a minimum level of quality and performance, as do many plans and construction standards designed to protect our health and safety. The problem arises when standards intended for health and safety overstep their bounds and lose their grounding in objective measures of goodness, or lose a connection with the original rationale for their existence. The residential environment is being shaped in a major way by standards that no one questions, but that have become part of a rigid framework closed to change. Land-consumptive requirements for large building lots, extensive road frontages, deep setbacks, and wide, paved roads have often restricted unconventional developments.

Why has this happened? Mainly because these standards have provided, through the years, an established, publicly approved framework that supposedly shields developers and cities from being liable.

Public Policies Provide Direct and Indirect Incentives for Sprawling Designs

Historical records of subdivision regulation development in the United States show a clear connection between public policies and prevailing, sprawling design manifestations. The past 70 years of federal financial assistance and mortgage insurance have resulted in the most ambitious suburbanization plan in U.S. history. To secure its investments, the federal government, through the Federal Housing Authority (FHA), established a comprehensive system of appraisal procedures designed to eliminate risk and failure. To qualify for a loan, lenders, borrowers and developers had to submit detailed plans and documentation of their projects to the administration, which would determine whether or not they had sound prospects. Thus, the

Photograph © Eran Ben-Joseph.

Figure 1. At least one-third of all urban development is devoted to roads, parking lots and other motor vehicle infrastructure. Much built road space is actually wasted, considering that local residential streets compose 80 percent of the total national road miles while they carry only 15 percent of total vehicle miles. Photograph © Alex S. MacLean/Landslides.

FHA underwriting procedure soon turned into the prevailing standard; with monetary support at stake, developers preferred to comply with the published standards. Soon FHA officials found themselves in a powerful position, far greater than any planning agency, to direct and shape development for generations to come.

FHA minimum standards and design regulations set the groundwork for modern subdivision practice. They shaped the practices employed by the Federal Public Housing Authority and its wartime housing projects, provided the basis for

SMARTER STANDARDS AND REGULATIONS

the post-World War II suburbanization drive and established the foundation for local government subdivision regulations. In 1934, nearly 4,000 financial institutions, representing more than 70 percent of all of the country's commercial banking resources, had FHA insurance plans. By 1959, FHA mortgage insurance had helped to provide homes for 5 million families and helped to repair or improve 22 million properties. Three out of every five U.S. families were helped by the federal government to purchase a home, most single-family dwellings (FHA 1959).

In January 1935, the FHA's first technical standards publication appeared in a series of five circulars: *Standards for the Insurance of Mortgages on Properties Located in Undeveloped Subdivision—Title II of the National Housing Act*. Circular number 5, *Subdivision Standards* (1937), was the basis for further publications by the agency's Technical Division. Setting the framework for regulation through written standards, the FHA also provided suggestions and recommendations for development layout. The circular illustrated the measures needed to build an ideal "well-balanced, carefully planned subdivision" (Figure 2).

Figure 2. FHA's first publication of a recommended street width illustrates the way street improvements on an 80-foot right-of-way could be increased gradually as the neighborhood grows. Simple engineering handbooks of street design standards have had a major impact on the American landscape. Presented as absolute and indisputable, they have become a rigid framework that allows little creativity and variation. They have shaped the overall pattern of neighborhoods and communities, as well as the quality and character of individual residential lots and streets. Drawing courtesy of the Federal Housing Authority (1937).

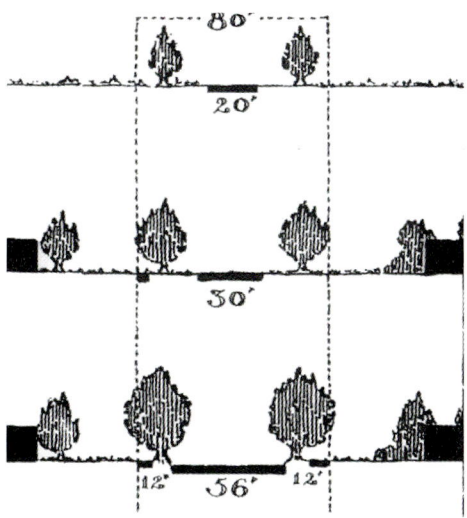

The federal government was thus able to exercise tremendous authority and power through the simple act of making an offer that one could not refuse. James Moffett, the FHA administrator in 1935, told his advisory board in a confidential meeting to "make it conditional that these mortgages must be insured under the Housing Act, and through that we could control overbuilding insertions, which would undermine values, or through political pull, building in isolated spots, where it was not a good investment. You could also control the population trend, the neighborhood standards, and material and everything else through the president" (Weiss 1987, 153). By 1941, 32 states had passed legislation granting power of subdivision control through the establishment of local planning commissions. Once authorized and empowered by the community, these commissions adopted rules and regulations governing subdivision procedures within their jurisdictions, most of which were adopted from the federal government's established criteria, in particular those of the FHA (Lautner 1941).

Changes Within the Public Realm

The independence of local agencies, and their ability to perform away from the government's yardstick, is key to changing regulations and standards. In some parts of the United States, such trends are beginning to emerge. As more communities wrestle with quality of life problems due to uncontrolled growth, traffic congestion and failure of existing infrastructure, they begin to take a stronger interest in local power, and some are establishing their own physical design initiatives and regulations. In 1991, the city of Portland, Oregon, adopted new local street standards as part of its comprehensive transportation plan. The Skinny Street Program, which reduces local residential street width by as much as 12 feet, has become a cost-effective way to preserve livability and neighborhood integrity. Moreover, reducing the standards has lowered the impact of grading slopes, lessened storm water runoff and resulted in less spending (Figure 3).

The Skinny Street Program has enjoyed a high level of support from both residents and state officials. It won the 1995 Award for Excellence from the League of Oregon Cities and generated such interest that Oregon's Land Conservation and Development Commission (LCDC) adopted a rule compelling other jurisdictions within the state to adopt the program. The appeal of the skinny street design is slowly gaining acceptance across the country. According to a recent survey, more than 30 jurisdictions in 16 states allow some form or another of narrow street standards (Table 1).

Figure 3. Portland, Oregon's Skinny Street Program allows new residential streets to be 20 feet wide with parking on one side, or 26 feet wide with parking on both sides. The city notes that such streets maintain neighborhood character, reduce construction costs, save vegetation, reduce stormwater runoff, improve traffic safety, and make it possible to use scarce land for purposes other than motor vehicle use. The Portland Fire Department finds that skinny streets provide adequate access for emergency vehicles. Photograph courtesy of the City of Portland.

While narrow streets challenge the prevailing physical mold of street standards, a more comprehensive venture can be found in various attempts by states to remove regulatory barriers to affordable housing. The Massachusetts Comprehensive Permit Law, established 30 years ago "to increase the supply and improve the regional distribution of low- and moderate-income housing by allowing a limited suspension of existing local regulations that are inconsistent with the construction of such housing," has allowed more flexibility locally in this important arena (Massachusetts Department of Housing and Community Development 1969). The permit process allows municipalities and developers to propose developments that differ radically from those possible under as-of-right zoning ordinances. Higher densities, varied housing types and cluster configurations are all possible and are not subject to traditional subdivision regulations. Thirty years after its passage, it is estimated that about 1,000 proposals, which include affordable housing

Table 1.
Narrow Streets Data

State	Jurisdiction	Standard
Arizona	Phoenix	28' - parking both sides
California	Santa Rosa	30' - parking both sides, <1000 ADT
		26'-28' - parking one side
		20' - no parking
		20' - neck downs @ intersections
	Palmdale	28' - parking both sides
	San Jose	30' - parking both sides, less than 21 DU
		34' - parking both sides, more than 21 DU
	Novato	24' - parking both sides, 2-4 DU
		28' - parking both sides, 5-15 DU
Colorado	Boulder	32' - parking both sides, 1000-2500 ADT
		30' - parking both sides, 500-1000 ADT
	Ft. Collins	30' - parking both sides
		24' - alley
Delaware	Delaware DOT	Mobility friendly design guideline
		200'-500' blocks required; network connectivity
		21' - parking one side, one travel, cueing for local subdivision
		22'-29' - parking one side, minor collector
		12' - alley in 20' row
Florida	Orlando	28' - parking both sides, residential lots less than 55' wide
		22' - parking both sides, residential. lots more than 55' wide
Maine	Portland	24' - parking one side
Maryland	Howard County	24' - parking unregulated, <1000 ADT
Michigan	Birmingham	26' - parking both sides
		20' - parking one side
Montana	Helena	33' - parking both sides
	Missoula	28' - parking both sides 81-200 DU
		32' - parking both sides 81-200 DU
		12' - alley
New Mexico	Albuquerque	27' - parking one side
	Santa Fe	34' - parking unregulated
Oregon	Beaverton	28' - parking both sides, less than 750 ADT
	Eugene	12' - one-way alley
		16' - two-way alley
		20' - no parking
		21' - parking one side, less than 750 ADT
		28' - parking both sides , more than 750 ADT
	Forest Grove	28' - parking both sides if not >16 single family or 20 multifamily
	Gresham	20' - no parking, more than 150' or more than 11 DU
	Hilsboro	28'-30' - parking on both sides
	McMinnville	26' - parking both sides
	Portland	26' - parking both sides
		20' - parking one side
	Tigard	28' - parking one side <500 ADT
	Tualatin	32' - parking both sides
	Washington County	28' - parking both sides

Tennessee	Johnson	22' - parking not regulated, <240 ADT 24'-28' - parking not regulated, 240-1500 ADT 28' parking not regulated, >1500 ADT
Vermont	Burlington	30' - parking both sides Washington Kirland 20' - parking one side 24' - parking both sides - low density only 28' - parking both sides
West Virginia	Morgantown	22' - parking one side
Wisconsin	Madison	27' - parking both sides less than 3 DU/AC 28' - parking both sides 3-10 DU/AC

Source: Adapted from Cohen 2000.

components, have been presented to local zoning officials. Yet few in the private market—and in particular those developers who are eager to change restrictive zoning and regulations—have taken full advantage of the freedom in design and physical planning that the law allows.

Changes Within the Private Realm

Challenges and modifications to existing subdivision standards and regulations are more apparent in privately owned and operated communities. As of 1998, there were about 205,000 neighborhood associations in the U.S., with almost 42 million inhabitants, or about 15 percent of all residents. In the 50 largest metropolitan areas, more than half of new housing is now built as part of a neighborhood association. In California, particularly in the Los Angeles and San Diego metropolitan areas, this figure exceeds 60 percent. If private development continues to spread at this rate, the result will be an unprecedented transition from the traditional, individual ownership of property to collective ownership of most residential and business private property in the United States (Treese 1999). Robert Nelson (1999a) suggests that the growth in popularity of private development and property ownership is due to new economic forces of the second half of the twentieth century, including the high cost of land (and thus the motive to increase higher densities of development), the desire for more control over neighborhood character, more economical private provision of common neighborhood services, and greater interest in common recreational and other facilities.

The establishment of a separate legal mechanism such as a neighborhood association within the community not only allows collective control over the neighborhood's common environment and the private provision of common services, but it also creates a de facto deregulation of municipal subdivision standards and zoning. Most cities and towns allow for a different, more flexible set of standards to be implemented on a private or semiprivate development. Because the local government has no legal responsibility, and thus no liability concerns, the developer can introduce different configurations and standards. The results are often innovative spatial and architectural layouts (Figure 4).

Belmont, Virginia, is a good example. Conceived as a planned unit development around 1988, the plan originally incorporated a curvilinear loop street system that conformed to the Virginia Department of Transportation's (VDOT) subdivision street requirements. In that same year, the Loudon County Board of Supervisors adopted a new initiative for neotraditional neighborhood design principles in response to the typical suburban development that had occurred in the region over the previous two decades. After prolonged and unsuccessful negotiations with VDOT, the developer received approval for a street system that the homeowners association would maintain privately. Only three collector and arterial streets were built to VDOT standards; the rest of the street system was placed in private hands and designed to different, narrower configuration (Wells 1993).

Figure 4. Private developments are pushing the design envelope while answering market demands. Many are increasing densities while maintaining the feeling of privacy and openness. Privacy is a key concern of potential home buyers and must be addressed in site and unit design to achieve market acceptance. The limitations of small yard size are mitigated by unit designs that maximize the perception of open space through generous unit glazing and open floor plans. Drawing courtesy of the Urban Land Institute (1994).

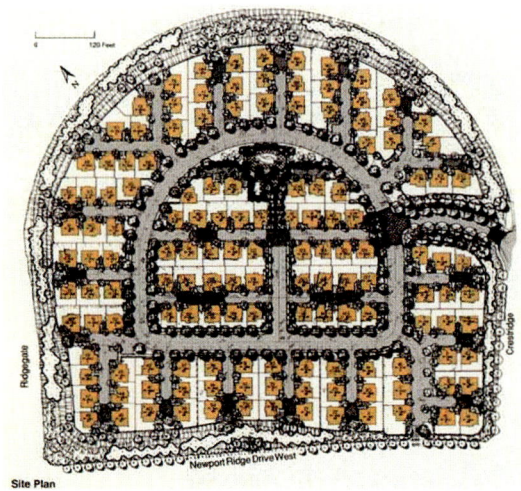

Figure 5. Some developments combine aspects of the cul-de-sac and cluster layouts. Houses are arranged around paved and landscaped courts that serve both pedestrians and vehicles, and are connected to an open space network. Such a configuration allows for greater flexibility in arrangement and reduces construction cost. Photograph courtesy of Michael Southworth.

At the Sancerre development in Newport Beach, California, the developer planned to build a single-family residential development to a net density of 9.4 dwelling units per acre, by using an innovative spatial configuration. But the local planning authority could not allow such modification under its current single-family subdivision ordinance. By opting for a private, gated development, the developer was able to lay out four- to six-unit clusters around private drives with a zero lot line to maximize the usable open space. Furthermore, the developer determined that the legal framework for condominium ownership would be advantageous. As condominiums, each four- or six-unit cluster would be developed as a single lot, wherein the buyer would get title to the house and to the side and rear yards as defined by the condominium plan. The concept is similar to townhouse ownership, an idea buyers readily understand and accept (ULI 1994). The result is a small-lot, zero-lot-line, courtyard community that pushes the single-family home density to the limit in order to meet market demand for this type of housing. Dwelling units are approximately 35 feet wide, most units have a 10- to

15-foot-wide yard on one side, which wraps around the unit and flows into a 15-foot-wide rear yard (Figure 5).

To maximize the benefit of the limited yard areas, Sancerre's designers extended substantial patio glazing from the units into the yards. Rooms are typically open to each other, so that both the side and rear yards are simultaneously visible from within the units. Thus, the private open space seems more expansive than its square footage would suggest. At the same time, to preserve privacy in the side yards, the adjacent zero-lot-line unit wall is windowless at the first floor, and second-floor windows are placed high on the wall to permit the entry of light, but preclude views into the neighbor's yard. The design flexibility inherent in the cluster layout leaves room for integrating the open lands into and around the groupings of structures. This ensures ready access to considerably more open land than would be possible with a conventional pattern.

Private development should serve as a catalyst in changing subdivision standards and regulations. Public officials should realize that the current practice of allowing a different set of standards on private developments acknowledges the inadequacy of their applied standards to public developments, and validates the assumption that what should guide change is actual performance and good design.

Mitigating Subdivisions' Spatial Deficiencies Without Sacrificing Market Appeal: A Smart Growth Approach

In 1927, while designing Radburn, Clarence Stein called for a "revolution in planning." He challenged existing practices that were geared toward facilitating the automobile and proposed a "radical revision of relation of houses, roads, paths, gardens, parks, blocks, and local neighborhoods." (Stein 1951, 42) Stein's call for change is as important today as it was 70 years ago. Yet, as we assess the physical form of the modern suburb, we should also acknowledge the market appeal of the predominant configuration, and learn to modify it through imperceptible spatial transformations. Ways to accomplish such spatial changes include the following approaches.

Integrate the Open Space Network as an Ecological Backbone that Connects to Existing Systems

Too often open space systems are developed from leftover land. A developer can satisfy a requirement for a percentage of open space by using residual spaces such as those on the periphery of the development, by the edge of a highway or adjoining another subdivision, or on steeply sloping land. Open space and natural corridors should be defined before the site is divided into lots and roads are laid out. Riparian systems, wetlands, ridges and sensitive environmental features should be conserved and incorporated as an integral part of development. Surface drainageways and water reclamation that use biological systems should be incorporated into the open space system. Such complex systems may also be more economical in the long run. They are multiuse, providing more benefits such as recreational and wildlife connections, while also purifying storm and surface water runoff (Figure 6).

Cluster or Contain Units Around an Open-ended Common, and Integrate It with the Overall Open Space System

The marketable appeal of the traditional cul-de-sac is capitalized on to develop small manageable pods (Ben-Joseph 1995a). The design flexibility inherent in cluster layout leaves room for integrating the open space into and around the groupings of structures. This ensures ready access to considerably more open land than would be possible with a conventional pattern. Units are then grouped more

Figure 6. Open space corridors that rely on natural systems, such as drainage ways, should be laid out before the site is subdivided into lots and streets. They should guide the development pattern to ensure minimal grading and visual intrusion while allowing for a pedestrian network. Photograph courtesy of Holly Ben-Joseph.

closely together around a public common space that is connected both by vehicular and pedestrian systems.

Design Flexible Lot Shapes and Configurations
The standardization of site works, infrastructure and housing units typically dictate a rectangular lot. Deviation from standards will allow for greater flexibility and opportunities to create topographical and ecologically fitting layouts.

Increase Density by up to 30 Percent
A 30 percent increases in density is almost indecipherable with good design, especially when it aligns with the preceding principles. With the ability to add more units without imperiling the typical desirable features of a detached suburban layout, the development retains its attractiveness to the buyer while lowering costs and providing an efficient land use pattern.

Reduce the Street Right-of-Way and Tame Traffic
Excessive street standards that require wide streets and large setbacks have major social and economic impacts. They waste land, drive up home costs and affect residential livability. The prevailing right-of-way (ROW) width for a residential subdivision street, as specified by the Institute of Transportation Engineers, has remained at 50 to 60 feet for the last 40 years (Southworth and Ben-Joseph 1997). There is no justification for ITE's ROW width, especially at the local street level that carries little or no traffic. Narrow streets as little as 26 feet wide and tight, right-angled corners are easily managed by pedestrians and those with disabilities, and they are safer because they force drivers to slow down.

Taming traffic through street redesign, using the shared street concept, is another mechanism that encourages pedestrians and social activity in the residential areas and reduces the amount of paved surfaces. The narrow paved area, with no curb or raised sidewalk, reduces the amount of nonporous surface while also slowing the movement of vehicles (Ben-Joseph 1995b).

Keep Amenities Within a Quarter-Mile Walking Radius
If given a choice, people tend to walk, rather than use other modes, to a destination within a quarter-mile from their point of origin. Unterman (1990) found that 70 percent of Americans will walk 500 feet for daily errands, and 40 percent will walk one-fifth of a mile. Only 10 percent will walk half a mile. Similarly, Barber

(1986, 73–90) found that the distance people walked for typical trips varied between 400 and 1,200 feet. It is important that clusters of public amenities, such as playgrounds, recreation and sport facilities, are located within such distances.

Diversify Form and Scale

Unit sizes, facades, architectural details, setbacks and entries (pedestrian and vehicular) should be diversified to provide variety and interest. Good architectural design can camouflage and mitigate many of the negative attitudes toward multi-unit dwellings. Duplexes in particular can be designed to fit the architectural language of a single-family style community. Variation in the size of the units and the ability to purchase a home at different finished phases allow for greater market affordability and a wider base of home buyers (Figure 7).

Public Understanding of Alternatives

The phenomenal growth of urban development has inspired a renewed discussion about the character and physical nature of this expansion. Yet, as architects and planners are generating new design paradigms, there is little or no public under-

Figure 7. Compatibility of architectural styles, materials and colors can mitigate many of the stigmas associated with higher-density housing, and allow for better integration of compatible uses. Photograph © Alex MacLean/Landslides.

standing of these alternatives. Designers and planners need to communicate better the changes they envision, in order for the layperson to adequately understand how these changes will affect their lives. While modes of imaging technologies—from two-dimensional maps, charts and diagrams to computer models—allow professionals to explain their designs and interventions more clearly than ever before, few outside the profession can interpret them entirely, or understand what it would be like to live in such spaces.

The rapid development of imaging technologies and the simple, free interface delivered by the Internet provide a unique platform for such interaction. This platform should provide a tangible representation where envisioning tools are incorporated into the decision-making process. Such tools afford visualization of otherwise abstract environmental impacts, consideration of a broader range of alternative scenarios and the integration of analytic tools, relevant media and cognitive information. VIC, a Visual Interactive Code, is one of these prototypes.[1] Developed at Pennsylvania State University, this computer-based system enables local governments to convert land use regulations and planning data into a single, visually based format using photographs, illustration and maps. Utilizing an easy and engaging graphic interface, with pictures and data that correlate to one another and are interchangeable, local governments can show the different effects of various regulations. With a click of a mouse, end users can view the different configurations of various developments, density measurements, street widths and setbacks, and related precedents (Figure 8).

Designers and planners need to address the public's difficulty in visualizing the physical ramifications of land use and subdivision regulations. Readily available imaging tools, as well as newly developed computational interfaces that integrate digital and physical information, can now introduce communities to the variety of choices available and help them visualize the effects of these choices. Such public education efforts promise to diversify the spatial character of monotonous subdivisions (Figure 9).

---

1   VIC and its original application PA BLUEPRINTS (Best Land Use Principles & Results, Interactively Shown) are available in a CD format from the Department of Landscape Architecture, Pennsylvania State University, University Park, Pennsylvania. It can be accessed on line at: *http://www.vicgroup.com/*. Other planning visualization tools can be viewed online at: *http://yerkes.mit.edu/DOT/TitlePage/Title.html* and *http://web.mit.edu/ebj/www/research.html*.

Smarter Standards and Regulations

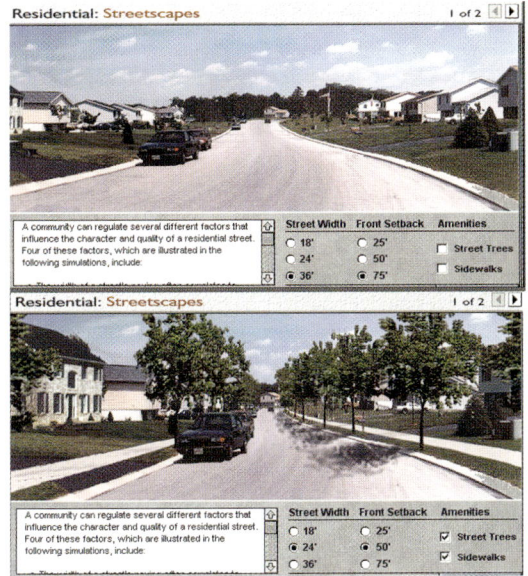

Figure 8. Simple, interactive and tangible representations that afford visualization of otherwise abstract standards, consideration of alternative scenarios and integration of information are essential components of change. Photograph courtesy of Kellean Foster.

Figure 9. Illuminating Clay, developed at the Massachusetts Institute of Technology, combines digital and physical interfaces to create a tangible simulation tool. Ideas, changes and suggestions, as well as their resulting impacts, can be seen and explored in real time allowing both the designer and the public to be better informed and involved. Photograph courtesy of Ben Piper.

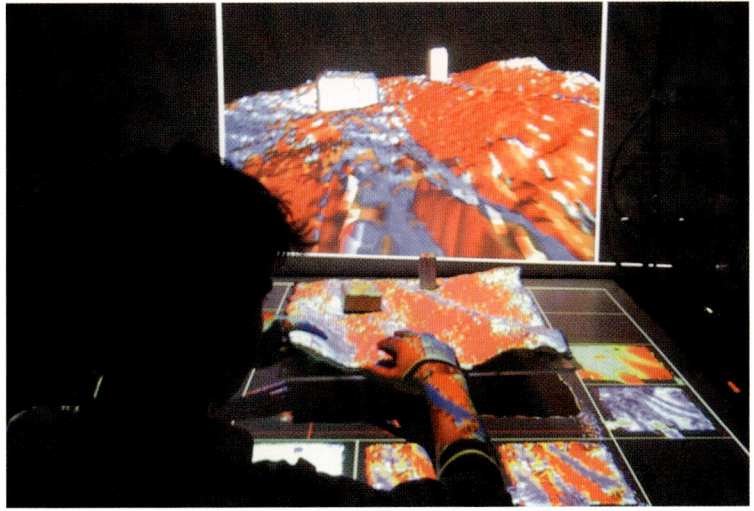

References

Barber, Gerald. 1986. Aggregate characteristics of urban travel. In *Geography of urban transportation.* Susan Hanson, ed. New York, NY: Guilford Press.

Ben-Joseph, Eran. 1995a. *Livability and safety of suburban street patterns: A comparative study.* Working paper 641. Berkeley, CA: Berkeley Institute of Urban and Regional Development and University of California Institute of Transportation Studies.

_____. 1995b. Changing the suburban street scene: Adapting of the shared street (Woonerf) concept to the suburban environment. *Journal of the American Planning Association* 61(4).

Cohen, Alan. 2000. *CNU narrow streets database* at: http://www.sonic.net/abcaia/narrow.htm

Federal Housing Administration (FHA). 1937. *Subdivision standards.* Circular no. 5 (May 1; revised August 15, 1938, and September 1, 1939). Washington, DC: FHA.

_____. 1938a. *Planning profitable neighborhoods,* Technical bulletin no. 7. Washington, DC: FHA.

_____. 1938b. *Principles of land subdivision and street layout.* Washington, DC: FHA.

_____. 1939. *Subdivision standards*, Circular no. 5. Washington, DC: FHA.

_____. 1959. *The FHA story in summary, 1934–1959.* Washington, DC: FHA.

Lautner, Harold W. 1941. *Subdivision regulation: An analysis of land subdivision control practices.* Chicago, IL: Public Administration Service.

Massachusetts Department of Housing and Community Development. 1969. See Housing Appeals Committee website at: http://www.state.ma.us/dhcd/components/hac/.

Nelson, Robert. 1999a. Contracting for land use law: Zoning by private contract. In *The fall and rise of freedom of contract.* F.H. Buckley, ed. Durham, NC: Duke University Press.

_____. 1999b. Privatizing the neighborhood: A proposal to replace zoning with private collective property rights to existing neighborhoods. *George Mason law review* 827.

Southworth, Michael, and Eran Ben-Joseph. 1997. *Streets and the shaping of towns and cities.* New York, NY: McGraw-Hill.

Stein, Clarence S. 1951. *Toward new towns for America.* Cambridge, MA: MIT Press.

Treese, Clifford. 1999. *Community association factbook.* Alexandria, VA: Community Associations Institute.

Unterman, David. 1990. Accommodating the pedestrian: Adapting towns and neighborhoods for walking and bicycling. In *Personal travel in the US, vol. II, A report of the findings from 1983–1984, Nationwide Personal Transportation Survey source control programs.* Washington, DC: U.S. Department of Transportation.

Urban Land Institute (ULI). 1994. Residential prototypes—Sancree, Newport Beach, CA. *ULI Residential Prototype Cases,* vol. 24/15. Washington, DC: ULI.

Weiss, Marc. 1987. *The rise of the community builders: The American real estate industry and urban land planning.* New York, NY: Columbia University Press.

Wells, Martin J. 1993. *Neo-traditional neighborhood development: You can go home again.* Arlington, VA: Wells & Assoc., Inc.

8

Brian W. Blaesser

Smart Growth

Legal Assumptions and Market Realities

> [A]s long as zoning codes favor low-density development over the creation of compact communities, developers will not be able to shake their reputation as land rapists, as they turn farm after farm into cookie-cutter sprawl. This is why one can buy a bumper sticker that reads: "Leaving Town? Take a Developer with You."
> —Andres Duany, Elizabeth Plater-Zyberk, Jeff Speck,
> *Suburban Nation: The Rise of Sprawl and the Decline of the American Dream*

> Duany, Plater-Zyberk, and Speck are so fixed on physical determinism that they seem to overlook the importance of social mores, the economy, and preexisting behavior patterns.
> —Paul Goldberger, *The New Yorker*

From the national press coverage that smart growth has received, everyone knows that the target of smart growth is *sprawl*—defined by many as poorly planned, noncontiguous, low-density residential and commercial development extending outward from urban areas into rural areas. This pattern of land use, it is argued, is wasteful of both land and natural resources and costly to serve with public facilities. Smart growth is the current antidote to sprawl. Of course, smart growth is not new. It has been around since the early 1970s, when there were initial efforts at growth management techniques designed to control the rate, amount, type, location and quality of growth. Now we have smart growth.

I think of smart growth as essentially growth management with an attitude. I say attitude, because it is my experience that many of the proponents of smart growth have the rather singular view that sprawl is almost criminal. The words used to describe smart growth initiatives are adversarial in tone. For example, Web sites devoted to the issue of sprawl frequently speak of combating and arresting sprawl. The national press has reported how the smart growth debate has turned land use law into a sexy specialty, and that there is now a boom in sprawl lawyers dedicated to stopping sprawl (El Nasser 2000). There is almost a ghost-busters quality to the whole discussion. Indeed, in the current zeal of the new urbanists and others to combat sprawl, they tend to overlook market realities and often make generous assumptions about what is legally possible in the name of smart growth.

With the intense focus on sprawl, insufficient attention is being given to what those who don't like sprawl also say in the same breath. For example, the governor of Oregon—whose state is often touted as a smart growth model—has noted candidly, "Oregonians don't like sprawl, but they don't like high density either."[1] A recent poll of citizens in major metropolitan areas of the United States confirms that a significant percentage of the American public shares the ambivalence toward sprawl remedies expressed by Oregonians. The poll, conducted by the Pew Center for Civic Journalism, found that 52 percent of the respondents believed that "local government should continue to plan for growth and new development in *all* areas," while 40 percent stated that "local government should try to limit growth in less-developed areas and encourage growth in areas that are already built up."[2]

The effort of smart growth initiatives to control the rate, amount, type, location and quality of growth can go too far or, to use the smart growth vernacular, smart growth can be "too smart"—bumping up against constitutional protections. The realities of the marketplace and constitutional limitations should be well understood by everyone in the smart growth debate if we are to have growth management results that truly reflect the intelligence implied by the term *smart growth*. The purpose of this chapter is to define some of these market realities and outline the constitutional limitations that should inform any government effort to introduce smart growth policies and techniques.

Before discussing some of the legal implications of smart growth policies and techniques, some further remarks about sprawl and the marketplace, the meaning of growth management and the underlying problem of the term *smart growth* are in order.

The Many Faces of Sprawl and Smart Growth

As I have said, sprawl is essentially unlimited, noncontiguous, low-density residential and commercial development extending outward from urban areas into rural areas. This pattern of land use, in addition to being seen as wasteful of resources and costly to serve, is also viewed by some as physically unattractive. But for others, the face of sprawl is not so bad. After all, sprawl in many respects is the product of U.S. affluence, enabling people to have a low-density residential environment that allows property owners to "borrow" and enjoy the open space that surrounds them. Sprawl also includes workplaces located within reasonable distances of affordable housing. As the saying goes, "You drive until you qualify." The relative ease of commuting and shopping also makes suburban sprawl attractive to many families.

---

1 Governor John Kitzhaber of Oregon in his State of the State Address (1999).
2 *Straight Talk from Americans—2000*, by the Pew Center for Civic Journalism (issues related to growth and crime were cited by 18 percent of the respondents). Available online at *www.pewcenter.org*.

The Euphemism of Smart Growth

It should be acknowledged that smart growth is really a euphemism—used by all sides in the debate in order to be able to say that they do not support sprawl and to give an attractive label to whatever they may say. It also hides a basic conflict of interest between what may be good for a metropolitan area as a whole and what often seems good for an individual locality. I am referring, of course, to the Ramapos of this country that adopt specific controls in order to defer development, and other communities that adopt UGBs without regard to the impacts of those actions on regional growth and infrastructure needs.[3]

The Other Euphemism: Sustainable Development

In 1999, the Sustainable Development Act was introduced into the Massachusetts state legislature. Under the proposed legislation, the term *sustainable development* was broadly defined as:

> development purposefully designed to bring about efficient, safe healthy, prosperous and livable communities (local, regional, and state) while simultaneously maintaining and enhancing the environment, the natural resource base and the ongoing functioning of natural ecosystems that are fundamental to sustaining life for current as well as future generations.[4]

At the same time, the proposed legislation, in circular fashion, defined sprawl as "unmanaged, unsustainable development"[5] and empowered the regional planning agencies (RPAs) in Massachusetts to do a sustainability review of local plans. The proposed act stated that an RPA must consider three criteria in determining whether a plan is sustainable.

1. The plan is designed to bring about safe, healthy, prosperous and livable communities while simultaneously maintaining and enhancing the environment, the natural resource base and the ongoing functioning of natural ecosystems that are fundamental to sustaining life for current as well as future generations.

---

3 *Golden v Ramapo Planning Bd.*, 285 N.E. 2d 291 (N.Y. 1972) (upholding development timing restrictions). For a discussion of this case from a perspective critical of the regional implications of the Ramapo program, see Bosselman (1975, 102–119). The problems created by local urban growth boundaries are discussed in National Association of Industrial and Office Properties (1999, 29–32).
4 The Sustainable Development Act (1999) at Section 2 (a)(16).
5 *Id*. at Section 2 (a)(12).

2. The plan is compatible with approved plans of abutting municipalities and the relevant regional plan, if adopted.
3. The municipality has proposed appropriate land use regulations necessary to implement the elements of the plan.[6]

These criteria are fundamentally flawed—they are too vague and therefore open to wide interpretation by an RPA. The criteria are simply inadequate guidance for RPA determinations of whether a town is eligible for state reimbursement funds for the preparation of sustainable town plans and land use regulations that are appropriate for implementing the plan. The problem stems from the term *sustainable development* itself. The term is generally understood to mean that our current generation should plan its communities and develop land in a manner that does not compromise the needs of future generations. But at the more specific level, much like smart growth, the term *sustainable development* encompasses a broad and varied agenda from person to person, neighborhood to neighborhood, and community to community. As the American Planning Association (1996, 7) acknowledges:

> For some, sustainability can be achieved by living in compact communities, using public transit, minimizing energy consumption, and recycling waste. For others, it conjures up images of communal living in small, organic-farm-oriented communities with a strong sense of community and surrounded by wide open spaces. Still others feel that true sustainability cannot be achieved at the local level given the constraints posed by global population growth and associated environmental ills.

The goal of achieving sustainability in development is laudable. But as the proposed Massachusetts legislation illustrates, the goal does not translate easily, if at all, into land use and development standards and regulations that can be determined to achieve sustainability in any meaningful sense.[7]

Smart Growth and the Constitution—Is There a Conflict?

The answer, of course, is that clearly there is the potential for conflict, and there always is tension between smart growth policies and the legal protections guaran-

---

6 *Id.* at Section 2 (d)(2).
7 Although sustainability may be one of the most salient examples of a planning goal whose implementation suffers from vagueness, no doubt the goals of other statewide planning models are difficult to translate into meaningful land use and development standards and regulations for the same reason.

teed by the Constitution. If we return for a moment to the essential elements of growth management (i.e., control of the rate, amount, type, location and quality of growth or development), I suggest that the areas where regulatory policies and techniques are most vulnerable to constitutional challenge are those that seek to control, rather than influence, the rate, amount, type, location and quality of growth, particularly those that attempt to control the amount and location and the quality of development. I address these areas of regulatory control next.

Constitutional Principles and Doctrines Implicated by Smart Growth Initiatives

Smart growth initiatives potentially implicate four constitutional principles and/or doctrines when they attempt to control rather than influence the rate, amount, type, location and quality of growth. These principles and doctrines are:

1. The Fifth Amendment's Takings Clause
2. The Fourteenth Amendment's Substantive Due Process Clause
3. The Void for Vagueness Doctrine—also derived from the Due Process Clause of the Fourteenth Amendment
4. The Right to Freedom of Mobility

I will define briefly each of these constitutional principles and/or doctrines and then apply them, as applicable, to smart growth regulations directed at controlling the rate, amount, type, location and quality of growth.

The Fifth Amendment's Takings Clause

Most people would agree that many, if not all, of the goals behind smart growth policies make sense. In other words, if smart growth means protecting sensitive environmental areas, preserving truly agricultural areas outside the urban core, encouraging land uses to locate where existing infrastructure already exists, encouraging redevelopment or infill of passed-over sites in urban areas—these are, in fact, legitimate governmental interests. This is important because as the U.S. Supreme Court instructed us in its discussion of the Fifth Amendment's takings test in *Agins*, a taking of property can occur if a regulation fails to "substantially advance a legitimate state interest."[8] The Court's subsequent decisions in the *Nollan* and the *Dolan* cases have reinforced and developed the takings test. *Nollan* tells us that there must

---

8   *Agins v City of Tiburon*, 447 U.S. 255 (1980).

be an "essential nexus" between the legitimate state interest that the government seeks to achieve through its land use regulation and any development conditions that are imposed by that regulation.[9] Unlike the *Nollan* case, where the California Coastal Commission could not demonstrate an essential nexus between the stated purpose of preserving the ocean view from behind the house by requiring a public easement in front of the house, most smart growth regulations will probably satisfy the essential nexus test if it can be demonstrated that those regulations are a means to protect sensitive environmental areas, preserve rural areas, encourage growth to locate where infrastructure is available, and so on.

But a community can run afoul of the essential nexus test when it fails to properly design some of the regulatory methods for implementing growth management policies. For example, one common growth management tool for assuring the availability of infrastructure for new development is impact fees. In those states that do not have state enabling legislation for impact fees—a common technique used to have new growth pay for infrastructure—some communities will adopt an impact fee ordinance that, apart from the lack of authority question, is constitutionally deficient because it allows the fee collected to be placed in a general revenue fund instead of an earmarked fund devoted to funding the infrastructure improvements for which the fee was imposed. In such a case there is no essential nexus between the government's stated purpose for imposing the fee—for example, to pay for new road construction in a particular area—and the costs for which the fees are assigned, such as paying for operational costs of a city department using general revenues.

But even assuming that the essential nexus test is satisfied by the smart growth type of regulation, the *Dolan* case added a second test to address what the *Nollan* case did not address—namely, "the required degree of connection between the exaction and the projected impact of a proposed development."[10] This second prong of the test defined in *Dolan* was "rough proportionality"—meaning that a local government must make some sort of individualized determination that an exaction is related both in nature and extent to the impact of the proposed development.[11] This test means that local governments cannot constitutionally justify conditions imposed on development based upon speculative and hypothetical impacts that a particular development project may generate on existing resources.

---

9   *Nollan v California Coastal Commission*, 483 U.S. 825, 837 (1987).
10   *Dolan v City of Tigard*, 512 U.S. 374, 386 (1994).
11   *Id.* at 391.

In other words, smart growth regulations must quantify anticipated impacts and only exact conditions that are roughly proportional to those impacts. This test may not always be easy to satisfy, as the following examples show.

Impact fees In 1999, the U.S. Supreme Court held in *City of Monterey v Del Monte Dunes*,[12] that it had not extended the rough proportionality test beyond the special context of exactions, which the Court defined as the "conditioning of land use approvals on the dedication of property."[13] Therefore, as a matter of federal constitutional law, monetary development exactions such as impact fees may not be challenged under the rough proportionality test of *Dolan*.

However, because the imposition of development exactions is a matter of state law, the constitutional test may vary across state jurisdictions. The U.S. Supreme Court's pronouncements on the federal constitutional test for development exactions do not prevent state courts in reviewing the constitutionality of monetary development exactions, whether imposed by ordinance or on a case-by-case basis, from imposing a test that may afford property owners more constitutional protection. In other words, federal law only sets the "floor" of constitutional protection; state courts can and do apply the rough proportionality test based on *Dolan*. So, for example, if the actual fees are based on generalized, statewide or national trend data, rather than making an individualized determination of the impacts that are caused by the specific project under consideration, a state court could reasonably find that such an impact fee regulation violates the *Dolan* rough proportionality test. And, in fact, state courts are beginning to apply the two-prong *Nollan/Dolan* test to impact fees.

For example, in a case of first impression in Ohio, the Ohio Supreme Court expressly addressed whether the *Nollan/Dolan* test applies in a challenge to a legislatively adopted impact fee ordinance.[14] The court concluded that the heightened scrutiny of the federal test for development exactions should apply to impact fee ordinances, explaining:

> Although impact fees do not threaten property rights to the same degree as land use exactions or zoning laws, there are similarities. Just as forced easements or zoning reclassifications can inhibit the desired use of property, an

---

12   *City of Monterey v Del Monte Dunes*, 526 U.S. 687 (1999).
13   *Id.* at 702.
14   *Homebuilders Association of Dayton and The Miami Valley v City of Beavercreek*, 729 N.E.2d 349 (Ohio 2000).

unreasonable impact fee may affect the manner in which a parcel of land is developed. Further, impact fees are closer in form to land use exactions than to zoning laws. Both forced easements and impact fees, while imposing a condition on the use of land, do not necessarily deny a landowner his or her intended use of the land. Zoning laws, to the contrary, may alter the classification of the land and, therefore, could deny the owner's intended use of the property.

…[T]he dual rational nexus test, is based on the Nollan and Dolan cases, and Hollywood, Inc. . . . It is our opinion that [it] balances both the interests of local governments and real estate developers without unnecessary restrictions. The trial court applied this test, and it is also the test we adopt for evaluating the constitutionality of an impact fee ordinance when a Takings Clause challenge is raised.[15]

The Ohio court's reference to the *Hollywood, Inc.,* case reflects the reality that state court litigation over impact fees generated a constitutional test long before *Nollan* and *Dolan* shaped U.S. regulatory takings jurisprudence. Much of this litigation was in Florida, and resulted in what the Ohio court properly refers to as the "dual rational nexus" test.[16]

There are two prongs to the dual rational nexus test. The first prong requires that there be an identified nexus (connection) between the new development and the need for the improvements for which a fee is imposed. In order to satisfy the first prong, the nexus must be substantial, rationally linked and direct between the new development and the identified need for the improvements. The second prong requires that the development that has been assessed the cost (fee) must receive a substantial benefit from the improvements constructed with a fee. This is the constitutional test followed in the majority of the states in which impact fees are legally authorized. The Supreme Court's decisions in the *Nollan* and *Dolan* cases have reinforced the use of the dual rational nexus test by state courts in assessing the validity of impact fee programs.

Natural resource protection   Communities increasingly are imposing resource protection and landscaping measures in order to preserve or enhance community character. Devices frequently used are the requirement of buffer areas around nat-

---

15   *Id.* at 356.
16   *Hollywood, Inc. v Broward County*, 431 So.2d 606 (Fla. App. 1983).

ural resources and enhancement requirements to compensate for resources that are affected by development impacts. When buffer zone damage and enhancement requirements exceed those needed to protect the resource or to mitigate damage, these types of regulations run afoul of *Dolan*'s rough proportionality requirement. For example, in the *Del Monte Dunes* case decided by the Ninth Circuit before it went up to the U.S. Supreme Court, the Ninth Circuit Court of Appeals found a taking where the zoning body had rejected a development proposal because of alleged impacts to species habitat, and where the agencies actions were "disproportional to both the nature and extend of the project."[17] In another case out of the Eighth Circuit, the court held that a subdivision developer was entitled to recoup a portion of the funds that he had to pay for an area-wide drainage system that was "in excess of its pro rata share."[18]

Land dedications Certainly *Nollan* and *Dolan* make it clear that if a regulation compels the dedication of private property to public use, such as public access for general public use, the regulator must demonstrate not only how the dedication confers a benefit on the property owner who has been exacted, but also identify the burden specifically created by the new development to justify the dedication.

Smart growth regulations may also, in some instances, deny all economically viable use of land, in which case the *Lucas* per se rule requires compensation. This is not likely to be easy to prove in most instances. However, it is important to recognize that there are principles embedded in *Lucas* that raise issues for smart growth initiatives that become effective after a landowner has purchased property or after properties have already been subdivided into individually recorded lots, each taxed as separate units under state law. The Court in *Lucas* held that in order for the government to enjoin so-called nuisances without being liable for a taking, it must "identify background principles of nuisance and property law that prohibit the use intended."[19] Justice Scalia said that putting land to productive use such as building a home could not be considered a nuisance. He said, "It seems unlikely that common law principles would have prevented the erection of any habitable or productive improvements on [Lucas's] lands; they rarely support prohibition of the 'essential use' of land."[20] Some court decisions help illustrate the application of these *Lucas* principles.

---

17 *Del Monte Dunes at Monterey, Ltd. v City of Monterey*, 95 F.3d 1422, 1432 (9th Cir. 1996).
18 *Christopher Lake Development Co. v St. Louis County*, 35 F.3d 1269 (8th Cir. 1994).
19 *Lucas v South Carolina Coastal Commission*, 505 U.S. 1003 (1992).
20 *Id*. at 1031.

In a Michigan State case,[21] the court held that generalized legislative statements regarding the conservation of wetlands and public resources could not render construction in the wetland a nuisance under background principles of state law. In a federal claims court case,[22] the plaintiff brought a successful takings claim against the denial of a permit for development of wetlands under the federal Clean Water Act because it prohibited development on small single lots.

In addition to the principles in the *Lucas* case that are relevant in assessing smart growth regulations, there is the "ad hoc factual test" from the U.S. Supreme Court's decision in the *Penn Central* case. Under this test, the court examines factors such as (1) the character of the government action; (2) the economic impact of regulation on the property owner; and (3) the extent to which the regulation interferes with the property owners "distinct investment–backed expectations."[23] For example, in *Florida Rock Industries, Inc., v United States*[24] the court stated: "Nothing in the language of the Fifth Amendment compels a court to find a taking only when the government divests the total ownership of the property." The Court in *Lucas* also expressly left open the possibility that a court may find compensation is appropriate where depravation caused by the regulation is "one step short of complete."[25]

The latest land use decision by the U.S. Supreme Court in the *Palazzolo* case[26] has added a dose of practicality to deciding the futility exception under the finality requirement of the so-called ripeness doctrine. As developed by the U.S. Supreme Court in response to regulatory takings claims, the ripeness doctrine requires a court to inquire whether a local government's decision regarding the application of its regulations to a particular property was sufficiently final to enable the court to properly assess whether the regulation has gone too far and constitutes a taking under the Fifth Amendment.[27] In order for this constitutional determination to be made, the decision must be definitive enough so that a court knows "the extent of permitted development."[28]

In order for that decision to be sufficiently definitive, the finality requirement requires that a property owner have applied for and received a decision on a

---

21 *K&K Construction Inc. v Department of Natural Resources*, 551 N.W.2d 413 (Mich.App. 1996).
22 *Bowles v United States*, 31 Fed.cl.37 (1994).
23 *Penn Central Transp. Co. v New York City*, 438 U.S.104 (1978).
24 *Florida Rock Industries, Inc. v United States,* 18 F.3d 1560 (Fed. Cir. 1994).
25 *Lucas v South Carolina Coastal Commission*, 505 U.S. 1019 n.8.
26 *Palazzolo v Rhode Island et al.*, 533 U.S. 606 (2001).
27 *Williamson County Regional Planning Commission v Hamilton Bank*, 473 U.S. 172 (1985).
28 *MacDonald, Sommer & Frates v Yolo County*, 477 U.S. 340 (1986).

particular development plan and, if necessary, seek such variances or other modifications as would possibly overcome the local government's objections to the project. The property owner may also have to seek reapplication of the proposed development, unless he or she can demonstrate that such reapplication would be futile—known as the futility exception.

The 5–4 *Palazzolo* decision written by Justice Kennedy addressed two key points of contention in the ongoing takings debate: (1) when a land use regulatory decision is sufficiently final to satisfy the ripeness doctrine; and (2) whether a regulatory taking claim is automatically barred when the enactment of a restrictive regulation predates the owner's acquisition of the property. This second point is particularly relevant to the issue of resource protection regulations, discussed above.

In 1959, Palazzolo and some associates formed Shore Gardens, Inc. (SGI), for the purpose of investing in three undeveloped, adjoining parcels consisting of approximately 22 acres along the coastline in the Rhode Island town of Westerly. Eighteen acres of this coastal land are a salt marsh, subject to tidal flooding—for example, a classic wetland—requiring fill up to six feet in some places before significant structures could be built. SGI subdivided the entire property into 80 lots. In 1960, Palazzolo became the sole shareholder of SGI. By 1969, following various lot transactions, SGI had 74 lots remaining, totaling about 20 acres.

Beginning in 1962, Palazzolo sought to develop the property and submitted an application to the Rhode Island Division of Harbors and Rivers (DHR) to dredge from the adjacent Winnapaug Pond and to fill the entire property. The application was denied for lack of essential information, and in 1963, Palazzolo submitted a second application. While the second application was still pending, Palazzolo submitted, in 1966, a third application to do a more limited fill to allow the construction of a private beach club. In 1971, DHR approved the second and third applications, giving Palazzolo the option of either constructing a bulkhead and filling the marsh or constructing a beach facility. However, seven months later, the DHR revoked its assent, which Palazzolo did not appeal.

In the meantime, two important events occurred. First, in 1971, Rhode Island established the Coastal Resources Management Council (CRMC), with authority to regulate coastal wetlands. In 1977, the CRMC promulgated regulations that prohibited the filling of coast wetlands without approval of a special exception by the CRMC. Second, in 1978, SGI's corporate charter was revoked for failure to pay corporate income taxes, and title to the property passed to Palazzolo by operation of law.

In 1983, Palazzolo, now the fee owner, filed an application with the CRMC similar to the 1962 application, requesting permission to construct a bulkhead and to fill the entire salt marsh. It was rejected, and Palazzolo did not appeal. In 1985, with an application similar to the 1966 application to build a private beach club, he again applied to the CRMC—specifically to fill 11 acres with gravel to accommodate "50 cars with boat trailers, a dumpster, port-a-johns, picnic tables, barbecue pits of concrete, and other trash receptacles."[29] This application was also denied by CRMC for failure to meet the special exception "compelling public purpose" standard under the regulations.

This time Palazzolo appealed, bringing an inverse condemnation action, and seeking damages in the amount of $3,150,000, based on the estimated value of a 74-lot subdivision. He lost at trial, and the Rhode Island Supreme Court affirmed on the grounds that Palazzolo (1) had not satisfied the finality requirement of the ripeness doctrine and hence his takings claim was not ripe; (2) had no right to challenge regulations predating 1978, when he became the owner by operation of law; and (3) had not been denied all economically viable use because of the undisputed fact that he had $200,000 in development value on the upland portion of the property.[30]

The U.S. Supreme Court disagreed with the Rhode Island Supreme Court's conclusions that Palazzolo's takings claim was not ripe and that he was barred from bringing a takings claim because the 1978 restrictive regulations predated his succession to ownership of the property. The Court did agree with the Rhode Island Court's conclusion that Palazzolo was not deprived of all economic use of his property because the upland portions of the property still had development value, but remanded the case for consideration of Palazzolo's claims under the multifactor takings test of *Penn Central*,[31] which had not been examined fully by the Rhode Island Court because it had found Palazzolo's takings claim under *Penn Central* barred.[32]

The Court concluded from CRMC's interpretations of its regulations to deny Palazzolo's various applications, the briefs, and the candid statements of counsel for both sides, that it was clear that the state had no intention of allowing any fill in the wetlands nor any use involving substantial structures or improvements: "[N]o fill for any ordinary use. . . .[N]o fill for its own sake; no fill for a beach club, either rustic or upscale; no fill for a subdivision; no fill for any likely or foreseeable use.

---

29   *Palazzolo v Rhode Island et al.*, 533 U.S. at 615.
30   *Id*. at 616.
31   *Penn Central Transp. Co. v New York City*, 438 U.S. 104, 123–25 (1978).
32   *Palazzolo v Rhode Island et al.*, 533 U.S. at 615 and 632.

And with no fill there can be no structures and no development on the wetlands. Further permit applications were not necessary to establish this point."[33]

The second issue addressed by the Court was whether a regulatory taking claim is automatically barred when the enactment of a stringent regulation predates the owner's acquisition of the property. The argument in favor of this result is that since property rights are created by the state, new legislation shapes and defines property rights and reasonable investment-backed expectations. So owners of property subsequent to the enactment of such legislation take title with notice of the limitation and cannot claim injury for lost property value.

At the time Palazzolo became the owner by operation of law, the wetlands regulations were already in place. Hence, the Rhode Island Supreme Court had held that Palazzolo's postregulation acquisition was fatal to both his *Lucas* and *Penn Central* takings claims. The U.S. Supreme Court rejected this result, reasoning that such a "single, sweeping, rule" would "absolve the state of its obligation to defend any action restricting land use, no matter how extreme or unreasonable." Such a rule would, in effect, allow the state "to put an expiration date on the Takings Clause."[34]

Instead the Court looked to its prior decision in *Nollan*,[35] striking down as unconstitutional a California Coastal Commission requirement that oceanfront landowners provide lateral beach access to the public as a condition of development approval. In that case, the majority held that "[s]o long as the Commission could not have deprived the prior owners of the easement without compensating them, the prior owners must be understood to have transferred their full property rights in conveying the lot."[36]

The dissent in *Palazzolo* argued that *Nollan* had been limited by the decision in *Lucas*,[37] in which the Court had cautioned that the landowner's ability to recover for government deprivation of all economically viable use was limited by "those restrictions that background principles of the state's law of property and nuisance already place upon land ownership."[38] But the *Palazzolo* Court rejected the proposition that any new regulation, once enacted, becomes a background principle of property law, which cannot be challenged by those subsequently acquiring title to property.

---

33 *Id.* at 621.
34 *Id.* at 626-627.
35 *Nollan v California Coastal Commission*, 483 U.S. 825 (1987).
36 *Id.* at 834, n. 2.
37 *Lucas v South Carolina Coastal Council*, 505 U.S. 1003 (1992).
38 *Id.* at 1029.

Without attempting to define the "precise circumstances when a legislative enactment can be deemed a background principle of state law or whether those circumstances are present here," the Court held that *Lucas* did not overrule its holding in *Nollan* and that "the determination whether an existing, general law can limit all economic use of property must turn on objective factors, such as the nature of the land use proscribed."[39]

The Court's decision in *Palazzolo* leaves clarification of some of its opinion for a later day—particularly the "objective factors" relevant to a determination of whether a legislative enactment becomes a background principle of property law. But it has finally added a degree of practical focus to determining when enough is enough under the ripeness finality requirement by holding that an applicant need not make meaningless permit applications when the government's interpretation of its regulations make clear the extent to which it will permit development on a site. Also, *Palazzolo* does away with the notice defense to takings claims. Property owners will now be able to bring takings claims despite having purchased property with notice of restrictive regulations.

Moratoria   One of the techniques frequently used by communities intending to implement growth management measures is to impose a "planning pause," otherwise known as a moratorium, while the community gets smart about what it wants to do in particular geographical areas. The U.S. Supreme Court made it clear in the *First English* case[40] that compensation is not precluded as a remedy simply because a government land use restriction is temporary. If the temporary restriction is sufficiently onerous, it is a taking—"not different in kind from permanent takings, for the which the constitution clearly requires compensation."[41] Of course, the Supreme Court's statement does not really tell us when a temporary restriction affects a taking.[42] But the facts in some cases are instructive. For

---

39 *Palazzolo v Rhode Island et al.*, 533 U.S. at 629-630.
40 *First English Evangelical Lutheran Church of Glendale v County of Los Angeles*, 482 U.S. 304 (1987).
41 *Id.* at 318.
42 To the surprise of many practitioners and commentators, the U.S. Court of Appeals for the Ninth Circuit recently distinguished a development moratorium from the type of temporary taking in *First English*. In *Tahoe-Sierra Preservation Council v Tahoe Regional Planning Agency*, 216 F.3d 764, *reh'g denied,* 228 F.2d 998 (9th Cir. 2000), *cert. granted,* 121 S.Ct. 2589 (2001), the Ninth Circuit held that a temporary development moratorium should not ever be considered a taking under the holding in *Lucas*. This holding, it seems to me, begs the question of when a moratorium extended over time incrementally, in fact, constitutes "extraordinary delay" in government decision-making. The Ninth Circuit's holding effectively precludes property owners denied economically viable use of their property during an extended moratorium from pursuing the compensation remedy under *First English*. The U.S. Supreme Court has granted certiorari in this case. The case will give the Court the opportunity to clarify temporary regulatory takings law in light of its decisions in *First English* and *Lucas*.

example, in *Corn v City of Lauderdale Lakes*,[43] the property owner proposed building a 900-unit mini-warehouse on a parcel zoned for such a use. The city rejected the proposal because of a change in zoning and an enactment of a moratorium. It was apparent that the moratorium was consciously designed to stop the project and not truly in the public interest. The Court decided: "The moratorium seems nothing more than an attempt at post hoc rationalization. In short, the city council was motivated solely by an irrational desire to thwart Corn's plans."[44]

Municipalities frequently assert that the power to impose a moratorium is a tool that is essential to its power to regulate land use—a legitimate governmental purpose. However, a recent decision by the Pennsylvania Supreme Court flatly rejected that position.[45] In that case, the township had enacted a moratorium on certain types of subdivision and land development approvals while it completed the process of revising its comprehensive plan. The township had no express statutory authority to enact such a moratorium, relying instead on the premise that such power was implicitly granted or incidental to the zoning powers conferred on municipalities by statute.

The Pennsylvania Supreme Court concluded in *Naylor* that the "power to *enact* a zoning ordinance, for whatever purpose, does not necessarily include the power to *suspend* a valid zoning ordinance to the prejudice of a land owner." The court went on to conclude that the "power to *suspend* land development" is a power "distinct from and not incidental to any power to *regulate* land development," and was not permissible without express legislative authorization.[46] The reasoning of this decision is significant in that it underscores the importance of establishing by express legislation the authority for local governments to adopt moratoria, and defining what are deemed legitimate purposes for moratoria. This limits the potential for a municipality to use a moratorium under the guise of growth management as a post hoc rationalization for an arbitrary purpose such as occurred in *Corn*.

The Fourteenth Amendment's Substantive Due Process Clause

It is important to remember that, as originally conceived, zoning was supposed to require very little exercise of discretion. Instead, it was intended to be a self-administering land use allocation system, that is, a system of prestated land use

---

43 771 F. Supp. 1557 (S.D. Fla 1991).
44 *Id.* at 1569.
45 *Naylor v Township of Hellam*, 773 A.2d 770 (Pa. 2001).
46 *Id.* at 774.

classifications and rules under which only cases of particular hardship would require administrative (variance) or legislative (zone amendment) action to resolve. This original premise was driven by a desire to avoid legislative or administrative interference with the land market (Krasnowiecki 1970; Kmiec 1982). In other words, concern for property rights and the goal of maximizing the productivity of private actors in the land market led the founders of zoning to design a "zoning by rules" system of land use control.

Zoning and land use controls have hardly remained faithful to that original property rights-based concept. In their effort to manage growth, protect natural resources, preserve community character, provide for infrastructure needs, and secure public amenities, local governments have gone far beyond the original limited concept of the variance procedure. Today they rely heavily upon discretionary review and approval procedures to address development proposals. Discretion is nothing more than the exercise of judgment. In the context of land use and development approvals, discretion means the substantive and procedural choices made by a legislative or administrative body for the purpose for which the power was delegated.

At issue in these discretionary review and approval procedures is fundamental fairness—the heart of due process. This is the central principle of the fifth and fourteenth amendments to the U.S. Constitution and requires that citizens be protected from the fluctuations of legislative policy.[47] Because the right to develop property is a valuable property right,[48] the failure to articulate clear, workable standards reduces the property owner to a state of uncertainty and effectively deprives the owner of that right. Failure to establish standards to guide the exercise of discretion at the administrative level also risks uneven treatment, a denial of equal protection.

Substantive due process When discretionary decision-making goes awry and judgment is exercised arbitrarily, there is abuse of discretion that may amount to a constitutional violation in the form of substantive due process—actionable under federal law. Substantive due process refers to the fact that the Fourteenth Amendment to the U.S. Constitution imposes both substantive and procedural requirements when it prohibits any government action that deprives "any person

---

47 *West Main Assocs. v Bellevue*, 720 P.2d 782 (Wash. 1986), citing *The Federalist* No. 44, at 301 (J. Madison), (J. Cooke, ed. 1961).
48 *Louthan v King County,* 617 P.2d 977 (Wash. 1980).

of . . . liberty or property without due process of law." This substantive component of the Due Process Clause bars "certain arbitrary, wrongful government actions 'regardless of the fairness of the procedures used to implement them.'"[49]

One regulatory approach that most frequently results in abuses of discretion in land use regulations designed to achieve growth management objectives and can result in substantive due process violations is regulations directed at development project impacts that allow as-of-right uses to be converted to special or conditional uses and subjected to discretionary review.

Automatic conversions to conditional use An example of local government administrative actions that attempt to convert a permitted use to a conditional use and impose conditions through design review after an applicant has demonstrated compliance with all zoning code requirements for a permitted use permit is found in a Minnesota case.[50] In that case, an applicant sought approval for a convenience food restaurant, which was listed as a permitted use in the zoning district, subject to specific performance standards. The application complied with all site plan requirements for curb cuts, safety signage, lighting, landscaping, parking, screening of view and architectural appearance. However, at the public hearing, neighborhood residents expressed the desire that the property be used for residential use rather than a commercial use and argued that the restaurant was inconsistent with the area's proresidential comprehensive plan. Following a discussion of how the proposal was inappropriately commercial and inconsistent with the comprehensive plan, the planning commission voted to deny the building permit on the basis of noncompliance with the following provision of the Minneapolis Zoning Code:

> The architectural appearance and functional plan of the building shall not be so dissimilar to existing buildings as to cause impairment in property values within reasonable distance of applicant's zoning lot.

However, no facts regarding dissimilar architectural design or impairment of property values were presented at the hearing to rebut the applicant's evidence on these issues. In the subsequent mandamus proceeding brought by the developer, the city argued that the conditions placed on the approval of the permit under the ordinance recharacterized the requested use as conditional, which gave the city

---

49 *Zinermon v Burch,* 494 U.S. 113, 125 (1990) (quoting *Daniels v Williams,* 474 U.S. 327, 331 (1986)).
50 *Chase v City of Minneapolis,* 401 N.W.2d 408 (Minn. App. 1987).

discretion to consider it in light of the general welfare and city's planning goals. The court, however, ruled that the city could not arbitrarily convert the permitted use to a conditional use in such a manner. Because the application complied with the zoning code in all respects, approval was required as a matter of right.[51]

Another one of the more flagrant examples of a legislative attempt to automatically convert permitted uses to conditional uses in wholesale fashion was the proposed Model Traffic Management Ordinance prepared for the DuPage Mayors and Managers Conference of Illinois. The ordinance's controlling concept was traffic impact. It provided:

> All other development of lots of record which are not otherwise classified as Planned Unit Development, Special or Conditional Uses, Zoning Variations, or Zoning Amendments, but which create a traffic impact as defined and determined by this Ordinance, shall be considered and reviewed procedurally as a Special or Conditional Use.[52]

If implemented in the municipal jurisdictions of DuPage County, such a provision would surely be challengeable as violative of due process and the uniformity[53] and special use provisions of the zoning enabling legislation, consistent with holdings in other jurisdictions.

Substantive due process and moratoria In a New York case,[54] the plaintiff, HBP, owned a 6.8-acre parcel within the boundaries of a sewer district under county jurisdiction and sought to develop a 15-lot subdivision. HBP obtained preliminary subdivision approval from the village planning board and all necessary county and state approvals for development of the subdivision, except a DEC sewer main line extension permit. Even though the county had approved HBP's sewer design, the county denied the permit because of a moratorium imposed by the state's Department of Environmental Conservation in 1986, a moratorium that had

---

51 *Id.* at 413.
52 Section 3.0–6 of the Draft Model Traffic Management Ordinance for DuPage County Municipalities (August 8, 1990). Section 3.0–5 of the ordinance also automatically converted any subdivision that creates a traffic impact to a planned unit development, subject to the standards and procedures for processing PUDs.
53 The uniformity provision found in most zoning enabling statutes requires that the regulations within each zoning district must be uniform, while regulations in the various zoning districts may differ from one another.
54 *HBP Associates v Marsh,* 893 F. Supp. 271 (S.D.N.Y. 1995).

remained in effect for almost nine years pending the county's demonstrating adequate plant capacity—which it hadn't been able to do. Here is an example of where the substantive due process protections of the Fourteenth Amendment become relevant. HBP was able to demonstrate to the court's satisfaction that in fact it had a protectible property interest in the benefit of the sewer services because it had paid a special assessment. Having demonstrated its property interest, HBP alleged that the DEC had never required the county to expand, upgrade or replace the treatment plant or to reduce sewage flow, and the county had never taken steps to demonstrate adequate capacity for future growth—all while at the same time providing sewage capacity to municipalities outside the boundaries of the sewer district.

Another regulatory approach found in growth management programs is the reliance on design review to address community character as part of the quality of life concern of growth management policies. This approach implicates the void for vagueness doctrine.

The Void for Vagueness Doctrine

The Void for Vagueness Doctrine is derived from the procedural due process requirement of notice and concerns the lack of clarity or certainty in the language of regulation. Its purpose is to place a limit upon arbitrary and discretionary enforcement of the law.[55] Most courts when presented with a void for vagueness challenge to a regulation will echo the U.S. Supreme Court's language,[56] namely, that "[a]n ordinance is unconstitutionally vague when men of common intelligence must necessarily guess at its meaning."[57] In other words, due process of law in legislation requires definiteness or certainty.

From a legal perspective, nothing could be less definite or certain than the new urbanism (Katz 1993; Duany, Plater-Zyberk and Speck 2000), which is touted as the way to combat urban sprawl and return to a village tradition—the traditional neighborhood design (TND).[58] Neotraditionalists criticize the rigidity and complexity of traditional zoning and subdivision regulations, and what they

---

55 *Burien Bark Supply v King County*, 725 P.2d 994, 996 (Wash. 1986) (vagueness found) citing *State v White*, 640 P.2d 1061 (Wash. 1982). See also Blaesser (2000).
56 *Broadrick v Oklahoma*, 413 U.S. 601 (1973).
57 *Union National Bank & Trust v Village of New Lenox*, 505 N.E.2d 1, 3 (Ill. App. 1987).
58 The term *new urbanism* encompasses a variety of design theories, including traditional neighborhood development, neotraditional development, transit-oriented development, pedestrian-oriented development and communities of place. See Sitkowski (1999).

believe those regulations have fostered—the suburban pattern of low-density residential and commercial development extending outward from urban areas into rural areas.

Neotraditionalists prefer instead to regulate through design codes that emphasize visual design archetypes rather than textual standards. The new urbanist view of our existing land use regulatory structure is not surprising since the land use patterns represented by neotraditional villages predate zoning in this country. The design of neotraditional communities emphasizes compact, higher-density, pedestrian-friendly, mixed-use communities, with single-family homes on small lots interspersed with multifamily townhouse and apartment developments. A grid pattern of streets is favored over cul-de-sacs in order to promote the village experience.

Neotraditional codes emphasize flexibility over precision. Also, these codes are often imposed through private covenants, which must be accepted by homeowners upon purchase. As a development option, the neotraditional development has clearly had an impact on the marketplace. However, when a local government tries to make these private codes into public codes and to zone for or mandate neotraditional patterns of development, the void for vagueness problem and other due process concerns arise. In their *Lexicon of the New Urbanism* (1999), Duany, Plater-Zyberk and Speck characterize an ordinance as the translation of a private code into legal language and the formal adoption of that code by a local government. It is not so simple, and the new urbanism design codes raise a number of the due process concerns already described.

Void for vagueness Neotraditional villages are supposed to be places of distinctive character, and whether a particular use is compatible in such a village context, or whether the village design is consistent with an ordinance that relies on visual aids and flexible standards, are highly subjective determinations. The overt design emphasis of neotraditional codes amounts to aesthetic regulation that most frequently fails the due process requirement for discrete and meaningful standards and therefore is likely to violate the void for vagueness doctrine. As noted previously, the purpose of the doctrine is to place a limit on arbitrary and discretionary action.[59] A developer must know or, in effect, have notice of what standards will apply. There must be consistency in the application of those standards from

---

59 *Burien Bark Supply v King County*, 725 P.2d 994, 996 (Wash. 1986) (vagueness found) citing *State v White*, 640 P.2d 1061 (Wash. 1982).

application to application, and a court must be able to evaluate the evidence with sufficient clarity to be able to judge whether or not the decision was arbitrary.

Is process the antidote for this area of subjective decision-making? The long accepted argument has been that where there are subject matters that are not amenable to definite standards, local governments can compensate for that with process, that is, with review procedures and findings of fact. However, since before the U.S. Supreme Court's decision in *Dolan*, experts have noted the impatience of an increasing number of state courts with so-called pretty committees and development review procedures based on subjective standards, and a growing movement toward more objective development standards.[60] If the standards used to make the decision in the first place are defective, the appellate process will also falter, because the standards at that level are not adequate to make up the deficiencies in the original standards. In other words, it is not enough to appendage an appeal process to a set of vague standards.[61] Hence merely adding a special review process for neotraditional design review is unlikely to cure the problem.

Spot zoning and uniformity The doctrine of spot zoning prohibits a local government from rezoning a parcel of land from a less-intensive-use classification to a more-intensive-use classification that is inconsistent with the surrounding uses.[62] The uniformity requirement found in most zoning enabling statutes requires that the regulations within each zoning district must be uniform, while regulations in the various zoning districts may differ from one another. The flexible design needed for a village may mean that a more intensive use should be inserted in the village—the equivalent of spot zoning. For example, it is generally recognized that local neighborhood commercial uses, such as hardware or ma and pa grocery stores found in many residential neighborhoods, although deemed nonconforming uses, are, in fact, compatible with the neighborhood. But a zoning amendment by a local government in order to authorize such a neighborhood commercial use in a neotraditional village is questionable under the spot zoning doctrine. The uniformity requirement is also implicated by the distinct design of neotraditional villages.

---

60   See symposium comments of Norman Williams, Orlando Delogu, Clyde Forrest and Richard Babcock in Blaesser and Weinstein (1989, 22–26).
61   *Anderson v City of Issaquah*, 851 P.2d 744 (Wash Ct. App. 1993) discussed at Section 8.04[2] *supra*.
62   *Burkett v City of Texarkana*, 500 S.W.2d 242 (Tex. Civ. App. 1973); *Griswold v. City of Homer*, 925 P.2d 1015 (Alaska 1996).

The spot zoning and uniformity issues are not necessarily insurmountable. Zoning enabling legislation can be amended to authorize use flexibility to achieve neotraditional village designs. But with the enactment of such enabling legislation to set the regulatory stage for innovative development patterns, there also must be market demand for alternatives to conventional development. Without such market demand, few developers will take the financial risk to pursue alternative forms of development.[63]

The Right to Freedom of Mobility

Freedom of mobility in order to seek greater opportunity has been inherent in America's growth as a country. For the last 200 years, our national government has encouraged migration throughout this country. The right to migrate and settle anywhere in this country is constitutionally protected by the fundamental right to travel—a right that the U.S. Supreme Court has found implicitly imbedded in the Constitution.[64]

Freedom to move also means freedom to choose. Growth management policies that seek to change growth and development patterns must accept this fundamental premise in the context of a market economy. Some advocates of growth management argue that growth control is needed to restrict outward movement of future development in order to force people into more compact urban forms. But development decisions are not made through a process of coercion. Rather, they result from market indicators—a reflection of freely made decisions by homeowners, businesses, commuters and shoppers about where to live, work and purchase goods. Developers respond to the demand of the consumer/users. Growth follows demand and will continue to follow it. Through education, consumers can hopefully choose to make decisions in a new direction, possibly toward more compact forms of living, but they will not be forced. Freedom to move is freedom to choose.

In the aftermath of the attack on the World Trade Center in lower Manhattan, this fundamental freedom to choose where to live and work has become even more palpable in the face of growth management objectives to

---

63 Surveys such as those conducted by American LIVES, Inc. (1995), suggest that at least as to residential development, there is an emerging market of empty nesters, smaller families, singles and seniors who are prepared to accept smaller lot sizes and clustered housing in exchange for open space. Their demand is consistent with the general trend nationally toward smaller lot sizes and increasing acceptance of mixing lot sizes and housing types (for example, townhouses and single family homes) both within developments and also within streets and blocks.

64 *Crandall v Nevada*, 73 U.S. (6 Wall) 35 (1867); *Edwards v California*, 314 U.S. 160 (1941); *United States v Guest*, 383 U.S. 745 (1966); *Griffin v Breckenridge*, 403 U.S. 88 (1971).

either encourage or force people into more compact urban forms. Since September 11, 2001, many firms are signing long-term leases for new locations in suburban communities. This dispersal of business functions means that employees will follow, reinforcing the outward movement of development. Such a phenomenon does not preclude the possibility that compact forms of development will be achievable in the suburbs and, indeed, may be necessary to achieve affordable housing solutions for the influx of new workers. But it does mean that with major urban centers facing a new period of uncertainty and competition from smaller towns and suburbs (Kotkin 2001), viewing the growth management debate in terms of the simple dichotomy of the benefits of compact urban form in cities versus the sprawl of suburbs is not very helpful for addressing the realities that will face suburban locations as the market adapts to security concerns caused by the terrorist attack.

Simply put, firms consciously seeking to decentralize their functions to the extent possible will create increased demand for a horizontal built environment that can also accommodate the automobile needs of workers. Whatever problems suburbs may have from the perspective of new urbanists and smart growth advocates, they must now be viewed as also containing the ingredients for solutions to the realities of the new living and working environments created by the events since September 11.

Smart Growth Efforts to Control the Amount and Location and Quality of Development

Smart growth strategies that attempt to control the rate, amount, type, location and quality of development generally fall into four categories of controls (Kelly 1993, 16):

1. Adequate public facilities (APF) programs that prohibit programs that prohibit development unless adequate public facilities are available;
2. Phased growth programs that determine when to allow development;
3. Urban growth boundary (UGB) programs that set limits on urban growth; and
4. Rate-of-growth programs that establish a defined growth rate.

Within these categories, regulatory strategies that are most vulnerable to constitutional challenge are those that seek to *control*, rather than influence, the amount and location and the quality of development.

Control of the Amount and Location of Development: The Urban Growth Boundary

Use of a spatial control device such as the urban growth boundary (UGB) to control the amount and location of development is a departure from the traditional land use regulatory system in this country. UGBs significantly affect the spatial arrangement of development patterns in ways that are not typical in the United States (Mandelker 1962; 1999, 4–5) By contrast, the British green belt program has been in place for almost half a century. The green belt limits growth of cities to preserve agricultural land and prevent sprawl. But it should also be remembered that Great Britain does not have the fifth and fourteenth amendments. Under the legal system in Great Britain, development rights are controlled essentially by the government, making development of property more in the nature of a privilege. In this country, however, when the goal of a UGB such as Portland's is designed to preserve agricultural and other natural resources areas, the UGB policy could raise a taking issue under the Fifth Amendment, when development is prohibited on lots that have already been subdivided.[65]

Urban growth boundaries in this country have had a major impact on the land market because they prevent development from occurring where developers have traditionally invested. Indeed, some argue that a cause of urban sprawl is investment in outlying areas—mere speculation according to some. But from the developer's perspective, this phenomenon is not speculation but rather investment in land induced in large part by the federal and state policies, including (1) construction of the interstate highway system and state and federal transportation investment policies that generally favored extension of that system over alternative transportation modes; and (2) restrictive land use regulations in the urban core making low regulatory environment in rural areas more attractive for development and other preferential assessment policies, such as green belt taxation and the undervaluation of land for property tax assessment purposes. In addition, it can be argued that federal tax policy that allows first home mortgage and property tax deductions on taxable income favors single-home ownership over other housing types that might support infill, rehabilitation and redevelopment of urban areas. One of the arguments of those who favor smart growth is that the market is imperfect and government intervention is necessary in order to manage those

---

65   *Bowles v United States*, 31 Fed. Cl. 37 (1994) (successful takings claims against denial of permit for development of wetlands under federal Clean Water Act).

imperfections. But I would suggest that without developers who are, by nature, risk takers, there would be no real estate market.

Quality of Growth: Community Character and Tree Preservation

One of the regulatory results under smart growth initiatives directed at the quality and character of communities is a new generation of tree preservation ordinances (Shae 1997). The underlying premise of these new tree preservation ordinances is that all trees are a public resource. The assumption is that government may control all public resources. If that assumption is true, then government may also control all trees. This is a tremendous shift from the concept of private ownership for trees growing on private property to the perception of community ownership of trees growing on private property.

Traditionally, tree preservation ordinances limited their scope to the protection of trees located in public rights-of-way, streets, avenues and public parks. Such ordinances also provided for the regulation of privately owned trees when they are dead, diseased or constitute a threat to public safety. The legal authority for this type of tree ordinance is derived from the common law of nuisance[66] and the police power—the legislative power that resides in each state and is delegated to municipalities to establish laws and ordinances to preserve the public order and to promote the public health, safety and morals and other aspects of the general welfare.

The new variety of tree preservation ordinances seeks to regulate privately owned trees for reasons that have nothing to do with abating nuisance, preventing disease, transmission or avoiding injury to the public. Typical language in a statement of purpose for a new tree ordinance is:

> To protect *public health* by absorbing air pollutants and contamination, by providing buffering to reduce excessive noise, wind and storm impacts, then by maintaining visual screening with its accompanying cooling effect during the summer months;
>
> To provide for *public safety* through the prevention of erosion, siltation and flooding;

---

66 The term *nuisance* refers to the use of one's property in a manner that seriously interferes with another's use or enjoyment of his or her property (a private nuisance) or is injurious to the community at large (a public nuisance). Unlike the concept of trespass to land, nuisance does not require a physical invasion of others' property (Blaesser and Weinstein 1989, 9).

> To contribute significantly to the *general welfare* of the City by providing natural beauty and recreational opportunities for existing and future residents.[67]

Based on these statements of purpose, this new type of tree ordinance typically requires that for each tree removed from the landowner's property, another tree like it be replanted elsewhere on the site.[68] If that is not feasible, the ordinance may also require payment of a fee in lieu to a community tree preservation fund. Some ordinances also provide that removing, cutting, or severely overpruning a tree deemed protected under the ordinance constitutes a public nuisance, punishable by criminal penalties.[69] Another typical tree preservation ordinance provision is that which prohibits property owners from removing trees on their land prior to or in anticipation of development.

If a person owns property in fee simple absolute, that ownership means that the person possesses a full and unrestricted right to use the property, provided that he does not commit a nuisance against his neighbor. In fact, this fee simple ownership is generally recognized as broadly including the right to make any use of the land, including cutting timber (Tiffany 1940). It can be argued that the new tree ordinances, by authorizing the local government to monitor and impose penalties on property owners who remove trees on the site essentially are downgrading the property owner's fee interest to that of a life estate. A life estate in property means that one has use of the property during one's lifetime, subject to the rule that the holder of the life estate interest must not commit waste on the property—that is, a duty owed to the owner of the balance of the fee interest, the remainderman. In effect, tree removal on private property is now waste for which the remainder persons must be compensated. The remainder persons are the people in the community—present and future. In effect, local government by intervening on behalf of the community, has created a constructive easement in trees over the private property owner's property.

It seems to me that this regulatory circumstance is no different than the circumstance presented in the *Nollan* case, where the California Coastal Commission imposed a constructive easement as a condition for granting a permit. The Court

---

67 City of Sterling Heights, Macomb County, Michigan, Ordinance No. 292, Article III, Tree Preservation (1991) (emphasis in original).
68 See Georgetown County, South Carolina, Tree Protection Regulations, Article IX, §§ 1102-1103 (Draft of Proposed Regulations dated June 14, 1999).
69 City of Jacksonville, Florida, Landscape and Tree Protection Regulations, Part 12, Chapter 656, Section 656.1210 (proposed amendments to regulations dated July 7, 1999).

in *Nollan* said that the Coastal Commission could require an easement, but it had to pay for it. The new generation of tree preservation ordinances that are sprouting up around this country do not provide for payment for the easements they create on private property. They merely assume that the control of privately owned trees is a public resource for which no compensation is required.

Conclusion

If there is consensus as to the target of smart growth, there certainly is lack of consensus as to the meaning of smart growth. This circumstance is due in part to the lack of consensus over what sprawl is, its causes, and what are ideal patterns of development. In 1973, a Rockefeller Brothers Fund task force concluded that no ideal pattern of development exists (Reilly 1973). The most important goal, in the view of the task force, was quality of development. The task force wrote:

> Quality is marked by respect for human and natural values. It is harder to create quality than to preserve it, for creation requires more choices and its goals are inherently complicated. In conservation, quality values are readily translated into physical ideals and in many cases, the ideals already exist—a community in harmony with its surroundings, a valley preserved in wilderness.
>
> If the community or valley is instead to be transformed by development, there are no convenient ideals. At what population level is there likely to be the greatest concern for the humanity of each inhabitant? Is it better that people live close together or far apart? That they walk to work, drive, be carried by mass transit, or perhaps by elevator within a futuristic megastructure? How much social contact should we aim for among people of different temperaments, incomes, races, and ethnic backgrounds?
>
> No consensus exists on these issues, and none is likely to be forthcoming soon.... For the foreseeable future, the decisions that create and shape our communities and regions will continue to be made without ideal development patterns, social or physical (Reilly 1973, 177–178).

Unfortunately, many proponents of smart growth, including the new urbanists, convey the view, with uncompromising zeal, that compact urban form and neotraditional villages are the only responsible patterns of development, ignoring market realities, preexisting behavior patterns and the principle so important to this country's development—freedom of choice. Their view is unfortunate and diverts attention from what, in my view, is the more important goal as identified by the Rockefeller Brothers Fund task force: quality of development.

Quality development can be achieved through various patterns of development that provide people with the choices needed in our increasingly technology-based economy—and now, the need for security. Those different development patterns can also be designed to be in harmony with their surroundings and the communities of which they are a part. Smart growth and traditional neighborhood development regulations rely heavily upon discretionary land use controls to achieve their objectives. It can be expected that such regulations will increasingly tie development approvals to adequate public facility determinations and impact fee programs, raising some of the legal issues covered in this chapter.

The fifth and fourteenth amendments place important constitutional limitations upon these and other potential smart growth initiatives. The legal principles I have discussed should be used to ensure that local government land use decision-making processes encourage a synthesis of viewpoints regarding appropriate or ideal development patterns, and that they provide certainty and consistency in the review of development proposals—necessary ingredients if smart growth initiatives are to be successful in this country.

References

Blaesser, Brian W. 2000. *Discretionary land use controls: Avoiding invitations to abuse of discretion, third ed.* Chapter 8. Eagan, MN: West Group.

Blaesser, Brian W., and A. Weinstein, eds. 1989. *Land use and the Constitution.* Chicago, IL: American Planning Association Planners Press.

Bosselman, Fred P. 1975. Town of Ramapo: Binding the world? In *Management and control of growth, vol. 2.* Washington, DC: Urban Land Institute.

Duany, Andres, Elizabeth Plater-Zyberk and Jeff Speck. 1999. *Lexicon of the new urbanism.* Miami, FL: Duany Plater-Zyberk Architects.

———. 2000. *Surburban nation: The rise of sprawl and the decline of the American dream.* New York, NY: North Point Press.

El Nasser, Haya. 2000. Development spawns hot new legal specialty: Sprawl. *USA today* (February 29).

Goldberger, Paul. 2000. It takes a village: The anti-sprawl doctors make a manifest. *The New Yorker* (March 27):128.

Katz, Peter. 1993. *The new urbanism: Toward an architecture of community.* New York, NY: McGraw Hill.

Kelly, Eric Damien. 1993. *Planning, growth, and public facilities: A primer for local officials.* Chicago, IL: American Planning Association, Planning Advisory Service Report no. 447.

Kmiec, Douglas. 1982. Deregulating land use: An alternative free enterprise development system. 130 *U.Pa. law review* 28, 50.

Kotkin, Joel. 2001. Cities must change to survive. *Wall street journal* (October 24):A22.

Krasnowiecki, Jan. 1970. The basic system of land use control: Legislative preregulation versus administrative discretion. In *The new zoning: Legal, administrative, and economic concepts and techniques, vol. 3*, N. Marcus and M. Groves, eds. New York, NY: Praeger Publishers.

Krizek, Kevin J., and Joe Power. 1996. *A planner's guide to sustainable development.* Chicago, IL: American Planning Association, Planning Advisory Service, Report No. 467.

Mandelker, David R. 1962. *Green belts and urban growth: English town and country planning in action.* Madison, WI: University of Wisconsin Press.

———. 1999. Managing space to manage growth. 23 *William and Mary environmental law and policy review* (Fall):801.

National Association of Industrial and Office Properties (NAIOP). 1999. *Growing to greatness: A growth management manual.* Herndon, VA: NAIOP.

Reilly, William K., ed. 1973. The use of land: A citizen's policy guide to urban growth. Rockefeller Brothers Fund task force report. New York, NY: Thomas Y. Crowell, Co.

Shae, Ruthmarie. 1997. A shorter cut to forestation: The constitutionality of local tree ordinances. *State & local news* 20(4)(summer). American Bar Association.

Sitkowski, Robert. 1999. The new urbanism for municipal lawyers. Paper presented to the International Municipal Lawyers Association. Washington, DC (April 12).

Tiffany, Herbert Thorndike. 1940. *A treatise on the modern law of real property and other interests in land.* Chicago, IL: Callaghan.

9

Jerold S. Kayden

The Constitution Neither Prohibits Nor Requires Smart Growth

The United States Constitution neither prohibits nor requires governmental efforts to achieve smart growth.[1] Among the various factors—political, institutional, economic, social and legal—that hinder or promote the realization of smart growth, constitutional law ranks low. The U.S. Supreme Court has interpreted the federal Constitution as granting government great leeway in fashioning land use regulatory instruments, even if such instruments substantially impinge upon the exercise of private property rights. On its face, the regulatory regime that implements smart growth respects this constitutional framework. Indeed, many of the regulatory instruments have endured legal vetting as stand-alone techniques, well before the present smart growth era. Although smart growth regulatory instruments, applied in individual cases, may from time to time go "too far," as Justice Oliver Wendell Holmes, Jr., would have it,[2] that possibility should not obscure the facial constitutionality of the general regulatory approach. At the opposite end of the spectrum, there is nothing in the federal constitutional schema that impels government to seek smart growth.

This article first defines smart growth and its implementing regulatory regime. It then sets forth the relevant constitutional framework governing the use of such a regime. Finally, it measures the regulatory regime against the framework, concluding that, smartly applied, the implementing tools satisfy the Constitution.

Definition of Smart Growth and its Regulatory Regime

Often situated as the opposite of sprawl, a land development pattern commonly produced by the real estate market under conventional local land use regulations, smart growth describes a normative pattern of land development that preserves open space, reduces reliance on automobiles, mitigates the need for new infrastructure, and otherwise contributes to assertedly better environmental, social and fiscal outcomes. The goals of Maryland's smart growth program are typical of those announced by programs across the country: "to save our most valuable remaining natural resources before they are forever lost, to support existing communities and neighborhoods by targeting state resources to support development

---

1   This article addresses the impact of the U. S. Constitution, rather than that of state constitutions, on governmental efforts to achieve smart growth. State constitutions may have provisions that may be interpreted as impeding or requiring aspects of smart growth above and beyond the U.S. Constitution. See *infra* note 9 and accompanying text.
2   *Pennsylvania Coal Co. v Mahon,* 260 U.S. 393, 415 (1922).

Photograph © Jerold S. Kayden.

in areas where the infrastructure is already in place or planned to support it, and to save taxpayers millions of dollars in the unnecessary cost of building the infrastructure required to support sprawl."[3] Smart growth sometimes includes a redistributive social agenda that favors affordable housing and jobs for poor families (Pollard 2000). In physical planning terms, development that is compact, high-density, and served by existing public transportation and capital infrastructure is smart growth; development that is spread out, low-density, and far from public transportation and capital infrastructure, is not.

Because the private real estate market does not inherently favor smart growth, and because conventional land use regulations such as zoning and subdivision controls, conventionally employed, not only do not mandate smart growth, but may affirmatively prevent it, some state, regional and local governments have adjusted existing or adopted special regulatory instruments to mandate or encourage smart growth. In general, these instruments control the location, type, density, layout, design, social/economic composition, associated infrastructure, and pace of private development in ways that produce smart growth. They say develop here, not there; develop this way, not that way; develop then, not now; and internalize negative externalities along the way. It is worth recognizing, however, that the smart growth regulatory regime is not a synthetic, command-and-control, comprehensive master plan in which property owners are required to build whatever government dictates.

Although the list of specific instruments making up the smart growth regulatory regime is not self-defining, it typically includes a number of usual suspects implemented by government:

- *Traditional zoning* is tweaked to encourage high-density development near public transportation nodes (APA 1998, 36).
- *Mixed-use zoning* encourages combinations of retail, residential and small office uses in the same structure (APA 1998, 30-32).
- *Inclusionary zoning* secures affordable housing as part of a new private market-rate housing development (Morris 2000, 29-45; Mallach 1984, 11-21).

---

3   *Smart Growth in Maryland* (2001) at *http://www.op.state.md.us.smartgrowth*.

- *Cluster zoning* authorizes tighter layouts of housing units than traditional single-family zoning would otherwise permit, securing open space throughout the rest of a land parcel.[4]
- *Agricultural zoning, floodplain, wetlands, and habitat protection controls, and other land use/environmental laws* protect sensitive land from inappropriate development, thereby preserving open space (Beaumont 1996, 165-167).
- *Historic preservation ordinances* protect landmark structures and historic districts in existing built-up areas, downtowns and main streets (Beaumont 1996, 17-43).
- *Planned unit development (PUD)* (APA 1998, 43-44) and *traditional neighborhood development (TND)* (Hoke 1994, 91-92) *ordinances* seek mixtures of land uses over large land areas.
- *Urban growth boundaries* promote development within and limit development outside built-up areas.[5]
- *Exactions* and *impact fees* condition land use regulatory approval on the developer's agreement to provide or pay for roads, water and sewer facilities, schools, open space, and other physical and social infrastructure needed by the proposed development (Frank and Rhodes 1987; Nelson 1988).
- *Adequate public facilities* and *concurrency* rules prohibit development until it can be demonstrated that public infrastructure and services are sufficient to meet the needs of the proposed development (DeGrove 1992, 16-20).
- *Infrastructure turndowns*, such as no curb cuts on this road or no hook-up to the water and sewer system, effectively control if and when development occurs (Beaumont 1996, 313).
- *Growth caps* restrict the amount of development permits in a given year or time period (Pierce 1997, 102-105).
- *Moratoria* temporarily halt land development while government prepares land use or capital infrastructure plans or otherwise works to ensure the availability of adequate infrastructure to service anticipated growth (Garvin and Leitner 1996, 3).

---

[4] Mass. G.L. ch. 40A, Section 9; Arendt (1996, *passim*).
[5] See, e.g., Knaap and Nelson (1992, 39-42); Nelson (1994, 299, 302); Oregon State Senate Bill 100 (1973).

Constitutional Law Framework

To the extent that smart growth is implemented primarily by state and local governments, the federal Constitution plays no affirmative role in establishing the authority of government to seek it.[6] Instead, it is the so-called police power of states, that residual font of authority attached to state sovereignty, that provides the basis for smart growth's regulatory regime. The police power allows state and local governments to enact regulations promoting and protecting the harmonious quartet of health, safety, morals and general welfare. The federal Constitution gains relevance when government efforts to achieve smart growth adversely affect constitutionally protected interests (some would say rights) of individuals. Put simply, is society's (read the majority's) attempt to secure smart growth fundamentally at odds with constitutionally protected choices individuals are allowed to make about how they use their private property, whom they associate with, how they express their ideas, and other such choices?

Before answering that question, it is interesting to inquire whether the federal Constitution's protection of individual rights may be read to "require" smart growth regulations. Parties have challenged sprawl-inducing, large-lot suburban zoning that prohibits construction of smart growth, higher-density, affordable housing on the grounds that it violates the due process and equal protection clause rights of racial minorities. The Supreme Court has been notably unreceptive to these arguments, erecting high evidentiary bars for parties attempting to show that they have actually been injured by such zoning,[7] and requiring evidence that the local government actually had an *intent* to discriminate, rather than that the zoning had the *effect* of discriminating.[8] State constitutions may be more availing. In its well-known *Mount Laurel* series of cases, the New Jersey Supreme Court has interpreted the due process and equal protection components of its state constitution to require that suburban zoning ordinances permit development of housing that accommodates a fair share of the relevant region's lower income housing needs.[9]

---

6   The federal government plays a supporting role, principally through its environmental and transportation laws. See Kayden (2000b, 445, 453-65).
7   *Warth v Seldin,* 422 U.S. 490 (1975).
8   *Village of Arlington Heights v Metropolitan Housing Development Corp.,* 429 U.S. 252 (1977).
9   See, e.g., *Southern Burlington County NAACP v Township of Mount Laurel,* 67 N.J. 151, 336 A.2d 713, *appeal dismissed and cert. denied,* 423 U.S. 808 (1975) (first in series of *Mount Laurel* cases); Haar (1996); Kirp, Dwyer and Rosenthal (1995). Other state constitutions have clauses that arguably could, but need not, be interpreted as creating an enforceable right to something like smart growth. See, e.g., Pennsylvania State Constitution, Article I, Section 27 ("The people have a right to clean air, pure water, and to the preservation of the natural, scenic, historic and esthetic values of the environment.").

Federal constitutional law chiefly enters the fray when the smart growth regulatory regime diminishes, denies, delays, or otherwise negatively affects an owner's wish to develop her private property, leading to the assertion that the constitutional right to private property has been impermissibly infringed. Although a number of constitutional clauses—just compensation, due process, equal protection—could serve as foundations for challenges to such regulatory impacts, a series of U.S. Supreme Court decisions announced over the past 25 years has effectively collapsed the relevant analytical framework into the Fifth Amendment's Just Compensation Clause.[10] That clause commands, "nor shall private property be taken for public use, without just compensation."[11] Its primary purpose is to guarantee that individuals do not "bear public burdens which, in all fairness and justice, should be borne by the public as a whole."[12] In its most obvious meaning, the clause assures that government will compensate owners when it exercises its sovereign power of eminent domain and physically takes property, lock, stock, and title, for construction of a new road or other desired public facility. While there may be disputes about whether the amount of just compensation is constitutionally sufficient (Orgel 1953, 70-171), or whether the use for which the land is taken is, indeed, a public use,[13] the underlying proposition of government power is universally accepted.

When government regulates, rather than physically seizes, private property, however, the applicability of the clause has been less clear. In 1922, U.S. Supreme Court Justice Oliver Wendell Holmes, Jr., was the first to put the just compensation ball in play when, on behalf of the Court, he wrote in *Pennsylvania Coal Company v Mahon*, "if regulation goes too far it will be recognized as a taking."[14] Although there is scholarly dispute over whether Justice Holmes meant "taking," as in "nor shall private property be *taken*," or whether he slung it more loosely to convey substantive due process, rather than just compensation, constitutional concerns,[15] subsequent Supreme Court decisions have endorsed the view that

---

10 See, e.g., *Palazzolo v Rhode Island,* 533 U.S. 606 (2001); *City of Monterey v Del Monte Dunes, Ltd.,* 526 U.S. 687 (1999); *Dolan v City of Tigard,* 512 U.S. 374 (1994); *Lucas v South Carolina Coastal Council,* 505 U.S. 1003 (1992); *Nollan v California Coastal Commission,* 483 U.S. 825 (1987); *First English Evangelical Lutheran Church v County of Los Angeles,* 482 U.S. 304 (1987); *Agins v City of Tiburon,* 447 U.S. 255 (1980); *Penn Central Transportation Co. v New York City,* 438 U.S. 104 (1978).
11 U.S. Const., am. V.
12 *Armstrong v United States,* 364 U.S. 40, 49 (1960).
13 See, e.g., *Poletown Neighborhood Council v City of Detroit,* 410 Mich. 616, 304 N.W.2d 455 (1981).
14 *Pennsylvania Coal Co. v Mahon,* 260 U.S. 393, 415 (1922).
15 See Brauneis (1996); Bosselman, Callies and Banta (1973, *passim*). This is not an inconsequential point. See *infra* note 51 and accompanying text.

regulatory actions, under certain circumstances, can effect just compensation clause *takings* for which compensation must be paid.[16]

It has been far simpler for the Court to assert the general proposition, however, than to define with precision its contours. Intermittently issuing self-effacing confessions describing the difficulty it has had in enumerating comprehensible standards to gauge regulatory takings,[17] the Court has come forth with three tests having potential consequences for smart growth's regulatory regime.[18] A regulation or regulatory action effects a taking if: *one*, it denies an owner all economically viable use of her property;[19] *two*, it imposes too great an economic impact, interferes too greatly with the owner's distinct investment-backed expectations, and/or lacks a sufficiently redeeming governmental character;[20] or *three*, it does not substantially advance legitimate state interests.[21] Meeting any of these three tests, standing alone, is enough to produce a regulatory taking.

Economic Tests

The first economic test, denial of all economically viable use, comes from the 1992 *Lucas v South Carolina Coastal Council* case.[22] David Lucas purchased two beachfront parcels of land on the South Carolina coast for $975,000,[23] and wanted to build two single-family houses.[24] Shortly after his purchase, the South Carolina legislature enacted the Beachfront Management Act, empowering the South Carolina Coastal Council to draw a line in the sand establishing where development could and could not occur.[25] Unfortunately for Lucas, his parcels fell on the ocean side of the line and, although he could use his property for outdoor recreational purposes, such as camping out, he could not build his houses.[26]

---

16   See, e.g., *First English Evangelical Lutheran Church v County of Los Angeles,* 482 U.S. 304 (1987).
17   See, e.g., *Kaiser Aetna v United States,* 444 U.S. 164, 175 (1979); *Penn Central Transportation Co. v New York City,* 438 U.S. 104, 123, 124 (1978).
18   Other regulatory takings tests, such as the permanent physical occupation test outlined in *Loretto v Teleprompter Manhattan CATV Corp.* 458 U.S. 419 (1982), and tests related to the taking of various strands of the property bundle, for example, in *Hodel v Irving,* 481 U.S. 704 (1987) (striking down provision of Indian Land Consolidation Act restricting escheat rights), and in *Andrus v Allard,* 444 U.S. 51 (1979) (upholding law restricting right of sale of Indian artifacts of bird feathers), are not relevant for the purpose of examining the smart growth regulatory regime.
19   *Lucas v South Carolina Coastal Council,* 505 U.S. 1003, 1015-16, 1019 (1992).
20   *Penn Central,* 438 U.S. at 124.
21   *Nollan v California Coastal Commission,* 483 U.S. 825, 837 (1987); *Agins v City of Tiburon,* 447 U.S. 255, 260 (1980).
22   505 U.S. 1003 (1992).
23   *Id*. at 1006.
24   *Id*. at 1008.
25   *Id.*
26   *Id*. at 1008-09.

In the South Carolina state trial court, where Lucas brought his challenge, he conceded the legitimacy of the Act's purpose—to protect South Carolina beaches from erosion and other environmental degradations—but asserted that, because his property had been rendered worthless, it was constitutionally taken by the Council's action.[27] Although the U.S. Supreme Court strictly did not find a taking, sending the case back to the South Carolina Supreme Court for further review,[28] it announced the categorical rule that a denial of all economically viable, beneficial, productive, or feasible use of land, in this case a reduction in value from $975,000 to zero, would normally be a taking.[29] The South Carolina Supreme Court subsequently found a taking,[30] and the state ultimately purchased the two lots from Lucas.[31] The requirement that an owner must suffer a 100 percent value wipeout to avail herself of *Lucas'* categorical rule was affirmed most recently in *Palazzolo v Rhode Island*.[32] There, the Court declared that, while a regulatory action that leaves a "token interest" in a property will not insulate such action from a *Lucas* claim, a regulatory action resulting in a severe, but not complete, diminution of value, will.[33] This was the case in *Palazzolo*, where the regulatory action allowed Mr. Palazzolo to build a single residence on his 18-acre parcel, yielding a property value of $200,000, even though he asserted that, with regulatory approval, his property would be worth over $3 million.[34]

The second economic test for a regulatory taking addresses the more common scenario in which a regulatory action diminishes, rather than eradicates, an owner's economically viable use of property. Unlike the *Lucas* rule, the test here is not outcome determinative, meaning that it does not through its own words describe factual conditions under which a regulatory taking could be definitively declared. Indeed, as initially portrayed in *Penn Central Transportation Company v New York City*, the test is one of "essentially ad hoc, factual inquiries" rather than a "set formula."[35] In that case, Penn Central owned Grand Central Terminal, a

---

27 *Id.* at 1009.
28 *Id.* at 1031-32.
29 *Id.* at 1015-16, 1019. Even as it claimed to announce a *categorical* rule, the Court introduced an exception to that rule in cases where so-called "background principles of the State's law of property and nuisance" that predated enactment of the challenged regulation would have, if applied to the property, restricted its use in a manner similar to the challenged regulation. *Id.* at 1029.
30 *Lucas v South Carolina Coastal Council*, 309 S.C. 424, 424 S.E.2d 484 (1992).
31 Lehman (1993, 3G). The settlement amount totaled $1.5 million. *Id.*
32 533 U.S. 606 (2001).
33 *Id.* at 630-31.
34 *Id.* at 615-16, 630-31.
35 *Penn Central Transportation Co. v New York City*, 438 U.S 104, 124 (1978).

The *Penn Central* case affirmed New York City's refusal to allow construction of a tower immediately above Grand Central Terminal. All photographs in this chapter © Jerold S. Kayden.

building designated a landmark by the New York City Landmarks Preservation Commission.[36] The company sought to build a tower above the terminal which would generate millions of dollars in annual lease payments.[37] The Commission denied Penn Central's application to build a tower on the basis of harm to the landmark qualities of the Terminal building.[38]

To guide its inquiry into whether the Commission's action effected a regulatory taking, the Court announced three factors of special significance: the economic impact of the regulation, the extent to which the regulation interfered with the owner's distinct investment-backed expectations, and the character of the governmental action.[39] Applied to the Grand Central Terminal fact pattern, the Court held that a taking had not been established.[40] To begin with, the company admitted that it earned a reasonable return on the Terminal use of the property, a use embodying the owner's primary expectation.[41] Furthermore, the landmarks law granted Penn Central the opportunity to "transfer" the otherwise

---

36   *Id*. at 115.
37   *Id*. at 116.
38   *Id*. at 117–18.
39   *Id*. at 124.
40   *Id*. at 136–37.
41   *Id*. at 136.

unusable development rights above the Terminal to a number of adjacent parcels owned by Penn Central.[42] The "character of the governmental action" factor was not expressly applied in the case.[43]

The Supreme Court has cited with approval the *Penn Central* three-factor test on numerous occasions.[44] Both *Palazzolo* and *Lucas* expressly note its continued vitality for fact patterns involving less than a 100 percent wipeout.[45] For example, in *Palazzolo*, the Court sent the case back to the Rhode Island Supreme Court to determine whether, among other things, the alleged reduction in property value would be sufficient to establish a taking under *Penn Central*'s three factors.[46] Justice O'Connor's concurring opinion applauded *Penn Central* and its fact-specific, case-by-case approach, breathing new life into the "character of the governmental action" factor by reading *Penn Central* as endorsing a balancing test in which, one could suppose, the more important the governmental purpose, the more constitutionally sustainable an economic infringement under *Penn Central*'s two economic factors would be.[47]

What remains disturbingly unclear is how much economic impact and/or how much interference with distinct investment-backed expectations are tolerable before a court finds a regulatory taking. Property owners and government regulators alike seek predictability, if not certainty, in going about their business, yet the only thing predictable and certain about the *Penn Central* test is that there is no set formula. Lower federal and state court opinions applying the *Penn Central* test normally find that substantial diminutions in value, standing alone, will not be grounds for a taking.[48] Short of a severe and perhaps unfair swipe at property value, government and owners are left to resolve their conflicts in the legislative and executive branch arenas, where value is created and diminished on a daily basis. Resort to the legal branch will be reserved for play that is truly out-of-bounds.

---

42   *Id.* at 137.
43   The Court provided only one example to illuminate its "character of the governmental action" factor, suggesting that a regulation authorizing a "physical invasion" would more likely be found to effect a taking than a regulation "adjusting the benefits and burdens of economic life to promote the common good." *Id.* at 124.
44   See, e.g., *Palazzolo v Rhode Island,* 533 U.S. 606, 617 (2001); *Kaiser Aetna v United States,* 444 U.S. 164, 175 (1979).
45   *Palazzolo,* 533 U.S. at 630; *Lucas v South Carolina Coastal Council,* 505 U.S. 1003, 1019 n.8 (1992).
46   *Palazzolo,* 533 U.S. at 630.
47   *Id.* at 633-36 (O'Connor, J., concurring).
48   See, e.g., *Daddario v Cape Cod Commission,* 425 Mass. 411, 416-18, 681 N.E.2d 833, 837-38, *cert. denied,* 522 U.S. 1036 (1977).

The *Agins* case affirmed the City of Tiburon's right to restrict development on the Agins' land parcel.

Substantially Advance a Legitimate State Interest Test

The third regulatory takings test, that regulations must substantially advance a legitimate state interest, concentrates on the rationality of the regulatory action and the legitimacy of the purpose to which it is directed, without regard to economic effect on the owner. Initially announced in the 1980 *Agins v City of Tiburon* opinion[49] and subsequently burnished in 1987's *Nollan v California Coastal Commission* case,[50] the test surprised a number of scholars who argued it had been improperly imported into just compensation clause jurisprudence from due process cases (Echeverria 2000; Kayden 1991). Their argument was not just the stuff of academics, for if the test were available for just compensation as well as due process clause challenges, then owners could pursue the just compensation clause's express monetary remedy rather than settle for judicial invalidation of an offending regulation.[51]

What made the "substantial advancing" test especially provocative was the statement, first uttered in a footnote in *Nollan*, that the test was more demanding,

---

49 447 U.S. 255, 260 (1980).
50 483 U.S. 825, 837 (1987).
51 See *First English Evangelical Lutheran Church v County of Los Angeles*, 482 U.S. 304 (1987). It is worth observing, however, that a substantive due process challenge could seek money damages pursuant to a Section 1983 challenge. See 42 U.S.C. Section 1983.

The *Nollan* case prevented the California Coastal Commission from obtaining from the Nollans a right for the public to walk up and down their beach.

and thus tougher for government to pass, than the traditional "due process" test from which it had been hatched.⁵² That due process test only requires a rational relationship between legislative means and ends.⁵³ In *Nollan*, however, the Court expressly distinguished just compensation from due process formulations, stating that the word "substantially," as in "substantially advance a legitimate state interest," meant something more than "rationally" advance as used in due process cases, in effect creating a heightened scrutiny for land use regulations challenged under the just compensation clause.⁵⁴

The applicability and meaning of the substantial advancing test both remain uncertain. Only one land use fact pattern, involving government attempts to condition development approval on an owner's agreement to dedicate part of her land to public use, has inspired the Supreme Court to elaborate. For such cases,

---

52 *Nollan*, 483 U.S. at 834-35 n.3.
53 *Id.* Ever since the demise of the so-called *Lochner* era (named after a Supreme Court opinion), during which the Supreme Court saw its constitutional role as carefully scrutinizing legislative enactments and striking them down under a variety of constitutional labels, the Court had usually deferred to legislative judgments, declining to be a super-legislature and upholding legislative enactments as long as they had a conceivably rational basis. See, e.g., *Williamson v Lee Optical of Oklahoma, Inc.*, 348 U.S. 483, 487-88 (1955).
54 *Nollan*, 483 U.S. at 834-35 n.3.

the Court has introduced two subtests, "essential nexus" and "rough proportionality,"[55] to determine whether the regulatory action substantially advances legitimate state interests.

In *Nollan*, the Court held that land dedication conditions must be supported by an "essential nexus" between the asserted purpose of the condition and what the condition demands.[56] There, the Nollans wanted to demolish their existing beachfront bungalow and replace it with a larger structure.[57] The California Coastal Commission said yes, but only if they would agree to allow members of the public to walk up and down their private beach, between their house to the east and the mean high tide line of the Pacific Ocean to the west.[58] The Court held that this condition effected a regulatory taking because there was no "essential nexus" between the Commission's stated purpose—ensuring views from inland to the Pacific Ocean—and the condition's lateral, north-south public access requirement.[59] On the other hand, a viewing spot on the Nollans' front yard, providing felicitous vistas of the Pacific Ocean, would, apparently, have satisfied the Court's essential nexus test.[60]

In the 1994 *Dolan v City of Tigard* case,[61] the Court announced that there must also be a "rough proportionality" between conditions on development permission and harmful impacts caused by the development.[62] Mrs. Dolan, an elderly widow, wanted to demolish her 9,700 square-foot plumbing and electric supply store located in Tigard, a suburb of Portland, Oregon, and replace it with a 17,600 square-foot store, almost twice as large, and a parking lot on her one-and-two-thirds acre parcel of land.[63] The expansion would obviously have land use impacts, including increased storm water runoff from more impervious land surfaces and additional automobile trips generated by the larger store.[64] Tigard sought to condition approval of the store expansion on Mrs. Dolan's agreement to leave unbuilt and allow public access on that portion of her land falling within

---

55 *Dolan v City of Tigard*, 512 U.S. 374 (1994), introduced rough proportionality to the mix but did not expressly link that test to the substantial advancing test. Unless rough proportionality is to be understood as a stand-alone just compensation clause test, on a par with the economic and substantial advancing tests themselves, however, it would have to locate itself under the substantial advancing label.
56 *Nollan*, 483 U.S. at 838-39.
57 *Id*. at 827
58 *Id*. at 828
59 *Id*. at 838-40.
60 *Id*. at 836.
61 512 U.S. 374 (1994).
62 *Id*. at 394-96.
63 *Id*. at 379.
64 *Id*. at 381-82.

a 100-year flood plain, some 10 percent of the parcel, as well as her agreement to provide an additional 15-foot-wide strip for a pedestrian and bicycle pathway that would connect to a nascent city pathway network.[65] The Supreme Court found that these two conditions violated the just compensation clause because there was insufficient evidence that they were roughly proportionate to the impact of the store expansion.[66] Although no precise mathematical calculation was required, said the Court, the government "must make some sort of individualized determination that the required dedication is related both in nature and extent to the impact of the proposed development."[67]

More recently, in the 1999 *City of Monterey v Del Monte Dunes, Ltd.* case,[68] the Court appeared to support application of the substantial advancing test in a case involving a simple permit denial rather than a condition attached to permit approval, although the actual language of the test specifically endorsed by the Court was "reasonably related."[69] Does that mean that the heightened scrutiny threatened in *Nollan*'s footnote three is not relevant to permit denials and other land use regulations and regulatory actions, even if the substantially advance test is? In a confession evocative of its *Penn Central mea culpa*, the Court conceded that it has failed to provide a "thorough explanation of the nature or applicability of the requirement that a regulation substantially advance legitimate public interests outside the context of required dedications or exactions."[70] However, the Court noted that it has not extended *Dolan*'s rough proportionality test "beyond the special context of exactions—land use decisions conditioning approval of development on the dedication of property to public use."[71] Today, the substantial advancing test appears to be in great flux, with some Supreme Court justices expressing questions about whether the test belongs under the just compensation clause at all.[72] It would not be surprising for the Court to grant review to one of

---

65   *Id*. at 380.
66   *Id*. at 394-95.
67   *Id*. at 391.
68   526 U.S. 687 (1999).
69   *Id*. at 706.
70   *Id*. at 704.
71   *Id*. at 702.
72   See *id*. at 754 n.12 (Souter, J., concurring in part and dissenting in part, joined by Justices O'Connor, Ginsburg, and Breyer) ("I offer no opinion here on whether *Agins* was correct in assuming that [the substantial advancing] prong of liability was properly cognizable as flowing from the Just Compensation Clause of the Fifth Amendment, as distinct from the Due Process Clauses of the Fifth and Fourteenth Amendments," adding in the main text, *id*. at 753, that *Agins* cited *Nectow*, a substantive due process case); *Eastern Enterprises v Apfel,* 524 U.S. 498, 545 (1998) (Kennedy, J., concurring in the judgment and dissenting in part).

the increasing number of petitions brought by litigants challenging or supporting the test's continued vitality under the just compensation clause.[73]

Application of Constitutional Framework to Smart Growth Regulatory Regime

Today's smart growth regulatory regime comports comfortably with the relevant constitutional framework. As described above, the just compensation clause, today's preferred, all-encompassing vessel for challenging government regulation of private property, readily accepts the idea that government may significantly limit a property owner's choice of development options in order to promote social, economic, fiscal and environmental agendas. Broadly speaking, that is precisely what the smart growth regulatory regime does, restricting or influencing the location, type, density, layout, design, social/economic composition, associated infrastructure, and pace of private development in order to promote a government-preferred land development pattern.

When measuring smart growth regulations against the constitutional framework, it is important to distinguish between "facial" and "as applied" challenges. A facial challenge must demonstrate that a smart growth regulation *on its face*, without regard to any property-specific application, violates the Constitution. Thus, a court would have to find that a regulation axiomatically denies every owner within its reach all economically viable use of property; that it imposes too great an economic impact and/or too great an interference with distinct investment-backed expectations on all owners, and/or that it lacks the requisite governmental character, with regard to all owners within its reach;[74] or that it fails to substantially advance a legitimate state interest. An as-applied challenge need only show that the regulatory instrument, *as applied* to a particular property, effects an unconstitutional taking. The Supreme Court has time and again emphasized that facial challenges under the just compensation clause are enormously difficult to win,[75] and that, even in as-applied cases, property owners have an obligation before bringing their case to court to pursue all available avenues granted by the government, including variances, to secure a constitutionally adequate level of development possibilities.[76]

---

73   See, e.g., Petition for a Writ of Certiorari, *Cayetano v Chevron, USA, Inc.,* No. 00-1198, at 5-15 (2001).
74   Indeed, as a case-by-case inquiry, the *Penn Central* three-factor test is arguably inapposite for a facial challenge.
75   See, e.g., *Suitum v Tahoe Regional Planning Agency,* 520 U.S. 725, 736 n.10 (1997); *Keystone Bituminous Coal Ass'n v DeBenedictis,* 480 U.S. 470, 495 (1987).
76   See, e.g., *MacDonald, Sommer & Frates v County of Yolo,* 447 U.S. 340 (1986); *Williamson County Regional Planning Comm'n v Hamilton Bank,* 473 U.S. 172 (1985).

Facial Challenges

None of the smart growth regulatory instruments likely carries the necessary across-the-board irrationality or economic effect to rate a successful facial challenge. To begin with, smart growth's constellation of concerns easily qualifies as a grouping of legitimate state interests for which government power may be exercised. It assembles under one buzz phrase individual goals that have been pursued by governments and approved by courts for decades, including preserving open space,[77] saving environmentally sensitive land,[78] protecting landmark buildings and community character,[79] promoting affordable housing,[80] and reducing traffic congestion.[81]

Moreover, smart growth's regulatory instruments on their face advance these goals. These are not new or revolutionary schemes, springing full-blown from the heads of Zeusian regulators. Rather, they are long-standing, evolutionary approaches, with regulatory DNA that contains strands from previous efforts expressly fashioned, and sometimes expressly found, to be constitutionally acceptable. It is hard to imagine these instruments shocking the constitutional constitution of judges.

For example, growth management, one of smart growth's linguistic predecessors, decades ago introduced then novel regulatory mechanisms as part of a "quiet revolution" of land use controls that controlled where, when and how development would occur (Bosselman and Callies 1971). The reasonableness of two of the revolution's most famous foot soldiers received judicial vetting under due process and equal protection analyses that prevailed before the hegemony of just compensation clause jurisprudence. In *Golden v Planning Board of Ramapo*, the New York Court of Appeals upheld an 18-year capital infrastructure plan that delayed approval of much private development until it could be shown to be adequately served by specific physical infrastructure.[82] In *Construction Industry Association of Sonoma County v City of Petaluma*, the U. S. Court of Appeals for the Ninth Circuit approved the city's annual limit on the number of multifamily housing units that could be constructed.[83] If today's version of the substantial

---

77 *Agins v City of Tiburon,* 447 U.S. 255, 261 (1980).
78 *Lucas v South Carolina Coastal Council,* 505 U.S. 1003, 1022-23 (1992).
79 *Penn Central Transportation Co. v New York City,* 438 U.S. 104, 108, 129 (1978).
80 *Pennell v City of San Jose,* 485 U.S. 1, 12 (1988).
81 *Dolan v City of Tigard,* 512 U.S. 374, 387 (1994).
82 30 N.Y.2d 359, 334 N.Y.S.2d 138, 285 N.E.2d 291, *appeal dismissed,* 409 U.S. 1003 (1972).
83 522 F.2d 897 (9th Cir. 1975), *cert. denied,* 424 U.S. 934 (1976).

The *Petaluma* case upheld the ability of Petaluma, California, to cap the amount of development in any given year, and thus advance such goals as preservation of open space.

advancing test may be understood as applying heightened scrutiny to narrowly defined, case-specific applications of certain smart growth regulatory instruments, it is surely not a broad-brush invitation to judges to become super-legislatures substituting their views of good and bad into the smart growth debate.

For facial challenges based on the tests of *Penn Central* and *Lucas*, it is unlikely that courts would be able to conclude that a smart growth regulatory instrument, by mere enactment, had crossed the constitutional line. By definition, the *Penn Central* three-factor inquiry thwarts facial invalidation because it demands consideration of distinct, investment-backed expectations, an inquiry that is necessarily case-by-case and subjective. It is possible, however, that a *Lucas*-based facial challenge could be mounted against, for example, a ruthlessly styled urban growth boundary that permanently sterilized any development on one side of the line, or a total development moratorium that extended without limit of time into the future. The minute such laws would include economic hardship appeal procedures to allow, and thus effectively require,[84] owners to seek special relief from the relevant regulatory authority before going to court, however, their facial validity would be secured. Like the classic zoning variance (U.S. Department of Commerce 1924), this safety valve would offer the possibility that truly problematic cases could be resolved by government modification or rescission of the regulation or, perhaps, the decision to pay compensation. In all events, it would be impossible to state on the face of the law that the owner could not avoid a *Lucas* wipeout.

As-Applied Challenges

Smartly applied, smart growth regulatory instruments enjoy the same constitutional safe harbor as that afforded traditional land use regulatory instruments. In general, "smartly applied" means that owners are left with some economically viable use of their property, that owners are asked to provide no more than their fair share of public infrastructure, and that government decisions are supported by planning studies demonstrating a reasoned basis for the decision.

Vulnerability to as-applied constitutional challenges varies according to the type of smart growth regulatory instrument. For example, applications of environmental and open space restrictions, urban growth boundaries, moratoria and historic preservation ordinances that result in significant diminutions of financial value must take special account of the just compensation clause's economic tests. In cases where restrictions prohibit the owner from developing any land or otherwise realizing some financial value, a *Lucas* claim is possible. Where the restriction prevents only some development, and there is more than token property value left, the case moves into *Penn Central* territory.

Unlikely to trigger sufficient economic impact to warrant *Lucas* or *Penn Central* challenges, exactions, impact fees, and adequate public infrastructure and concurrency rules face their greatest vulnerability under the *Nollan* and *Dolan* essential nexus and rough proportionality tests. Although ambiguity clouds the applicability and meaning of such tests beyond the context of land dedication conditions placed on individual development permission cases, their rationale could be extended to cover non-land dedication conditions. Inclusionary zoning and other socially oriented regulations present similar concerns, especially when private market-rate housing developers ask why they are being asked to address a

---

84   See *Williamson County Regional Planning Comm'n v Hamilton Bank,* 473 U.S. 172, 186-94 (1985).

problem that, at first glance, appears not to have been of their own making (Kayden 2000a, 12-13). As a response to constitutional ambiguity, local governments may find it prudent to prepare planning studies identifying negative impacts of proposed development and documenting the proportionality of specific regulatory responses (Kayden 2000a, 13).

Conclusion

This article argues that, in its current form, the smart growth regulatory regime is consistent with the Supreme Court's constructed constitutional balance between public needs and private interests. Measured by the economic tests of *Lucas* and *Penn Central*, or the substantial advancing, essential nexus and rough proportionality tests of *Agins*, *Nollan* and *Dolan*, federal, state and local governments have sufficient latitude to influence land patterns toward smart growth, and private property owners have sufficient latitude to challenge restrictions that go too far. To the extent it plays a role, judicial intervention will be rifle-shot rather than shotgun, considering case-specific fact patterns documenting the allegedly unconstitutional impact of a smart growth regulation on this particular property owner. Put another way, the smart growth regulatory regime is vulnerable, when it is, to retail rather than wholesale attack.

One may speculate about the future. Imagine that smart growth regulatory efforts become far more aggressive than today's version, effectively cleaving the metropolitan landscape into classes of winners and losers. Winners would be owners located in or near developed areas, near public transportation stops, or inside growth boundaries, who are allowed, indeed encouraged, to build at high densities and who enjoy windfall profits from such newly minted revenue opportunities. Losers would be owners denied the opportunity to develop or use their property because such activities hinder realization of smart growth. Court battles become more common. The Supreme Court accelerates what some already deem its steady march toward greater protection of private property (Callies 1999; Berger 1987) and begins striking down government efforts that create losers.

No matter how fanciful, this scenario cautions that the constitutional validity of smart growth's regulatory regime partly depends on detaching the geography of winners and losers from the geography of smart growth. One approach worthy of renewed attention from planners and lawyers is imbedding compensatory mechanisms within some of smart growth's regulatory architecture. Mechanisms that palliate the "bitter" of restrictions with the "sweet" of density bonuses and other regulatory concessions, or, most promisingly in terms of winners and losers, the opportunity to sell through transfer of development rights (TDR) schema otherwise unusable development rights, will lessen the chance that regulations will be found to go too far.[85] As the smart growth regulatory regime matures, it is not too early to invent new or adapt old techniques to promote fairness and provide constitutional insurance across the land.[86]

---

85   See Kayden (1992); *Penn Central,* 438 U.S. at 113-14, 137.
86   As this book went to press, the U.S. Supreme Court announced its opinion in *Tahoe-Sierra Preservation Council, Inc. v Tahoe Regional Planning Agency,* 2002 U.S. LEXIS 3028 (April 23, 2002), upholding a 32-month moratorium imposed by the Tahoe Regional Planning Agency against a regulatory takings challenge brought by property owners under the Just Compensation Clause. The 6–3 majority opinion strongly endorsed the ad hoc, fact-based, case-by-case analytical framework of *Penn Central Transportation Co. v New York City,* reserving the categorical rule of *Lucas v South Carolina Coastal Council* for the extraordinary circumstance of a permanent deprivation of all beneficial use (see slip op. at 20, n. 9; 22 & n. 23). It would be hard not to read this broad constitutional approval of a moratorium—a member of smart growth's regulatory regime—as anything other than an indication that this Court is not about to undermine radically the smart growth regulatory apple cart.

References

American Bar Association. 1999. *From sprawl to smart growth: Successful legal, planning, and environmental systems.* Chicago, IL: American Bar Association.

American Planning Association (APA). 1998. *The principles of smart development.* Planning Advisory Service Report No. 479. Chicago, IL: American Planning Association.

Arendt, Randall G. 1996. *Conservation design for subdivisions: A practical guide to creating open space networks.* Washington, DC: Island Press.

Beaumont, Constance E. 1996. *Smart states, better communities.* Washington, DC: National Trust for Historic Preservation.

Berger, Michael. 1987. The year of the taking issue. 1 *Brigham Young university journal of public law* 261, 261-63.

Bosselman, Fred, and David Callies. 1971. *The quiet revolution in land use control.* Washington, DC: U.S. Government Printing Office.

Bosselman, Fred, David Callies and John Banta. 1973. *The taking issue.* Washington, DC: Council on Environmental Quality.

Brauneis, Robert. 1996. The foundation of our "regulatory takings" jurisprudence: The myth and meaning of Justice Holmes's opinion in *Pennsylvania Coal Co. v Mahon.* 106 *Yale law journal* 613.

Callies, David L. 1999. Regulatory takings and the Supreme Court: How perspectives on property rights have changed from *Penn Central* to *Dolan,* and what state and federal courts are doing about it. 28 *Stetson law review* 523, 525-26.

DeGrove, John M. 1992. *The new frontier for land policy: Planning and growth management in the states.* Cambridge, MA: Lincoln Institute of Land Policy.

Echeverria, John D. 2000. Takings and errors. 51 *Alabama law review* 1047, 1073.

Frank, James E., and Robert M. Rhodes. 1987. *Development exactions.* Chicago, IL: Planners Press.

Garvin, Elizabeth A., and Martin L. Leitner. 1996. Drafting interim development ordinances: Creating time to plan. *Land use law and zoning digest* (June):3.

Haar, Charles M. 1996. *Suburbs under siege: Race, space, and audacious judges.* Princeton, NJ: Princeton University Press.

Hoke, John Ray, ed. 1994. *Architectural graphic standards.* New York, NY: John Wiley & Sons.

Kayden, Jerold S. 1991. Land-use regulations, rationality, and judicial review: The RSVP in the *Nollan* invitation. 23 *Urban lawyer* 301, 314-15.

_____ 1992. Market-based regulatory approaches: A comparative discussion of environmental and land use techniques in the United States. 10 *Boston College environmental affairs law review.* 565, 568-59 (incentive zoning), 574-77 (transfer of development rights).

_____. 2000a. Inclusionary zoning and the Constitution. *National housing conference affordable housing policy review* 2 (1):12-13.

_____. 2000b. National land-use planning in America: Something whose time has never come. 3 *Washington university journal of law & policy* 445, 453-65.

Kirp, David L., John P. Dwyer and Larry A. Rosenthal. 1995. *Our town: Race, housing, and the soul of suburbia.* New Brunswick, NJ: Rutgers University Press.

Knaap, Gerrit, and Arthur C. Nelson. 1992. *The regulated landscape: Lessons on state land use planning from Oregon.* Cambridge, MA: Lincoln Institute of Land Policy.

Lehman, H. Jane. 1993. Case closed: Settlement ends property rights lawsuit. *Chicago tribune.* (July 25):3G.

Mallach, Alan. 1984. *Inclusionary housing programs: Policies and practices.* New Brunswick, NJ: Center for Urban Policy Research.

Morris, Marya. 2000. *Incentive zoning: Meeting urban design and affordable housing objectives.* Planning Advisory Service Report No. 494. Chicago, IL: American Planning Association

National Housing Conference. 2000. Inclusionary zoning: A viable solution to the affordable housing crisis. *National housing conference affordable housing policy review*, vol. 2, issue 1.

Nelson, Arthur C., ed. 1988. *Development impact fees.* Chicago, IL: Planners Press.

_____1994. Oregon's urban growth boundary policy as a landmark planning tool. In *Planning the Oregon way: A twenty-year evaluation,* Carl Abbot, Sy Adler and Deborah Howe, eds. Corvallis, OR: Oregon State University Press.

Oregon State Senate Bill 100 (1973).

Orgel, Lewis. 1953. *Valuation under the law of eminent domain,* 2d ed. Charlottesville, VA: The Michie Co.

Pierce, Tom. 1997. A constitutionally valid justification for the enactment of no-growth ordinances: Integrating concepts of population stabilization and sustainability. 19 *Hawaii law review* 93, 102-05.

Pollard, Oliver A. III. 2000. Smart growth: The promise, politics, and potential pitfalls of emerging growth management strategies. 19 *Virginia environmental law journal* 247, 282-84.

U.S. Department of Commerce. 1924. Standard State Zoning Enabling Act, Section 7. Washington, DC.

10

Timothy C. Weiskel

Ethical Principles for Smart Growth

Steps Toward an Ecological Ten Commandments

Ethics begins where the law and economics leave off. The ethical principles we adhere to are manifest in the sum total of the value judgments we make in our personal and collective lives. The assumption in Western culture is that the world exists as an environment outside the human sphere, distinct from it, external to it. The environment is thought of as something that—with the use of technology—we are both empowered and entitled to manipulate at will to meet ever-growing, ever-changing human needs.

In academic circles we are only now beginning to argue that we need to get smart about how we manage and manipulate the world. It's about time, don't you think? The appeal for smart growth has been slow in coming, but the consequences of "stupid" growth (unrestrained growth, aimless growth, anarchic growth) are becoming too apparent to ignore. Clearly the appeal for smart growth is the wave of the future. After all, who could possibly be against it, if all it is contrasted with is stupid growth? No one would deny that smart growth is an ethical imperative.[1] All we need bicker about from now on is, who gets to call what smart?

The difficulty with this whole framework, however, is that in an ecosystem, systemwide troubles are bigger than merely human problems. By pursuing what we have come to recognize and embrace as smart growth we may be missing a much larger point about the human prospect. Indeed, to the extent that we think we can manipulate the natural environment at will to maximize human benefit, we are in danger of fine-tuning disaster.

In short, the elegance of smart growth blinds us to its arrogance. Rather than avoiding extinction we may merely be making it more efficient. We may think we are growing in a smart fashion, but human growth itself may be the problem in the larger system. We need to have the courage to entertain the question: In a world already choked by the human enterprise, where so much of the natural world suffers from our collective species footprint, isn't smart growth an oxymoron, an arrogant contradiction in terms?

To be effective and enduring, smart growth needs to develop two fundamental attributes. First, it will require rethinking all priorities in light of the objective constraints of the biogeochemical processes of the ecosystem. Second, it will require a strong ethical foundation that grounds the human enterprise beyond the

---

1   The proposition that conventional patterns of economic growth should stop altogether has been forwarded by some as a moral imperative. This notion has gained prominence since the publication of the influential Report to the Club of Rome, entitled *Limits to Growth* (Meadows and Club of Rome 1972; Meadows, Meadows and Randers 1992). Many who challenged the notion of limits to growth did so in strong moral terms as well (Walter 1981; Beckerman 1995).

logic of energy efficiency, materials recycling and systems optimization. All these things will be required, but more is needed—much more. At the core, smart growth requires a new guiding metaphor for human existence based on self-imposed self-restraint—not merely enlightened self-interest or deferred gratification. If smart growth is going to mean anything more than a trendy phrase of the week for the *hipgeoisie*[2] a new kind of environmental ethic will need to take hold of the public mind. This new ethic needs in turn to be born of a newly informed awareness of place in the broader ecosystem, of which we remain only a single constituent species.

To achieve this sense of place we need to learn to acknowledge and accept four simple truths:

1. We did not create the world; we cannot control it; we should not destroy it.
2. We must learn instead to live as ecologically responsible citizens within Earth's ecosystem, rather than continue to struggle against it, seek vainly to dominate it, or strive pathetically to live as if we could ignore it.
3. We are embedded as participants in a patterned system of materials exchange and energy flow, governed by the second law of thermodynamics.
4. If we wish to survive as a species, we had better learn the house rules before—in our ignorance of them or our stubborn refusal to take them seriously—we drive ourselves into extinction.

In short, infinite growth in a finite system is not possible. Smart growth is by definition self-limiting. It is important to get the numbers straight in this regard, because the rhetoric of public discourse and daily economic life is confusing. It is not uncommon, for example, to hear phrases like "steady growth" or "sustained growth" in discussions about the economy. In the larger biological system, however, it becomes apparent that the illusion of steady, sustained or continuous growth is simply not possible. In the long run, all economies function as subsets of ecosystems, so it is important to establish the fundamental laws of ecosystems firmly in our minds. At the level of organisms and populations, growth is best understood as a phase phenomenon. Individual organisms or populations go through a growth phase in their development, but this is not—indeed it cannot be—a permanent state of affairs. Unrestrained growth is not feasible; nor is it

---

2   The self-styled "hip" bourgeoisie.

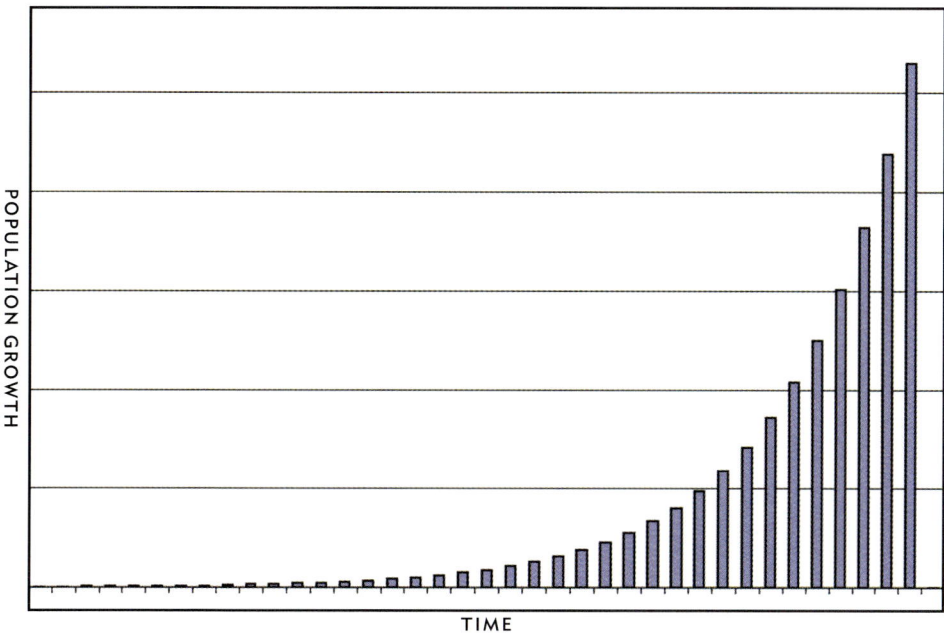

Figure 1   A model of a hypothetical exponential growth pattern of a population produces a J-shaped curve. This can lead to an explosive growth of a total population over time even though the growth rate (R) remains constant and low.

healthy. A steady growth rate is potentially explosive since a constant rate of growth (R) in reproducing organisms leads to an exponential growth of the population as a whole. The typical form of exponential population growth takes on the appearance of a J-shaped curve, with a long period of gradual growth followed by a rapid expansion of organisms in a very short period (Figure 1). No biological system can tolerate this kind of growth pattern on the part of one of its constituent species for very long. If the population itself shows no change in its reproductive behavior, sooner or later it is subject to the external limits of habitat or nutrient availability, and it overshoots, then rapidly collapses when the limit of the environmental carrying capacity (K) is exceeded (Figure 2).

Over time, there may be nothing fixed or permanently determined in what is referred to as the carrying capacity of a system, with reference to any one population. It could—at least in theory— expand or increase if the population were to adjust to another pattern of consumption or self-maintenance. In principle, this might mean that populations could periodically exceed their carrying capacity in a given system, but in subsequent periods they could enjoy an increased carrying capacity and expand to that new level before overshooting and collapsing.

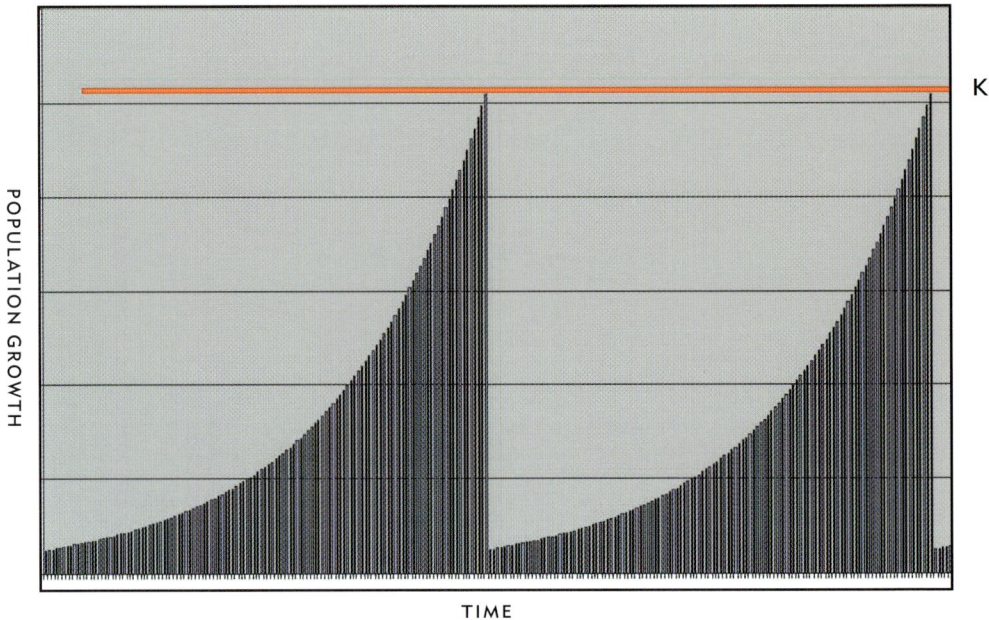

Figure 2 Populations that grow at a constant rate (R) experience a J-shaped growth curve followed by an abrupt collapse when the total population exceeds the environmental carrying capacity (K). If some reproducing individuals are able to survive, the pattern of overshoot and collapse can repeat itself again and again.

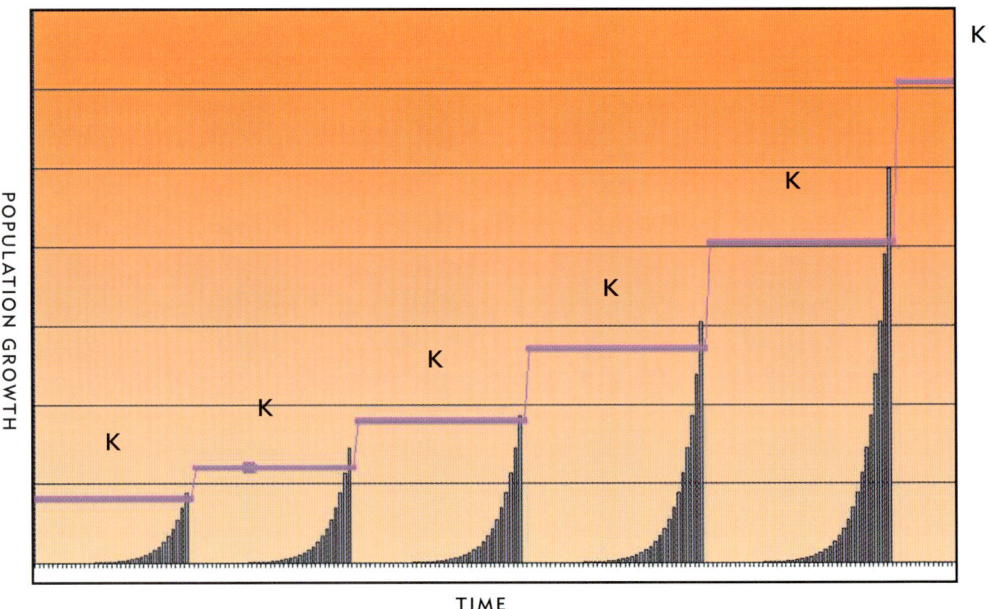

Figure 3 A population that grows at a constant rate (R) can expand over time *if* the carrying capacity (K) of the system increases. With a constant rate of growth it is still subject to boom and bust cycles of overshoot and collapse, and if the carrying capacity is momentarily increased, the amplitude of the boom and bust cycles can increase, even though the overshoot and collapse syndrome remains the same.

Mathematically, this can be modeled simply as a system with a population growing at a steady rate, but one within which the carrying capacity (K) expands over time after periodic episodes of population collapse (Figure 3).

Of course there is nothing in an ecosystem that assures that the carrying capacity of an individual species *will* expand over time. Quite the contrary. When populations overshoot and collapse, they can frequently be quite destructive to their life support systems—the complex web of organisms that provide the biogeochemical cycling required for the steady flow of nutrients, water and energy that each organism requires. So, it is quite often the case that the phenomena of constant growth—which leads repeatedly to a syndrome of overshoot and collapse—systematically diminishes the carrying capacity of a system over time with regard to a particular organism. Thus, although the fundamental population growth pattern (boom-bust) of a population may not change, its actual population can decline over time in response to a deteriorating carrying capacity caused, in part, by the environmental devastation of repeated overshoot and collapse events (Figure 4).

It follows from the basic dynamics of populations in ecosystems that if smart growth is to assure the long-term survival of the population concerned, growth must be self-limiting. Each population must stabilize at a level below the carrying capacity (K) of the system concerned. If the carrying capacity is declining, the self-limiting stabilization must occur rapidly, and for this to happen the rate of growth must decline to near zero. The net increment of population added at each interval takes on the shape of a bell-shaped curve, whereby the net increment builds to a maximum point and then declines to zero (Figure 5).

On the most fundamental level, smart growth must start with the affirmation that we need to design within the possible in the complex biogeochemical system that we inhabit. It is not smart to design systems that are not possible to sustain. There are no externalities in an ecosystem so we must abandon sectoral thinking (predicated on growth of particular sectors) for systems thinking (predicated on the stability and self-maintenance of the health of the system as a whole). Those who advocate smart growth will need to recognize and embrace the fact that in healthy populations, as in healthy individuals, growth is a phase through which life forms move on the way to maturity. Continuous growth is not possible in healthy organisms or healthy populations. It is, in fact, the sign of pathology and imminent death. Physicians point out that continuous growth is the ideology of a cancer cell. It is little wonder that urban policies predicated on the fiction of continuous growth leave us with a pattern of urban sprawl that resembles a form of cancer on

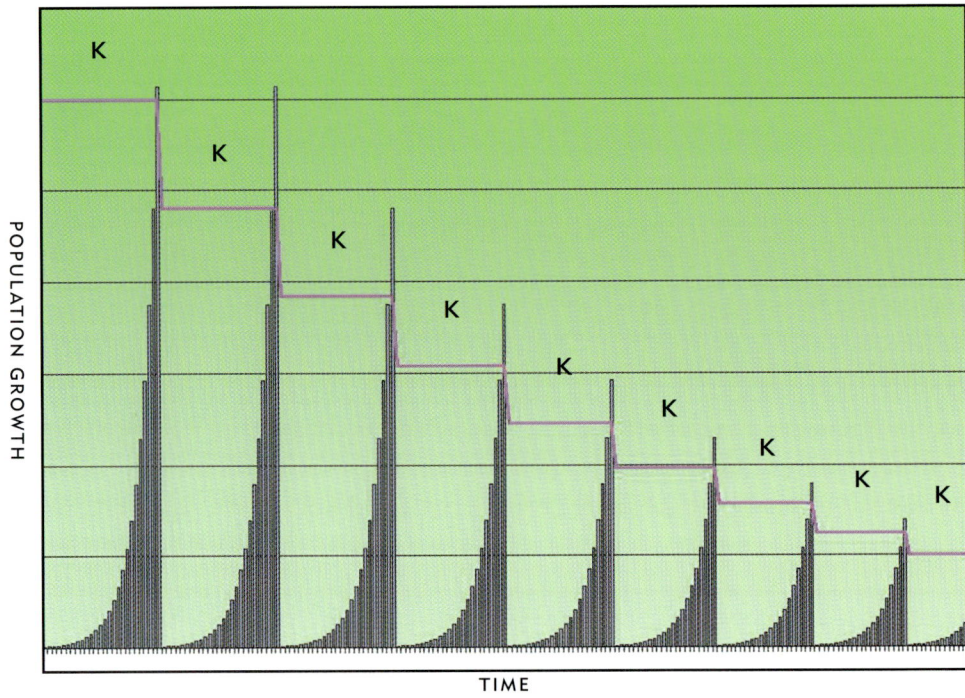

Figure 4 Carrying capacity (K) can also decline over time. The overall dynamics of a population can remain the same, but if each time it overshoots and collapses, the carrying capacity of its environment declines, then when it grows again it will not reach its former total before it collapses yet again. This can be said to be a constant growth pattern, but it does not appear to be smart growth because each boom and bust episode diminishes subsequent chances for survival over time.

the land.[3] The ethical principles for smart growth reflect a new and sober assessment of the problematic character of growth and a renewed sense of place for the human prospect in a complex ecosystem.

In 1949, Aldo Leopold wrote an essay entitled "The Land Ethic," which appeared as the last chapter in his famous work, *A Sand County Almanac*. In this essay he expressed the thought that ethical systems evolve as human communities extend their sense of responsibility:

> The extension of ethics…is actually a process in ecological evolution. Its sequences may be described in ecological as well as in philosophical

---

3   See the U.S. Geological Survey's cartographic representation of urban growth in the San Francisco Bay area at: *http://geo.arc.nasa.gov/esdstaff/william/urban.mpg.*

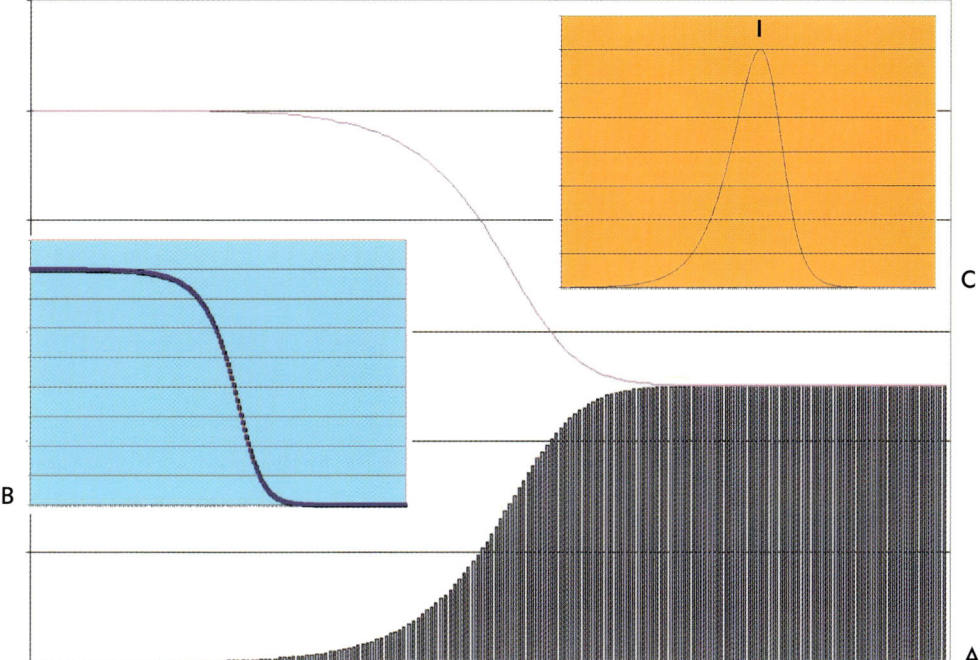

Figure 5 Growth is a phase in the evolution of an organism or a population as it moves toward maturity. In stable, sustainable populations the growth rate declines to near zero (A) and the population stabilizes without exceeding its carrying capacity (B). During the growth phase, average periodic increments in population reach a peak at the point of inflection (I), after which the increment added to the population declines in each successive period (C). Smart growth is self-limiting.

terms....The first ethics dealt with the relations between individuals....Later accretions dealt with the relation between the individual and society....There is as yet no ethic dealing with man's relation to land and to the animals and plants which grow upon it. Land...is still property. The land-relation is still strictly economic, entailing privileges but not obligations. The extension of ethics to this third element in human environment is, if I read the evidence correctly, an evolutionary possibility and an ecological necessity. It is the third step in a sequence. The first two have already been taken. Individual thinkers since the days of Ezekiel and Isaiah have asserted that the despoliation of the land is not only inexpedient but wrong. Society, however, has not yet affirmed their belief. I regard the present conservation movement as the embryo of such an affirmation. (Leopold 1966, 238-239).

Fifty years after these words were written, we would do well to reflect upon them with an eye to evaluating whether or not we have made significant progress in developing the land ethic of which Leopold wrote so passionately.[4]

Deriving a land ethic of this nature will of necessity involve a profound shift in the core metaphors of Western culture. For a long time we in Western cultures have come to believe that the environment is external to us; that we can exploit it at will; and that we are entitled, empowered and even anointed to do so. If we make a mess of things, so the thinking goes, we will be forgiven if we are contrite, and we will be entitled to make a new start—usually somewhere else further "west" or out on some putative frontier. This ideology of continuous linear expansion toward an ever-receding frontier leaves devastation in its wake, but we do not bother ourselves overly much with the waste stream in the wake of our civilization. Instead, some of the most intelligent and curious minds among us are encouraged by this culture of expansion to conquer new frontiers onwards and upwards in a seemingly unquenchable thirst for new space and resources to subdue.[5]

This species arrogance is not limited to Earth alone. The thrust of our popular mythology encourages us to believe that it quite natural "to boldly go where no man has gone before." In popular culture, we can no longer distinguish fact from science fiction. Serious scientist and technicians—not just Star Trekkies—talk about mining the moon or promising near-Earth asteroids. Most recently, the prospect of finding water on the moon or on Mars was portrayed by a breathless group of scientists and techno-boomers as an indication that we may be able to tap these water resources as a potential source of hydrogen and oxygen to fuel further expansion missions into space. The impulse to leave Earth and colonize other parts of the accessible solar system is now deeply engrained in the rhetoric surrounding our space program. Scientists talk of seeding Mars with microbial life to encourage the development of greenhouse gases and create an atmosphere more like what we have come to inherit on Earth. On some levels there are troubling signs that otherwise sober and serious individuals believe this is both possible and good.

Those of us more focused on the precariousness and fragility of life forms and their associated ecosystems here on Earth recognize that the spaceship dream and the colonization of Mars are sadly misguided delusions. Moreover, we feel passionately that the human prospect is still worth trying to preserve on Earth. After

---

4 The Harvard Seminar on Environmental Values devoted the year 1999-2000 to a reconsideration of Leopold's thoughts on the land ethic (Harvard University 1999).

5 For an extended discussion of the concept of nature and the importance of the frontier experience in Western cultures, see Weiskel (1983).

all, we already live on the largest inhabitable spaceship in the known universe. If we prove ourselves through our blindness or stubbornness incapable of sustaining human life on this precious, richly endowed sphere, on what grounds do we think we will be successful on barren rocks anywhere else?

Because of Western culture's technological arrogance and its collective fascination with perpetual expansion and growth, it is becoming increasingly apparent to the wider world that we will need a radical transformation of this culture's core values and ethics if human survival is to be assured. The transition involved in adopting new principles for survival may prove very difficult; cultures do not smile kindly on major challenges to their core beliefs. Nevertheless, despite the difficulty of implementing them, the principles themselves are clear to see and can form the basis of a new deontological approach to environmental ethics. Others should feel free to refine the following list, but it can at least serve as a starting point for discussion.

In our public and private lives we should always and everywhere seek to act personally and collectively (for example, tax, spend, regulate, legislate and litigate, etc.) so as to follow these proposed Ecological Ten Commandments:

1. Design within the possible; reinsert the human enterprise within Earth's biogeochemical cycles, sustained by throughput solar energy;
2. Substitute the consumption of nonrenewable resources with renewable ones;
3. Reduce the consumption of renewables to at or below their rate of renewal;
4. Enter nothing into the waste/nutrient stream that cannot be "eaten" safely by other organisms that you can live with;
5. Allocate the accumulated fruits of production in a more—rather than less—equitable and just fashion (large and growing inequities of assets and power are inherently destabilizing in an ecosystem and must be avoided);
6. Measure and monitor environmental conditions affecting the safety, health and welfare of all species (ecosystems must deliver benefits to all constituent species or they cease to be functioning systems and rapidly collapse);
7. Educate and inform the public about the circumstances it must confront and the "footprint" that human cultures generate in the broader ecosystem;
8. Entitle and empower local human communities to manage their resources sustainably (human communities cannot be salvaged "on average" or "in

general"; if they don't survive in their own unique and particular ways, the human enterprise cannot be sustained);

9. Cajole, exhort and convince those who do not follow these precepts of ecological citizenry to mend their ways; and

10. Expose, denounce, condemn and seek to punish those who consistently and intentionally violate these precepts of responsible ecocitizenry—including those who otherwise wish to present themselves as "respectable" public leaders.

Perhaps the notion of ten commandments is a bit of a misnomer. The ethical principles enumerated here are not the same as rules or policy prescriptions. They should be understood more broadly as guidelines to keep in mind in shaping specific rules, laws, economic incentives, tax provisions, citizen and community initiatives, and business and professional agreements. At any point we should ask ourselves whether specific proposals support or violate these basic principles of environmental ethics. The objective of ethical reflection in the context of smart growth is not to pretend we can achieve moral purity, but rather to urge each of us individually and collectively to devise effective guidelines for responsible behavior in socially equitable and ecologically sustainable communities.

References

Beckerman, Wilfred. 1995. *Small is stupid: Blowing the whistle on the Greens.* London, England: Duckworth.

Harvard University, University Committee on the Environment. 1999. *The land ethic revisited: Ownership, stewardship and moral responsibility in an ecosystem.* Harvard Seminar on Environmental Values, 1999–2000. Available at *http://ecoethics. net/hsev/sche1999.htm.*

Leopold, Aldo. 1966. *A Sand County almanac: with essays on conservation from Round River.* New York, NY: Ballantine Books.

Meadows, Donella H., and Club of Rome. 1972. *The limits to growth: A report for the Club of Rome's project on the predicament of mankind.* New York, NY: Universe Books.

Meadows, Donella H., Dennis L. Meadows and Jorgen Randers. 1992. *Beyond the limits: Confronting global collapse, envisioning a sustainable future.* Post Mills, VT: Chelsea Green.

Walter, Edward. 1981. *The immorality of limiting growth.* Albany, NY: State University of New York Press.

Weiskel, Timothy C. 1983. Rubbish and racism: Problems of boundary in an ecosystem. *Yale review* (Winter):225–244.

11

Harvey Gantt

Smart Growth and Urban Revival

The general public and many planners appear to support a smart growth strategy, and I think it is interesting that more and more conferences on this subject also include builders and developers. However, I have newfound concerns about equity in relation to smart growth. Does this movement actually represent a new turn in direction toward defining, controlling and conserving our environment, or will handling growth at the edge actually cause center-city revitalization efforts, such as they are, to continue to suffer as they have for the last 50 years?

What I mean by center-city involvement is, in fact, the reclamation, restoration or revitalization of inner-city, low-income neighborhoods. Much of what we hear today about smart growth relates to a strategy that calls for a more intelligent way to manage our resources and change the settlement patterns in emerging suburbia. Such planning, while important and inherently good, rarely appears to involve center-city neighborhoods, or even first-ring suburbs in the metro regions of tomorrow.

Most of the time, and generally around the country, what we hear about strategies related to smart growth are basically strategies about physical design. As an architect, I'm excited about that. But I am convinced that there's much more that we need to focus on than simply well-planned streets or properly designed streetscapes or lot layouts. We continue to hear a lot about design plans and alternative transportation modes. We hear much about preservation of open space, environmental issues, and density and zoning concerns. My friends in the new urbanist movement admit that they've developed quite a following on traditional neighborhood development (TND), and how the nostalgic characteristics of what our cities and neighborhoods used to be like, or still are, can be applied to the future planning of places.

The new application of these TNDs as a way to better organize new growth cells in suburbia is good idea. But in some cases this approach, absent other strategies, has led to the same lack of diversity in population and housing mix that we find in old suburbia. To me, what is missing in this national discussion are pressing social questions about the makeup of our metropolitan regions and, more specifically, issues of center-city revival as part of the smart growth movement.

Where will the working poor and moderate-income families live in tomorrow's smart growth regions and metros? What impact will the placing of development limits on metro areas have on affordable housing, if any? Can central cities become a viable settlement alternative for the middle class? If so, what happens to lower-income communities in declining neighborhoods as reformation and gentrification take place? Can we put in place transportation policies that allow

Infill middle-income housing adjacent to existing housing in an inner-city neighborhood being revived with selective clearance policies. Photograph courtesy of Gantt Huberman Architects.

Housing being destroyed by urban renewal projects. Site converted to parking lot or no man's land. Photograph courtesy of Gantt Huberman Architects.

greater accessibility to jobs and housing for a wide range of economic groups, including the poor? And what about the quality of urban public education and its impact on a diverse population in the metro region and in center cities?

I could go on asking questions like these, but I believe most readers will get the drift. The revitalization strategies for the central city, both social and physical in nature, can and must be the most significant elements in the development of the overall metro region. Once smart growth advocates start to deal with social development issues, as well as the pattern of physical development, three possible scenarios may occur in the next 10 to 15 years.

One scenario or approach would concentrate on smart growth purely as a need to better organize suburban expansion. The focus would be on physical design, accompanied by a marketing strategy that asserts that livable communities are better because we have designed them better, have handled land use policies better and have conserved open spaces. We've already accomplished things like urban growth boundaries and purchase of development rights. Through our transportation systems, both transit and the automobile, we have connected communities very well to major centers of employment. These kinds of efforts are reflected in discussions around the country today. But how will we better organize the edges of cities and metropolitan areas? Will we continue to talk about preserving some open space and slowing the pace of traffic and congestion? Or will we only talk about increasing density, perhaps only slightly in the end?

I don't want to leave the impression that it's not a good idea for us to organize new growth better for the metro region. On the negative side, however, I see such a scenario and approach to growth creating greater demands on the scarce public resources that we have available today. This approach would take dollars away from central-city constituencies without increasing political and economic leverage, and would direct those resources to new infrastructure and land acquisition, preservation of open space and construction of transportation systems. Further, the increasing rise of land prices will raise the cost of housing, without the needed expansion of affordable housing to provide suburban and center-city areas more diversity. Moreover, the 60-year trend of center-city abandonment will continue unabated if there is no plan for revival, leaving center cities further behind on a continuing path of what I call twentieth-century ruins—the abandoned neighborhoods and shopping areas that exist in the core city and even in some areas of the suburbs.

The smart growth strategy I've just described is no friend to the central city. It's the same social program that leaves behind a deprived central core. However, that is the perception of many urban thinkers about smart growth today. As I look at the audience that attends conferences about smart growth, I don't see very many representatives from the core cities. I don't see very many African American leaders sitting in the audience, because they don't perceive smart growth to be anything that deals with them and their issues. We need to be concerned about this perception.

A second scenario would continue much of the smart growth strategies I've just described, but with an eye toward developing urban downtown areas as a primary location for retail development, entertainment, sports events and culture. As a former mayor of Charlotte, North Carolina, I have some understanding of the mindset of mayors. We have worked on these kinds of things for years, to make our core cities the living room for the region, and to build skyscrapers, hotels, stadiums and arenas that represent a forward-looking community. While these kinds of initiatives are expensive to accomplish, they are relatively easy to do, and they can sometimes be accomplished in the time span of one's political career, adding glitz and at least perceived liveliness and vitality to center cities. We even see some mayors and cities working hard to attract residents back into the city.

Low-density housing that incorporates low-income and middle-income families. Photograph courtesy of Gantt Huberman Architects.

When this happens, and residential rehabilitation results, such areas are often settled by high-income residents or at least risk-averse persons who don't mind living next to poor people. These newcomers are often swingers and single; because of their life cycle, they find living in the city quite desirable. This process of neighborhood rehabilitation is a good thing, but the ironic twist is that nothing very good seems to happen to the surrounding poorer neighborhoods. As a matter of fact, many of these poorer neighborhoods feel threatened by expansion onto their turf. The neighborhood leaders in these poorer communities often are unable to influence public policy, and this leads to increased fear and distrust.

I visited Atlanta a few months ago. The main topic of conversation during my visit was urban housing, and it was quite interesting to note grassroots leaders reflecting all kinds of perceptions about what gentrification was going to mean to their neighborhoods, their livelihood and their life in the city. The second scenario, then, says let's keep the smart growth strategies applicable to the edge, but let's do something about fixing up downtown as well. This approach still leaves a lot of underutilized places and neighborhoods with a great deal of fear and distrust, and increases a lot of tension. In an ironic kind of way, it is unfortunate that those who want to help revitalize the city find such resistance, because of poor understanding of what the city and its leaders can do.

The third and most viable scenario, I believe, is one that seeks to grow intelligently both at the edge and at the core. It is an alternative that does not automatically assume that some neighborhoods will always be poor and declining, and that middle- and moderate-income families will never choose to live in the central city. I believe that we ought to work on a strategy that attracts a wide range of families back to the city without disrupting those who already live there. This strategy will drive urban leaders to build aggressively upon all the major assets of the city—its universities and colleges, its medical facilities, its cultural facilities, its civic architecture. The core usually has the largest employment center, and it has infrastructure in place, which, though often underutilized, merits attention. It has a network of both major and minor streets, and is often the most accessible location in the region.

The fact is that years of negative connotation and stigma can be associated with inner cities or central cities, yet people still look for opportunities to go there because they find it more interesting. I believe there are now fourth-generation suburban dwellers who may, in fact, be looking for something different. We have an opportunity to take advantage of the city's assets. With a strong program of infill housing, we can build inventory and drive down housing prices to affordable levels for the working poor.

While some existing neighborhoods have concerns about increasing density, there is evidence that higher density can be accommodated if the right neighborhoods are chosen and sound strategies are worked out in terms of design. Protective measures that offer incentives to homeowners and renters who live in areas targeted for redevelopment can often keep them in place, even as higher-income housing is built around them. The plan for city neighborhoods should be to reduce the impact of gentrification while encouraging more diversity—something that generally cannot be done in the suburbs.

We tried this approach in Charlotte. We said, let's find a way for the city to reward low-income homeowners and renters in an area that was prime for redevelopment. We did this by offering them loans and grants at very low interest rates, provided they would renovate their places, put on a new roof, paint and fix the front porch, add a room, or do whatever they wanted and needed to do. At the same time, we allowed developers to come in and build on vacant land that had grown valuable because of the growth of banking and utilities in the Charlotte area, and the tremendous expansion of new jobs and businesses. Public programs

High-density housing in a mixed development including retail and office uses. Photograph courtesy of Gantt Huberman Architects.

to improve streetscapes and the overall urban appearance were also important. Increasing the perception and reality of greater safety and security, while expensive initially, paid dividends by encouraging more development down the road. Accessibility to jobs, both in the center city and in other areas due to improved public transit, helped raise the economic outlook of the average family and enhanced the normal sphere of activity.

Perhaps most important to encouraging the resettlement of a diverse city is how we address urban public education. If cities can be freed to become innovative in restructuring public education, and to achieve the result of providing a high degree of success for its students (who in most cases today are poor children), then we can do something about turning around the existing cycle and encouraging middle- and upper-income families to move into the city. Of course, achieving this kind of smart growth scenario, which is inclusive of the entire metropolitan region and where the inner city is the core of appropriate development, will take a lot more time, a lot more perseverance, a large commitment of public and private dollars, and the political will to encourage such a vision. And yet, if we're not careful, *if we're not very careful*, this little thing we call smart growth today may come to be viewed as nothing more than simply organizing sprawl. It could degenerate into nothing more than a fad that we'll be talking about in 10 or 15 years as a movement that ultimately failed.

I think we've got the answer only half right if we concentrate only on making suburbia just a little bit better and more diverse. There's a great opportunity here for us to look at metro regions comprehensively, particularly since the country seems to want to focus on smart growth. It's an opportunity to address center-city problems, which have not been addressed in the last 50 years or so in a very serious manner. All of our goals for smart growth and smart development—conservation of open space, better utilization of the infrastructure, reducing traffic and air pollution, increasing accessibility to jobs, providing affordable housing—can be accomplished if we are willing to grapple with the really tough issues.

I will conclude by saying to my colleagues in planning and architecture that smart growth must be about more than just design. It must also be about dealing with tough social policy questions on race and economic class, and on the fact that we have developed a growth strategy without a clear understanding of the great potential of central cities to influence urban settlement patterns.

Afterword

Smart Words

It is safe to say that most of the contributors to this volume would join most of us who are engaged in the urban planning enterprise in agreeing that what we understand to be smart growth is indeed "smart." This speaks of a consensus in the field that may be attributable, at least in part, to the clever and politically astute choice of these two words as the sobriquet for a broad range of planning policies and practices. Yet some planners and critics remain troubled by the consequences of at least some dimension of the smart growth agenda, or about the term itself. For example, more than one of the authors in this volume has referred to the term smart growth as a euphemism. And at least one, Timothy Weiskel, has called it an oxymoron, an "arrogant contradiction in terms."

As I write this, the dictionary that comes most readily to my hand (*Webster's Ninth New Collegiate Dictionary*) defines euphemism as "the substitution of an agreeable or inoffensive expression for one that may offend or suggest something unpleasant." Utopia, another word pertinent to this discussion, is defined in three ways, each of which may be relevant to some observers: (1) "an imaginary and indefinitely remote place," (2) "a place of ideal perfection esp. in laws, government, and social conditions," and (3) "an impractical scheme for social improvement." Eutopia, disappointingly, is not to be found in the Collegiate Webster's (my computer spell-check program is equally puzzled by it), but readers of Lewis Mumford (or of Greek) know it to be the "good place" as opposed to the "no place" of utopia. Dystopia, again according to my Webster's, is "an imaginary place which is depressingly wretched and whose people lead a fearful existence."

So, fellow Pilgrims, are we progressing on the road to Eutopia, or lost in the Slough of Despond? In exploring the words of the advocates and analysts we will learn, among other things, that while Portland, Oregon, may be a planner's heaven, for others it is a hell under construction.

AFTERWORD

Smart Growth as Euphemism

The American Planning Association has proposed an ambitious set of model planning laws for the states under the rubric "Growing Smart," having concluded that "our tools are outdated for the times we live in....In some communities and regions since the 1970s, high rates of growth have prompted concern over cost of services, adverse impacts on the environment and quality of life, and the balance between jobs and housing" (APA 2002) In contrast, the Florida Sustainable Communities Center (FSCC) reports that Steve Seibert, the secretary of the state's Department of Community Affairs, is concerned "that the terms 'sustainable community' and 'smart growth' imply failure or 'dumb growth' on the part of those who choose not to embrace the strategy." Anthony Downs (2001) of the Brookings Institution has asked vis-à-vis smart growth, "Can groups as different as home builders and transit advocates be using the term in the same way? The answer is no."

Just what do such different groups mean by smart growth? From the National Association of Home Builder's website we are not too surprised to find the statement, "In its broadest sense, Smart Growth means meeting the underlying demand for housing created by an ever-increasing population and prosperous economy by building a political consensus and employing market-sensitive and innovative land-use planning concepts." In "The Path to Smart Growth: A Toolkit Developed by the Surface Transportation Policy Project and the Natural Resources Defense Council," on STPP's website, we learn, again perhaps not surprisingly, that smart growth is "compact, walkable, and transit-accessible." Downs (2001) has helpfully set out the main areas of agreement as well as disagreement among the various groups: Most agree on open space protection, core redevelopment, better urban design, and regional cooperation. But he finds wide disagreement about urban growth boundaries, infrastructure financing, and reducing reliance on the automobile.

Smart Growth as Dystopia

The cover story in the Fall 2001 edition of *Regulation* magazine (a.k.a. *The Cato Review of Business and Government*) is titled "The Folly of 'Smart Growth.'" Author Randal O'Toole, who hails from the Thoreau Institute in Bandon, Oregon, argues that smart growth policies around Portland are associated with "increases in traffic congestion, air pollution, consumer costs, taxes, and just about every other impediment to urban livability." In a sidebar titled "The Fruits of Smart Growth," he enumerates the following future outcomes for Portland:

increased gridlock and traffic congestion; reduction in the quality of current mass transit through diversion of resources to rail transit; increased housing costs; higher taxes to pay for rail and subsidize high density housing; higher consumer costs due to restrictions on shopping areas; and loss of valuable open space currently available for recreation in favor of inaccessible farms (O'Toole 2001).

Another dystopian, Samuel R. Staley of the Reason Public Policy Institute, takes issue with the "so-called Smart Growth movement" in the *Houston Chronicle* (July 22, 2001), and assails a Brookings index that relates sprawl to a rate of land consumption in excess of population growth. "This is an absurd standard; taken literally, it would suspend the dreams of millions of homebuyers and seriously compromise the quality of life for millions of families." Staley had earlier given an address at the 2001 national meeting of the American Planning Association with the searchingly interrogative title, "Why Am I a Smart Growth 'Contrarian?'" (Staley 2000). Brian Blaesser (this volume), perhaps more as anti-euphemist than dystopic, has called smart growth "growth management with an attitude" (based on "the rather singular view that sprawl is almost criminal"), while arguing for the freedom to choose uncompact development patterns.

Smart Growth as Oxymoron

Timothy Weiskel (this volume) asks, "In a world already choked by the human enterprise, where so much of the natural world suffers from our collective species footprint, isn't smart growth an oxymoron, an arrogant contradiction in terms?" World population is expected to peak at nine to ten billion by the end of the twenty-first century, more than a 50 percent increase over its present level of about six billion. And some feet are no doubt bigger than others, with those in developing countries leaving a footprint of about 2.5 acres per capita compared to 24 acres in the U.S. "For every person in the world to reach U.S. levels of consumption with existing technology would require four more planet Earths" (Wilson 2002, 23). How we grow (and consume), then, appears to be at least as important as how many of us we are.

While not antagonistic to global population control per se, pioneering regional planner Benton MacKaye analogized population growth at the regional scale to rainfall: you could not control its quantity, but you could manage its distribution. "The regional planner makes no attempt to control the flow of population into his region from other portions of the world; no more than the engineer attempts to control the flow of water into his river basin coming through rainfall from other portions of the world. The regional planner and the engineer, each

AFTERWORD

within his region or his river basin, accepts a given amount of quantity of flow, and then distributes it according to some plan" (MacKaye 1990, 157). Arthur (Chris) Nelson (this volume) has pointed out the challenge, and opportunity, for U.S. planners presented by the "given" that we will have 56 million new people by 2025 and will need about 25 percent new development and 20 percent reconfigured, totaling about 45 percent of development needed nationwide. Looking further ahead, using, as Nelson does, the middle projection of the U.S. Census Bureau, by 2050 another 66 million more people will be living in the U.S. and by 2100, a total of about 300 million new people, more than doubling the 2000 population of 281 million.

Richard Carson (2000), a former planning director of Portland's Metro, writing a Viewpoint piece for *Planning* magazine titled, "How Practical is Smart Growth?" states, "In reality, smart growth only slows growth, while New Urbanism simply makes increased density more enjoyable. Neither doctrine alone can change the fact that growth in metropolitan areas will result in overcrowding, traffic congestion, and poor air quality. … Yet planners rarely talk about limiting growth. That's because we don't have a politically marketable alternative that allows for rational growth."

I would like to conclude this Afterword, which I have served up as a little postprandial *digestif* to follow a banquet of carefully prepared dishes, by harking back to the first course, as it were, offered by my co-editor Terry Szold, who has left it for history to judge the ultimate success of smart growth, but not without a certain implied hopefulness in the result. Perhaps Eutopia is just around the corner.

Armando Carbonell
Senior Fellow and Cochairman
Department of Planning and Development
Lincoln Institute of Land Policy

References

American Planning Association. 2002. *http://www.planning.org/growingsmart/background.htm*

Carson, Richard. 2000. Viewpoint: How practical is smart growth? 66 *Planning* (August):54.

Downs, Anthony. 2001. What does "smart growth" really mean? 67 *Planning* (April).

Florida Sustainable Communities Center. *http://sustainable.state.fl.us/fdi/fscc/news/ index.html*

MacKaye, Benton. [1928] 1990. *The new exploration: A philosophy of regional planning.* Champaign Urbana, IL: The Appalachian Trail Conference and University of Illinois Press.

Meck, Stuart, ed. 2002. *Growing smart legislative guidebook 3: Model statutes for planning and the management of change.* Chicago, IL: American Planning Association.

National Association of Home Builders. *http://www.nahb.org*

O'Toole, Randal. 2001. The folly of 'smart growth.' 24 *Regulation* (3).

Staley, Samuel R. 2000. Presentation to Council on Urban Economic Development, Portland, Oregon (June 12).

———. 2001. Why Am I a Smart Growth 'Contrarian? Presentation to American Planning Association National Conference, New Orleans, Louisiana (March 12).

Surface Transportation Policy Project. *http://www.transact.org*

Thoreau Institute. *http://www.ti.org*

Wilson, Edward O. 2002. *The future of life.* New York, NY: Alfred A Knopf.

Contributors

Eran Ben-Joseph is a Hayes Career Development assistant professor of landscape architecture and planning at Massachusetts Institute of Technology in Cambridge, Massachusetts. Previously he was a faculty member at Virginia Institute of Technology and a visiting instructor at the Technion Israel Institute of Technology. Ben-Joseph is the founding principal of BNBJ, a multidisciplinary planning firm in Tel-Aviv, which specializes in new town site planning, landscape architecture and urban design. His current sponsored research includes a study of the impacts of streets and infrastructure standards on the built environment; technological developments in site planning; and new interfaces for urban simulation.

Brian W. Blaesser, Esq., is a partner and heads the Land Use and Development Group in the Boston office of Robinson & Cole LLP. He practices in the areas of commercial real estate development and leasing, residential development, land use and environmental law, planning law, condemnation law and litigation. He represents real estate owners, investors and developers in analyzing and securing requisite entitlements from governments and agencies, and negotiating and drafting development agreements. He also has extensive experience in state and federal trial and appellate courts in litigation involving the takings issue, impact fees, vested rights, condemnation, U.S. EPA enforcement actions, and violations of Section 1983 of the Civil Rights Act. He is the author or co-author of numerous publications on land use, growth management and real estate development.

Armando Carbonell is a senior fellow and cochair of the Department of Planning and Development at the Lincoln Institute of Land Policy. He also lectures in the Department of Urban Planning and Design at the Harvard University Graduate School of Design. Prior to his appointment to the Institute, Carbonell was executive director of the Cape Cod Commission, a regional planning and land use regulatory agency.

CONTRIBUTORS

John P. DeVillars is executive vice president of Brownfields Recovery Corporation in Boston. He served as administrator of the U.S. Environmental Protection Agency's New England office from 1993 to 2000. Prior to joining the EPA, DeVillars directed the Environmental Services Group for Coopers and Lybrand, an international accounting and consulting firm. He also served as Secretary of the Environment for the Commonwealth of Massachusetts and as chairman of the board of the Massachusetts Water Resources Authority. DeVillars is also a visiting lecturer in environmental policy in the Department of Urban Studies and Planning at Massachusetts Institute of Technology.

Harvey Gantt is cofounder of Gantt Huberman Architects, an architectural firm in Charlotte, North Carolina. As a former mayor of Charlotte, he has been interested in planning, revitalization of the inner city, housing and managed growth. His primary focus is to make the case that the problems of the urban areas of our country demand a more activist role for architects in shaping public policy.

Dolores Hayden, an urban historian and architect, is professor of architecture, urbanism and American studies at Yale University. She has written several award-winning books about the history of American urban landscapes and the politics of design. *The Power of Place* deals with Los Angeles and its public history, and *Redesigning the American Dream* offers a feminist critique of 1950s tract houses. She is currently writing a history of American suburbia and also developing *A Field Guide to Sprawl*.

Jerold S. Kayden, Esq., a lawyer and city planner, is associate professor of urban planning at the Harvard University Graduate School of Design. He specializes in planning and environmental law, public and private development, and the relationship between law and design. He writes widely on these topics, including his most recent book *Privately Owned Public Space: The New York City Experience*.

Alex Krieger is professor in practice of urban design and chair of the Department of Urban Planning and Design at the Harvard University Graduate School of Design. He is also a founding principal of Chan Krieger & Associates in Cambridge, an award-winning firm offering architectural, urban design and master planning services. Krieger was one of the original members of the Boston Civic Design Commission and a director of the Mayor's Institute in City Design.

Contributors

He is now involved in the planning of a number of American cities, including Boston, Pittsburgh, Cincinnati and Washington, DC. He is the author of several books, including *Mapping Boston*.

Glenna Matthews is an historian who specializes in both women's history and the history of California. She is completing "Silicon Valley, Women, and the California Dream," which draws upon her doctoral research at Stanford University on the Santa Clara Valley during the 1930s. Matthews is a visiting scholar at the Institute of Urban and Regional Development, University of California, Berkeley.

William J. Mitchell is dean of the School of Architecture and Planning at MIT. He was formerly director of the Design Studies Program at the Harvard University Graduate School of Design and head of UCLA's Architecture/Urban Design Program. Mitchell is a fellow of the Royal Australian Institute of Architects. His scholarly interests include design theory, computer-aided design and electronic media. He has also consulted and cofounded a software company and has served as president of The Urban Innovations Group in Los Angeles.

Arthur Christian Nelson is professor of city planning and urban design in the College of Architecture and professor of public policy in the College of Management at Georgia Institute of Technology, in Atlanta. He is also a member of Georgia Tech's Transportation Research and Education Center, located in the College of Engineering, and president of Growth Management Analysts, Inc. He has conducted pioneering work in land use planning, growth management and public facility finance, and has written many books and professional publications.

Terry S. Szold is principal of Community Planning Solutions, and has over 16 years of experience in land use, growth management, strategic and comprehensive planning. She served as planning director for the Town of Burlington, Massachusetts, from 1988 to 1994, and held other senior planning positions in Massachusetts and New Hampshire. Szold's scholarly interests have been in community planning, land use law and regulation, and transportation and design-related issues. Szold is also adjunct associate professor in the Department of Urban Studies and Planning at Massachusetts Institute of Technology, where she serves as a practitioner and educator in land use and growth management.

CONTRIBUTORS

Timothy C. Weiskel is a visiting scholar in the Institute of Liberal Arts and Interdisciplinary Studies at Emerson College, Boston. In addition he is the director of the Harvard Seminar on Environmental Values and the co-director of the Working Group on Environmental Justice at Harvard University. Trained as an anthropologist and as a historian, his scholarly interests include the connections between cultural values and environmental policy, environmental ethics, and the religious dimensions of the environmental crisis.

About the Lincoln Institute

The Lincoln Institute of Land Policy is a nonprofit and tax-exempt educational institution established in 1974. Its mission as a school is to study and teach land policy, including land economics and land taxation. The Institute is supported by the Lincoln Foundation, established in 1947 by John C. Lincoln, a Cleveland industrialist who drew inspiration from the ideas of Henry George, the nineteenth-century American political economist and social philosopher.

The Institute's goals are to integrate the theory and practice of land policy and to understand the multidisciplinary forces that influence it. Through its curriculum development, courses, conferences and publications, the Lincoln Institute seeks to improve the quality of debate and disseminate knowledge about critical issues in its departments of planning and development and valuation and taxation and in its program on Latin America and the Caribbean.

The Institute does not take a particular point of view, but rather brings together scholars, policy makers and citizens with a variety of backgrounds and experience to study, reflect and exchange insights on land and tax policies. The Institute's objective is to have an impact—to make a difference today and to help policy makers plan for tomorrow. The Institute is an equal opportunity institution in employment and admissions.

113 Brattle St. Cambridge, MA 02138-3400 USA

Phone	617.661.3016
	800.LAND.USE (800.526.3873)
Fax	617.661.7235
	800.LAND.944 (800.526.3944)
Email	help@lincolninst.edu
Web	www.lincolninst.edu